Illustrated Record of German Army Equipment
1939–45

ARMOURED FIGHTING VEHICLES

The Naval & Military Press Ltd

Published by

The Naval & Military Press Ltd
Unit 5 Riverside, Brambleside
Bellbrook Industrial Estate
Uckfield, East Sussex
TN22 1QQ England

Tel: +44 (0)1825 749494

www.naval-military-press.com
www.nmarchive.com

In reprinting in facsimile from the original, any imperfections are inevitably reproduced and the quality may fall short of modern type and cartographic standards.

ILLUSTRATED RECORD
OF
GERMAN ARMY EQUIPMENT
1939-1945

FOREWORD

1. The issue of this publication, two years after the end of the war in Europe, is designed to put on record essential information on the armament of the German Land Forces during the war. It includes some of the more interesting equipments which were developed, but which, due to the conclusion of hostilities, or to production difficulties, did not come into general service.

   The publication is primarily a photographic record, supported by a brief specification, and in some instances a short description. The material has been drawn from the large collection of matter compiled by the Technical Intelligence Services during and subsequent to the war. Much of it has appeared in the various Technical Intelligence Summaries and Bulletins issued by the War Office, and by G.H.Qs. overseas, supplemented by photographs and details added from German sources after the collapse.

2. Handbooks have already been published on some of the more important equipments. The volume of material and the scope of the present publication, have precluded detailed descriptions. For any recipient officially requiring fuller information on any particular subject, the records available can be consulted through M.I.10, The War Office, up to the end of 1947. Thereafter they will be disposed of.

3. This publication is laid out in the form of a reference album showing a photograph of each equipment, together with the specification or brief description. It has been divided into five separate volumes under the following subject headings:-

   Vol. I   Infantry Weapons

   Vol. II   Artillery

   Vol. III   Armoured Fighting Vehicles

   Vol. IV   Vehicles (other than A.F.V's)

   Vol. V   Mines, Mine Detectors, and Demolition Equipment

4. It will be noted that the sections dealing with mines, mine detectors, and demolition Equipment have been written up rather more fully, but in no case do these sections claim to be exhaustive.

5. It should be noted that all figures quoted are taken from German sources. It is appreciated that in many instances these differ from the figures quoted in official British and American reports.

6. In conclusion it is hoped that this publication will serve a purpose as a brief permanent record of the major German Army weapons and equipments developed and used during the 1939-1945 war.

The War Office   Director of Military Intelligence

VOLUME III - ARMOURED FIGHTING VEHICLES

GENERAL INDEX

Section One   -   Tanks

Section Two   -   Self propelled Artillery

Section Three -   Armoured cars

VOLUME III - A.F.Vs.

SECTION ONE - TANKS

INDEX TO SECTION ONE

1. Scope of Section One.
2. General.
3. Development history of tanks taken into operational use.
4. Tanks of foreign design used operationally by the German Army.
5. Unsuccessful and unfinished tank projects.
6. Main component development.
    (a) Armament
    (b) Armour and construction.
    (c) Power plant.
    (d) Transmissions.
    (e) Suspensions.
    (f) Tracks.
7. Specifications of tanks taken into service.
8. Table of leading data of tanks taken into service.
9. Photos of prototypes, projects and tanks taken into service.
10. Bibliography.

PART III A.F.Vs.

SECTION ONE - TANKS

1. **Scope of Section One**

    This section is concerned only with giving a general development history of German tanks and main tank assemblies since 1933, together with a series of general specifications and photographs of all tanks brought into operational service and a combined table giving leading data of these tanks incorporated as Appendices. Photographs of experimental models are also included.

2. **General**

    Before giving the main development history, it is necessary to explain the various code words used to describe tank projects in the design and development stage by the various departments concerned in their production, i.e., the Heereswaffenamt and the manufacturing firms. In the first stages, from 1933 to the outbreak of war, these code words (such as "Landwirtschaftliche Schlepper" (La.S.) meaning "Agricultural Tractor", Bataillonsführer Wagen" (B.W.) meaning "Battalion Commander's Vehicle" and "Zugfuhrer Wagen" (Z.W) meaning "Troop Commander's Vehicle") were used to hide the fact that any tanks were being built at all, and open reference was never made to tanks as such. With the operational use of tanks in the Spanish War and the occupations of Austria and Czechoslovakia, however, the need for secrecy came to an end, and they became publicly known as "Panzerkampfwagen" (Pz.Kpfw.) although the original code names died a very slow death within the manufacturing firms.

    A further system of code nomenclature was introduced to cover the numerous experimental vehicles ordered by the Heereswaffenamt. Each design of prototype was given a four-figure number, preceded by the letters "VK" (for Vollketten-kraft-fahrzeug), to denote that it was a fully tracked experimental vehicle. The first two figures represented the weight class of the vehicle and the last two the number of the particular prototype - e.g. VK.4501 would be the first prototype of a tank with a designed weight of 45 tons. It is of interest to note that the weight as specified by the Heereswaffenamt was nearly always exceeded by several tons in the production vehicle. When the vehicle was finally taken into service it was also allotted an Sd.Kfz. number ("Sonder Kraftfahrzeug" number) to distinguish it in the Ordnance Vocabulary.

    As orders to develop a tank in a given weight class were generally given to at least two firms, the "VK" number was usually followed by the initial letters, in brackets, of the firm responsible for the design, to distinguish between the various prototype vehicles.

    As the War neared its end, the need for a completely new series of tanks embodying the latest principles and refinements was foreseen as a long term requirement by Wa.Pruf.6, and accordingly, due to the increase of weight of heavy tanks to 100 tons or more and the consequent unwieldiness of the "VK" numbers, a new system of code nomenclature was introduced. This new system still indicated the desired minimum weight class of the tank but did not take into account the prototype number. The letters "VK" were dispensed with and the letter E (significance unknown but possibly means "Einheitsfahrgestell" (general purpose chassis) or "Entwicklung" (development)) substituted. Thus, a vehicle in this latest series known, say as "E 100" would be an experimental vehicle with a specified minimum weight of 100 tons.

/3. Development

3. Development History of Tanks in Operational use

Tank production in Germany proper started when the National Socialist regime came into being in 1933, although it is believed that secret assembly of German tanks took place at Kasan in Russia from 1926 to 1932, while various German firms had designed prototypes in Germany from 1921 onwards. As stated in the introduction above, the first tanks produced in Germany were known as "Landwirtschaftliche Schlepper" (La.S.) or agricultural tractors, and in 1933, the orders to design prototypes were given by the Heereswaffenamt (Wa.Prüf.6) to the firms of Krupp, M.A.N.(Maschinenfabrik Augsburg - Nurnberg), Henschel, Daimler Benz and Rheinmetall Borsig. Of the various designs submitted, the Krupp vehicle was accepted, (Krupp-Traktor) and orders for its production were given to Krupp, Henschel, Daimler Benz, M.A.N. and probably others. The first order given to Henschel was for 3 vehicles, and assembly of these commenced towards the end of December, 1933. The first vehicle ran on the 3rd February, 1934, and all three vehicles were inspected on 27th April, 1934. By the end of July, 1934, orders had been placed with Henschel for a total of 150 vehicles. This version of the La.S. was known as the Model A, and a second version, known as the Model B, was subsequently produced in the same year. The La.S. later took the official name of Panzerkampfwagen I (Pz.Kpfw.I Sd.Kfz 101), and was first used operationally in the Spanish War. A further model, the Model C or Pz.Kpfw.I/n.A, was ordered by the Heereswafenamt in September, 1939 under the nomenclature of VK 601. The chassis was designed by Krauss - Mafei of Munchen and the superstructure and turret by Daimler Benz of Berlin. One prototype was produced, but the further 40 vehicles ordered were subsequently cancelled.

Meanwhile, in July, 1934, Wa.Prüf. 6 placed an order for the design of a slightly bigger tank, in the 10-ton weight class, with Henschel, M.A.N. and Krupp, each of whom designed and produced prototypes. Trials of these prototypes took place at Ulm Proving Ground under the supervision of Wa.Prüf. 6 throughout 1935, as a result of which the M.A.N. version was accepted and subsequently put into production. This vehicle was known as the 'La.S.100' and was produced by the same firms (excluding Rheinmetall Borsig) as was the La.S. There followed a period of continual modification and improvement during which approximately 3000 vehicles were produced by Henschel, Alkett, M.A.N. and M.I.A.G.(Muhlenbau und Industrie,A.G.) in five different models, with chassis numbers as follows:-

Model	a 1	Nos.	20001 - 20025	)
	" a 2		20026 - 20050	)
	a 3		20051 - 21000	) M.A.N. version
	" b		21001 - 21100	)
	" c		21101 - 23000	)

These models were followed in 1937 by the Model A and in 1938 by Models B and C. Models D and E, designed by Daimler Benz, appeared in 1939 with normal armament, but by June, 1940 had all been converted to flamethrower tanks and redesignated Pz.Kpfw.II (F). The Model F, incorporating much thicker armour, was in production by June, 1941 and was the last direct development of the La.S.100. On being taken into operational use, the La.S.100 became known as the Pz.Kpfw.II (Sd.Kfz.121). The total number of Pz.Kpfw.I and Pz.Kpfw.II tank chassis (of which many were used as S.P. mountings) produced in the period 1940 - Jan, 1944 inclusive was 632, with a maximum monthly average of 25 in 1942.

A further development of the Pz.Kpfw.II, Models D and E, the VK 1,601, was designed by Daimler Benz in September, 1939. A prototype of this vehicle, having thicker armour, a redesigned turret (the basis of the Panther Model D turret) and a suspension consisting of 5 twin overlapping rubber tyred bogie wheels per side was produced, but was not accepted, owing to the comparatively weak fire power (2 cm. Kw.K.30 and coaxial M.G.) for the weight of 16 tons. This vehicle was subsequently converted into an A.R.V. and was captured in 21 A.Gp. Area in January, 1945. A second prototype, the VK 1602, mounted a 5 cm Kw.K39/1 in place of the

/2 cm.

2 cm. KwK.38. However, this project, to have been called 'Leopard'
(light), never progressed beyond the wooden mock-up stage (see below). A
lighter vehicle of similar design and with 2 cm. main armament was
accordingly designed in the autumn of 1941 by Daimler Benz and M.A.N.,
known as the VK.901. 3 prototypes were produced but were again turned
down, this time as being too light for reconnaissance. Wa.Prüf. 6 then set
a weight of 13 metric tons in a new order, again given to Daimler Benz
(turret and superstructure) and M.A.N. (hull and chassis) for the VK 1301,
a vehicle which was externally almost identical to the VK 901. A mild
steel prototype was produced at the end of April, 1942, was accepted, and
from it the VK 1303 (or Lynx) went into production in August 1942. On being
taken into service, this vehicle became known as the Pz.Kpfw.II Model L.
The original contract was for 800 vehicles, of which the first 100 were to
mount the 2 cm. Kw.K.38 and vehicles from number 101 onwards (from April, 1943),
the 5 cm. Kw.K.39 (L/60) as main armament. This latter version which was
to have been called the 'Leopard' (light) (VK 1602) was never produced, however,
and the turret (slightly modified) was subsequently used for the 8 wheeled
Armoured Car 'Puma' (Sd.Kfz.234/2) and also as a model for the small-fronted
'Panther' turret (Panther 'schmal' turm). 131 'Lynx' vehicles were
scheduled to be produced by 12 May, 1943. A further version of the
Pz.Kpfw.II weighing 22 tons, mounting a long 7.5 cm. gun (Kw.K.41) and to be
known as 'Leopard' (heavy) was intended to be produced from October, 1943,
but production was never started as this vehicle too nearly resembled existing
vehicles such as the Pz.Kpfw.IV and Panther.

Orders for the development of a tank in the 15-ton weight class had
meanwhile been placed by Wa.Prüf. 6 with M.A.N. Daimler Benz and
Rheinmetall Borsig in 1936. The three resulting prototypes were tested
at Kummersdorf and Ulm (nr. Muensingen) Proving Grounds from late 1936
to the end of 1937. Production of the Daimler Benz design, known as the Z.W.
(Zugführerwagen), was entrusted to Henschel, M.A.N. and Daimler Benz. There
followed a period of continuous development, 5 models, A, B, C, D and E
(of each of which only small numbers were produced) making their appearance
by 1939. It is believed that 10 of the Model A, 15 Model C, 55 Model D
(converted to Commander's tanks) and 100 Model E were produced. Production
of the Model F, of which 450 were produced, started in 1939, Models G and H
appeared in 1941, Models J, L and M in 1942 and Model N (mounting the 7.5
cm. Kw.K L/24) in 1943. The 'ZW' was first used operationally in Poland in
September, 1939 and became known as the Pz.Kpfw.III (Sd.Kfz.141). The total
number of Pz.Kpfw.III produced from 1940 to August, 1943, inclusive, was
5,644, 20 being produced in the last month, and the maximum production of 213
vehicles was attained in 1942.

In the spring of 1935, Krupp, Rheinmetall Borsig and M.A.N. submitted
tentative designs for a tank in the 20-ton weight class, the VK 2001 or
BW (Bataillonsführer Wagen), of which the Krupp version was accepted by the
Heereswaffenamt. The prototype underwent trials at Ulm and Kummersdorf in
1937, in which year the Krupp design was put into production. Three models
(A, B and C) had been produced by 1939, Models B and C being battle-tested
in the Polish Campaign. The resulting modifications were incorporated in the
Model D, which was produced in late 1940. Models E and F1 appeared in 1941,
Models F2 and G, mounting the 7.5 cm. Kw.K 40 (L/43), in 1942. The BW, which
was now known as the Pz.Kpfw.IV (Sd.Kfz.161) was still further upgunned
in Models H, produced in 1943, and J, produced in 1944, the length of the
7.5 cm. Kw.K.40 being increased from 43 to 48 calibres. Comparatively small
numbers only were produced of Models A, B and C (200, 100 and 200 respectively).
Of the other Models, however, from 1940 to February, 1945 inclusive, 280 were
produced in 1940, 480 in 1941, 964 in 1942, 3073 in 1943, 3366 in 1944 and
343 in January and February, 1945. The maximum monthly production was
334, attained in June, 1944. It should be borne in mind, however, that a
considerable proportion of these vehicles was converted to S.P. carriages.
Another VK 2001 was designed in 1942 by Daimler Benz, the main features of
which were later incorporated in their VK 3001 prototype, but was not
accepted by the Heereswaffenamt for production.

/The next.

The next tank to be introduced into service was the Pz.Kpfw. Tiger Model E, originally ordered by Wa.Prüf. 6 as a 45-ton tank under the code name of VK 4501. The design was placed with two firms, Henschel u. Sohn G.m.b.H., of Kassel and Dr.Ing. h.c.F. Porsche, K.G. of Stuttgart/Zuffenhausen. The origin of the final Henschel design can be traced back to the end of 1937, when Henschel were ordered to design and construct a 30 - 33-ton tank to be called the D.W.1. (Durchbruchswagen 1.). After one chassis had been built and trials commenced Wa.Prüf. 6, in 1938, ordered the design and construction of a 65-ton tank, the VK 6501 (also known as the 'SW' or Pz.Kpfw. VII), during which time work on the D.W.1. was suspended. Two prototypes were built and partial trials had been carried out when the order was cancelled, and trials of the D.W.1. were subsequently resumed until 1940, in which year Henschel developed from it a further tank, in the same weight class, known as the D.W.2. One prototype chassis was built and trials on this chassis were carried out until 1941, but it never went into production. A further order for another design of tank in the same weight class was then received in 1941 from Wa.Prüf. 6 under the code name of VK 3001, an order which was also given to Porsche K.G., Daimler Benz and M.A.N. The Henschel version was a development of the D.W.2, and 4 prototypes, differing only in detail, were produced, 2 in March, 1942 and 2 in October of the same year. Simultaneously an order for a 36-ton design, the VK 3601 had been placed, and a prototype of this vehicle was also produced in March, 1946. Design work on these projects, however, had to stop when the order for the VK 4501 was placed late in 1941. As the prototypes of this vehicle were ordered by Speer to be ready in time for Hitler's birthday on the 20th April, 1942, design time was limited and Henschel decided merely to incorporate the best features of the above-mentioned experimental tanks into a vehicle of the specified size and weight, known as the VK 4501(H) or Pz.Kpfw.VI (H).

The history of the VK 4501(P) designed by Porsche dates back to the order, given to Porsche K.G., Henschel, Daimler Benz and M.A.N., for the design of a 30-ton vehicle, the VK 3001. A prototype was designed and produced by Porsche and became colloquially known within the firm as the 'Leopard'. Before assembly had been completed, the order was cancelled by the Heereswaffenamt on the personal decision of Hitler that it required an 8.8 cm. gun instead of the 7.5 cm. (L/48) gun for which it was originally designed. A new design (colloquially known as Tiger) was therefore ordered under the code name of VK4501 (or Type 101 in Porsche nomenclature), although permission was given to complete the running trials of 'Leopard' as it incorporated several novel design features such as petrol-electric drive, longitudinal torsion bar suspension, etc. As the 'Leopard' running trials were successful, it was decided to incorporate the electric transmission and the suspension in the VK 4501 (P), a prototype of which was completed on the 17th April, 1942.

The demonstration of the VK's 4501(H) and (P) duly took place before Hitler at Rastenburg on the 20th April, 1942 as a result of which (and subsequent) trials the Henschel vehicle was adjudged to be superior and an order for its production, to start in August, 1942, was given. As however, an initial order for the construction of 90 Porsche vehicles was well under way, it was decided to complete this contract and convert the vehicles into S.P. carriages for the 8.8 cm. (L/71) gun, the resulting equipment being known, at first, as the 'Ferdinand' (after Dr. Ferdinand Porsche) and later as 'Elefant'.

/The Henschel

The Henschel design later became known as the Pz.Kpfw. Tiger, Model E (Sd.Kfz.181), and, in the two years (August, 1942 - August, 1944) of its production life a total of 1350 vehicles out of the 1376 ordered were produced, chassis numbers ranging in a continuous series from 250001 to 251350. Maximum production in any one month was attained in April, 1944, when 104 tanks were produced. It is of interest to note that the specified weight of 45 tons was exceeded, in the production model, by as much as 11 tons with the vehicle in action.

The next tank to be introduced into service was the Pz.Kpfw. Panther (Sd.Kfz.171), developed from the VK 3001 (D) and VK 3002(MAN) designed, by Daimler Benz and M.A.N. respectively, in 1941. The VK 3001(D) was based on the T.34, and was approximately the same size although mounting a 7.5 cm. (L/48) gun. The Daimler Benz design was chosen by Hitler personally in March, 1942 as being the better of the two, although stating that an increase in armament to a 7.5 cm. (L/70) gun was desirable, and an initial order for 200 such modified vehicles was given. However, the M.A.N. design was subsequently accepted by Wa.Prüf. 6 and was put into production as the Pz.Kpfw. Panther. The Panther weighed 45 tons in action, and was at first (November and December, 1942) produced only by M.A.N. and Daimler Benz; M.N.H. and Henschel (200 vehicles only, produced in 1943) coming into production in January, 1943. Production by M.A.N. started in November, 1942, and by May, 1943 the combined monthly production had reached 324 vehicles. A monthly production average of 154 vehicles in 1943 and 330 in 1944 was maintained. The total number produced up to and including February, 1945 (in which month 135 were built) was 4814 vehicles. 3 models of this tank were operationally used, Models D, A and G in that order, differing slightly as regards auxiliary armament, armour thickness, etc., and, in addition, an A.R.V. based on the Panther chassis, known as the Pz. Berge.Wg.Panther, was also produced in small numbers. The production figures of this latter vehicle are included in the overall Panther figures given above.

Meanwhile in the Autumn of 1942, Wa.Prüf. 6 had given Henschel the order to design a heavier development (the VK 4503) of the Pz. Kpfw. Tiger Model E, incorporating thicker armour, sloped plates as on the Panther and Russian T. 34, and an 8.8 cm. (L/71) gun as main armament. Porsche also redesigned his 'Tiger' to conform to this new specification, the new design being known as the Type 180. His first design, with the turret forward and engine at the rear was turned down due to the large overhang of the gun, so a second type with a rear turret and forward engine was submitted. This was also turned down due to the shortage of copper (required in the electric transmission) and Porsche turned his full attention to the 'Maus' (Type 205) mentioned in Section 4. Design work by Henschel was duly completed and a prototype Pz.Kpfw. Tiger Model B or Tiger II (Sd.Kfz.182), as this vehicle became known, was finished in October, 1943, three months behind the original schedule due to the insistence of Wa.Prüf. 6 that, for simplification of production, the vehicle should incorporate several components and design features of the experimental M.A.N. Panther II. Production of the Tiger Model B started in December, 1943, when one vehicle was produced. The first 50 vehicles to be completed were fitted with spare turrets originally intended for the Porsche Tiger (Type 180) but rendered

/superfluous

superfluous by the rejection of the latter vehicle. The remaining production vehicles were fitted with a modified turret, specially designed for the Tiger Model B, having thicker armour and eliminating the re-entrant angle under the trunnion axis. Production of this tank by Henschel continued up to the time of the German surrender. By 31st March, 1945, 485 vehicles had been completed as against 512 scheduled, the maximum production attained in any one month being 84 in August 1944. The total order was for 950 tigers Model B, to have been completed by September, 1945, and to attain this figure Henschel had to sub-contract to Nibelungenwerke of St. Valentin the production of 100 vehicles, to commence in May 1945. Chassis numbers allotted to the Tiger B commenced at 280001 and, in a continuous sequence, had reached 280485 on 31st March, 1945.

The foregoing paragraphs give a general picture of the sequence of development leading up to the design and introduction of all tanks taken into service as standard equipment in the German Army, as far as can be ascertained from the firms, documents and personalities to which we have had access. Information from Nibelungenwerke, Alkett, Daimler Benz and Vomag of Plauen has been scanty, as these firms are or have been, in the Russian Zone of Occupation. The various projects on the drawing board and in various stages of construction at the time of the German surrender together with those equipments which were built but never taken into service are mentioned in a subsequent section. A further section deals with the development of the main tank components such as engines, suspensions etc.

4. Tanks of foreign design used operationally by the German Army

Foreign tanks used by the Germans were chiefly those types designed and produced in countries under German occupation, very little use being made of British, American, or Russian vehicles captured in action. Tanks taken into use were generally those to which no similar type already existed in the German Army, and, on being taken into service, the nomenclature of the country of origin was dropped in favour of the German "Fremde Gerät" number of the particular vehicle. The German Heereswaffenamt had anticipated such a situation by classifying all foreign weapons and equipment ("Fremden Geräts") by a number, followed in brackets by the initial letter of the country of origin.

The foreign tank most used by the German Army was the Czech "L.T.H." light tank, known by the Germans as the Pz. Kpfw. 38 (t). This vehicle, modified in various forms, was used throughout the war either as a tank or as an S.P. Carriage, all production taking place at the Skoda Works near Pilsen. No other foreign tank was employed on such a scale, but limited use was made of certain French vehicles such as the Char B, Hotchkiss H.39, Renault A.M.C. 35 and R.35, Hotchkiss H.35, F.C.M., and Somua S.35 and S.40, as tanks (chiefly in the Balkans and Norway) and as S.P. Carriages.

/5 Unsuccessful

5. Unsuccessful and unfinished tank projects

Apart from those unsuccessful designs mentioned in Section 3 which were in the direct line of development of tanks taken into operational use, many other designs were produced from 1921 onwards to Wa.Prüf. 6 and OKH specifications or as provate ventures, which were never fully developed or taken into service.

Among the earliest and most important of these was the so-called 'Pz.Kpfw.V' and its successor, the 'Pz.Kpfw.VI', 23-ton tanks of which propaganda photographs were seen in 1938-1939 and again in the Norwegian campaign. The Pz.Kpfw.V. and VI are believed to have been designed in 1933, and 5 built, by Rheinmetall Borsig and Krupp, and were officially known as 'Nb.Fz' (neubaufahrzeuge). They were designed with a main turret and two auxiliary turrets rather on the lines of the Vickers 'Independent' tank and had little, if any, resemblance to earlier German designs. The armour was, however, very thin, and the armament too light for the overall vehicle weight, and a large crew was needed. The Nb.Fz. was never taken into service, except as a training vehicle at Putlos tank training school, a platform from which the Führer made speeches, and as a propaganda weapon in the Norwegian Campaign.

A heavier version of the Pz.Kpfw.I n.A. (VK.601), known as the VK 1801 or Pz.Kpfw.I n.A.(verst.), was ordered in December, 1939 and a complete prototype was delivered by Krauss - Maffei and Daimler Benz in June, 1940. The production series of 100 vehicles was subsequently cancelled, however.

Probably the tank which came nearest to being taken into service was the super-heavy (180 ton), Porsche-designed 'Maus' (formerly 'Mammut'), which had a long and chequered production career. The order for the design of a tank in the 150-ton weight class appears to have been given verbally to Dr. Porsche by Hitler on the 8th June, 1942 as some compensation for the rejection by the Heereswaffenamt of the Porsche 'Tiger', mentioned in Chapter 2. Design work was accordingly started under the project number of Type 205, several features (notably the longitudinal torsion bar bogie type of suspension and the petrol-electric drive) of the Porsche Tiger being incorporated. A model of this vehicle was shown to Hitler on 4th January, 1943, but, due to various modifications ordered in the armament, and delays in the supply of the engine, production was delayed. Assembly of the first prototype was begun by Alkett on 1st August, 1943, and it had its first trial run on 23rd December, 1943, with a massive weight in place of the turret. Trials then took place at Böblingen (near Stuttgart) until May, 1944, when, on receipt of the turret and armament from Krupp's final assembly was begun and finished by 9th June. A second prototype had also been built, meanwhile, and arrived at Böblingen on 20th March, 1944. Due to the deterioration in the war situation, however, work on the project was stopped and both prototypes were sent to Kummersdorf in October/November, where they were blown up before the proving ground there was overrun. Several hulls and turrets were found both on the Krupp proving ground at Meppen, where a specimen of the main armament in a proof mounting was also found, and in the Krupp's works at Essen after Germany's surrender, and it appears that production of at least 10 prototype vehicles was originally intended.

/The 'Maus'

The 'Maus' project appears to have been an unofficial one, the usual channels being short-circuited and the order given direct by Hitler to Porsche. The Heereswaffenamt, however, also had two projects for super-heavy tanks, one, the E.100, forming part of a whole new series of tanks to be introduced in late 1945/46 and the other 'Löwe' (Lion), or VK 7001 designed by Krupp. Both were ordered as a counterblast to the 'Maus' and were intended to mount the same main armament as that tank. The VK 7001 (also known as 'Tiger-Maus') never progressed beyond the drawing board, and consisted essentially of a Royal Tiger modified to mount the 12.8 cm. (L/55) and coaxial 7.5 cm. guns of the 'Maus'. The E.100, a heavier (140 tons) vehicle designed by Adler in co-operation with Henschel, was a new design, larger than, but bearing some resemblance to the Royal Tiger, and a prototype was, at the surrender, in process of assembly on the Henschel proving ground at Haustenbeck.

The series of tanks of which the E.100 formed part contained five other vehicles, the E.5 (weight in action approx 5 tons), the E.10 (in the Pz.Kpfw.38(t) Class) the E.25 (in the Pz.Kpfw.III and IV class), the E.50 (in the Panther/Tiger Class) and the E.75 (Royal Tiger class). The complete series was intended to replace all existing tanks and to make use of standardized components, although they never progressed further than the drawing board. The E.10 is believed to have been designed by Wa.Prüf. 6 and Klöckner - Humboldt - Deutz, the E.25 by Argus, and the E.50 by Argus and/or Auto-Union.

As an interim measure, to increase production of tanks in the Pz.Kpfw. III and IV class, the Pz.Kpfw.III/IV was designed, embodying the components of the III and IV. A large scale production of this vehicle was intended, but the programme was cancelled owing to the war situation before any had been completely assembled.

Further development of the Panther was also intended, and a small-fronted turret modelled on that (mounting a 5 cm. gun) of the VK 1602 was developed by Daimler Benz for the Panther Model F. This turret gave greater protection for the same weight. Numerous other refinements, such as a 1.32 metre-base range-finder and the latest type of periscopic sight (T.W.Z.F.), were also incorporated, and it was intended ultimately to mount the 8.8 cm. Kw.K.43 (L/71) in a larger turret. Only mock-ups and demonstration models of this turret were, however, produced.

Before the E.5 was projected, there were two other definite projects for a light, two-man tank in the 3-5 tons weight class, known as the VK 301 and VK 501. These were believed to have been designed by Weserhütte and Büssing NAG respectively. In addition, approximately 20 other designs for similar vehicles had been tentatively produced and subsequently rejected by Wa.Prüf. 6.

6. Main Component Development

(a) Armament

Briefly, the story of the development of German tank armament from 1933 to 1945 is one of continuous increases in calibre, weight of projectile and barrel length (and consequently, muzzle velocity). The main armament, in general, consisted of a high velocity anti-tank gun with a coaxial 7.92 mm. M.G., while an auxiliary M.G. was usually ball-mounted in the front vertical (or glacis) plate.

The Pz.Kpfw.I, being a light tank, was armed with two turret-mounted coaxial 7.92 mm. M.Gs. 13, while in the Pz.Kpfw.II the left-hand M.G. was increased in calibre to 2. cm. (2 cm. Kw.K. 30 or 38). The early models (A, B, C and D) of the Pz.Kpfw.III mounted a 3.7 cm.Kw.K (same ammunition and ballistics as 3.7 cm.Pak) with two coaxial 7.92 mm. M.Gs. 34 in the

/turret,

turret, and one M.G.-34 in a gimbal mounting on the offside of the front vertical plate. In Models E to early J inclusive, the main armament was increased to 5 cm. in calibre (5 cm. Kw.K (L/42)) with only one coaxial M.G. 34, while in later Models J to M inclusive, a longer 5 cm. gun (the 5 cm. Kw.K.39 (L/60)) was substituted. This had the chamber lengthened to take the 5 cm. Pak 38 cartridge. Final development of the Pz.Kpfw.III main armament came with the Model N, which mounted the short, low velocity, 7.5 cm. Kw.K (L/24) rendered superfluous by the up-gunning of the later Models of the Pz.Kpfw.IV.

The early models of the next tank to be introduced, the Pz.Kpfw.IV, mounted the 7.5 cm. Kw.K. (L/24) as stated above, together with a coaxial M.G. 34 and, in the case of Models A, D, E and F, an auxiliary hull-mounted M.G. 34. With the introduction of Models F2 and G the length of the 7.5 cm. gun was increased to 43 calibres (7.5 cm. Kw.K.40 (L/43)), thus altering its role from that of a low velocity H.E. firing weapon to high velocity anti-tank. Models H and J of this tank mounted a gun with an even longer barrel, 48 calibres long, the 7.5 cm. Kw.K.40 (L/48). The Kw.K.40 appears to have been designed to give the same ballistics as the Pak 40, but with a short, necked cartridge case instead of the long parallel-sided case of the A.T. gun.

The Pz.Kpfw.Panther replaced the Pz.Kpfw.III and IV in the armoured divisions, and although heavier than its predecessors, it retained the calibre of 7.5 cm. for its main armament (7.5 cm. Kw.K.42 (L/70)). The length of the gun (70 calibres) was, however, considerably greater than that of the latest Pz.Kpfw.IV. A coaxial 7.92 mm M.G. 34 was also provided in all models, but the hull M.G. was omitted in the earliest model, the Model D.

It is of interest to note here that the Germans found it necessary to provide a muzzle brake for all tank guns of 7.5 cm. calibre and above with a calibre-length of more than 40 when mounted in turrets, where recoil is relatively short. In early designs, a spherical single-baffle brake was used, but these were later replaced by a double baffle type, the inner baffle having a renewable insert.

With the introduction of the slower, heavy tank Pz.Kpfw. Tiger Model E, a change from 7.5 cm. to 8.8 cm. was made in the calibre of the main armament with the mounting of the 8.8 cm. Kw.K.36 (L/56), while the subsidiary armament again consisted of one coaxial 7.92 mm. M.G. 34 and a similar gun in a ball mounting in the front vertical plate. The 8.8 cm. calibre main armament and the subsidiary armament were retained in the Tiger Model E's successor, the Pz.Kpfw. Tiger Model B, although in the latter vehicle, the calibre length of the 8.8 cm. gun was increased to 71 (8.8 cm. Kw.K.43(L/71)). This gun represents the largest calibre and calibre length employed operationally by the Germans in a tank mounting. The Pz.Kpfw. 'Maus', 'Löwe', and 'E.100' were, however, to have mounted the 12.8 cm. Kw.K.82 (L/55) or 15 cm. Kw.K.44 (L/38) and a coaxial 7.5 cm. Kw.K.44 (L/36.5), while 7.5 cm., 8.8 cm., 10.5 cm. and even 15 cm. guns with calibre lengths up to 100 were in various stages of design, construction or trial.

All German tank guns had similar main features, such as electric primer firing, recoil gear consisting of hydraulic buffer and hydro-pneumatic recuperator, semi-automatic breech operation with spring opening and closing and vertical sliding wedge breech blocks. All guns (except the 12.8 cm. Kw.K.82 (L/55)) employed fixed Q.F. ammunition of H.E. (fuzed D.A. or Graze) and APCBC shell types. In most cases, composite-rigid, tungsten-carbide-cored projectiles were also originally provided, although supply of these projectiles was stopped later in the war owing to shortage of tungsten-carbide. In the case of the lower velocity guns, hollow charge and smoke ammunition was also fired. Balance of the main armament was achieved artificially by a coil-spring cylinder or a torsion bar in earlier vehicles (up to the Pz.Kpfw. Tiger model E) and by a hydro-pneumatic cylinder in subsequent tanks. A table of operational German tank guns appears at Table I below

/Sighting

Sighting of the main armament was accomplished by means of an articulated stationary-eyepiece, moving and illuminated graticule, telescope, monocular in the case of the Pz.Kpfw. I, II, III and IV, binocular in the Pz.Kpfw. Tiger Model E, Panther Model D and the first fifty Tiger Model B, with a magnification of approx. 2.5, field of 25° and an exit pupil diameter of 5 - 6 mm. On later models of the Panther, and the remainder of the Pz.Kpfw. Tiger Model B, the binocular sight was abandoned in favour of a monocular, dual-magnification telescope also a stationary eyepiece type. For future vehicles, a standard periscopic sight, the W.Z.F. (Winkelzielfernrohr) or T.W.Z.F. (when used in turrets) had been put into production, as well as a standard design of built-in stereoscopic range-finder. It was ultimately intended to stabilize the sight in elevation, and, if possible the turret, armament and sight in azimuth and elevation.

Full provision for indirect fire was never made on German tanks, although a clinometer was provided on the Pz.Kpfw.IV Models F2 and G and the Pz.Kpfw. Tiger Model E. Traverse indicators marked in clock hours from 1 to 12 were also provided for the commander (a ring in the cupola, driven from the turret rack) and the gunner (a small single or double dial, also driven from the turret rack). In some tanks the traverse indicator and a second dial, sub-divided into 100 mils for indirect fire.

A sighting vane or fixed open sight was usually provided on the turret roof in front of the commander. Ball mounted M.G's were invariably sighted by the cranked moving eyepiece telescope K.Z.F.2. A table of German telescopic tank sights taken into service is reproduced below as table II.

(b) Armour and Construction

Generally speaking, the aim of the German tank designer with regard to armour was always to make the front of the tank immune to its own gun (the calibre and length of which were stated first in the specification) at any given range, and the sides and rear immune at longer ranges only. Thus we find a continuous strengthening of German tank armour with each new tank introduced, and not infrequently, with new models of existing tanks. This strengthening was obtained in earlier tanks by face-hardening, bolted or welded appliqué armour and spaced plates. In later designs, thicker, well-sloped homogeneous rolled armour was employed, all joints being welded and interlocked, or pegged. This armour as a whole was softer than earlier, and thinner, homo-armour, and no face hardening was employed.

As protection against hollow charge projectiles, mild steel skirting plates, or wire mesh on the Pz.Kpfw.IV Model J, were introduced. The use of cast armour was restricted to gun mantlets, ball-mounting housings and other small parts.

(c) Power Plant

With the exception of the Pz.Kpfw.I Model A, which employed a 60 H.P. Krupp engine, the power plant of all operational German tanks was designed by Maybach Motorenbau G.m.b.H. of Friedrichshafen and built by Maybach and Nordbau of Berlin. This Maybach monopoly was no doubt due to the friendship between Dr. Maybach and Kniepkamp of Wa.Prüf. 6. All Maybach tank engines were of water-cooled carburetted petrol type, those fitted to the Pz.Kpfw.I and II being of 6-cylinder in line, and later ones of 12-cylinder Vee arrangement. The largest engine used operationally, the HL 230 mounted in the Tiger and Panther tanks, had an output of 594 BHP at 2,600 r.p.m. A table giving leading data of all German tank engines taken into service appears below as Table III.

TABLE I – GERMAN TANK GUNS TAKEN INTO SERVICE

a) Automatic weapons.

Weapon	Calibre	Used in	Weight	Overall length	Cyclic rate of fire	Cooling	Feed	Method of operation	M.V. (A.P.)	Remarks
M.G.13K (Dreyse)	7.92 mm.	Pz. Kpfw. I.	23.9 lbs.	55.75 ins (incl. butt)	625 (trials in England)	Air	Box (25 rds or 100 rds) or Drum (50 rds)	Recoil	2525 f.s.	Differences from M.G.13 ground model not known.
M.G.34	7.92 mm.	All subsequent German tanks.	25.5 lbs.	40.75 ins.	800-900 r.p.m.	Air	Metal link belts each containing 150 rds. (carried in belt bags. Also boxes containing 100 rds (Armd cars) or 50 rd belt drum.	Recoil assisted by muzzle blast.	2525 f.s.	Formerly saddle type magazine containing 75 rds. Differs from ground pattern in having thick (armoured) barrel casing.
Kw.K.30	2 cm.	Pz.Kpfw. II and Lynx, and Panther A.R.V.	139 lbs.	6 ft. 4¼ in.	280 r.p.m	Air	10 rd. mag.	Recoil	2625 f.s.	Shorter barrels than Flak 30 and 38. Lower M.Vs. Later models of Kw. K. 38 had some barrel length as Flak 38.
Kw.K.38	2 cm.		123 lbs.	6 ft. 4 5/8 in.	420-480 r.p.m.	Air	10 rd. magazine		2625 f.s.	Superseded 2 cm. Kw. K. 30.

b) Semi-automatic weapons.

Type and calibre of gun	3.7 cm.(1.46 in.) Kw.K.(L/45)	5 cm.(1.97 in.) Kw.K.(L/42)	5 cm. (1.97 in.) Kw.K.39(L/60)	7.5 cm.(2.95 in.) Kw.K(L/24)	7.5 cm.(2.95 in.) Kw.K.40(L/43)	7.5 cm.(2.95 in.) Kw.K.40(L/48)	7.5 cm.(2.95 in.) Kw.K.42(L/70)	8.8 cm.(3.46 in.) Kw.K.36(L/56)	8.8 cm.(3.46 in.) Kw.K.43(L/71)
Used in	Pz.Kpfw.III. Models A,B,C,D.	Pz.Kpfw.III. Models E,F,G,H, and early J.	Pz.Kpfw.III. Late Models J, L and M.	Pz.Kpfw.III. Model N. Pz.Kpfw.IV. Models A to F.	Pz.Kpfw.IV. Models F2 and G.	Pz.Kpfw.IV. Models H and J.	Pz.Kpfw.Panther. Models D.A.G.	Pz.Kpfw.Tiger Model E.	Pz.Kpfw. Tiger Model B.
Length of rifling (ins)	51.49	64.75	87.84	51.5	97.12	112.12	171.38	161.1	203.87
Length of chamber (ins)	10.20	11.1	17.1	10.23	20.03	20.03	27.12	23.6	33.87
Length of bore (ins)	61.69	75.85	104.94	61.73	117.15	132.15	198.50	184.7	237.74
Length of bore (cals)	42.3	38.5	53.2	20.9	39.7	44.8	67.3	53.3	68.7
Depth of breech opening (ins)	5.86	6.39	6.39	7.88	9.45	9.45	8.25	9.6	10.26
Length of piece (ins)	67.55	82.24	111.33	69.61	126.6	141.6	206.75	194.3	248
Length of piece (cals)	46.5	42	60	24	43	48	70	56.1	71.6
Additional length of muzzle brake (ins)	–	–	–	12	12	12	11.25	15.1	15.18
Overall length of piece (ins)	67.55	82.24	111.33	69.61	138.6	153.6	218	209.4	265.18
Weight of piece complete (incl. muzzle brake) (lbs)	430	492	672	628	1041	1094	2390	2932	3726
Rifling – No. of grooves	16	16	20	28	32	32	32	32	32
Depth of grooves (mm.)	0.45	0.7	0.76	0.85	0.9	0.9	0.3	1.05	1.2
Width of grooves (mm.)	4.765	5.82	4.57	5.1	3.86	3.86	3.86	5.34	5.04
Twist	Increasing R.H. 1 in 50 to 1 in 30	Increasing R.H. 1 in 42 to 1 in 30	Increasing R.H. 1 in 42 to 1 in 30	Increasing R.H. 1 in 35 to 1 in 36 (later uniform 1 in 25.8)	Increasing R.H. 1 in 29.39 to 1 in 19.84	Uniform R.H. 1 in 25.8	Uniform R.H. 1 in 27.57	Increasing R.H. 1 in 45 to 1 in 30	Uniform R.H. 1 in 27.57
Effective chamber capacity (c.cs.)	280	900	1250	1000	3170	3170	5100	3650	9000
Cartridge case design No.	6331	6317	6360	6354	6339	6339	6387	6347	6388
Weight of cart.case complete with primer (lbs)	1.17	1.9	2.5	2.1	6.06	6.06	6.75	14
Wt. of APCBC proj. (lbs)	1.5(AP)	4.53(AP)	4.53(APC)	14.9	15	15	15	20.75	22.25

M.V. of APCBC proj. (f.s.)	2445	2247	2700	1263	2428	2461	3063	2657	3340
Penetration at 500 yds/30° (mm.)	30	56	61	41	89	-	141	110	132
Max. recoil (mm.)	245 (normal)	335	335	455	505	505	420	580	570
Firing mechanism	Electric primer	Electric primer	Electric primer	Electric primer	Electric primer	Electric primer	Electric primer	Electric primer	Electric primer
Breech		SEMI		AUTOMATIC	SLIDING	WEDGE			
Types of ammunition	AP	AP	AP	APCBC	-	-	APCBC	APCBC	APCBC
	-	APC	APC	-	APCBC	APCBC	AP/CR	AP/CR	AP/CR
	AP/CR composite rigid	AP/CR	AP/CR	HE/AT	AP/CR	AP/CR	-	HE/AT	HE/AT
	H.E.	H.E.	H.E.	H.E.	HE/AT	HE/AT	H.E.	H.E.	H.E.
	-	-	-	Smoke	H.E.	H.E.	-	-	-
				Case Shot	Smoke	Smoke			

TABLE II - GERMAN TANK TELESCOPIC SIGHTS

A. TURRET SIGHTING TELESCOPES

Type	Used on	Guns and ammunition	Range Scales (Metres)	Mag. (X)	Field (Deg.)	Overall length (less eye guard) (Ins)	Weight (lbs.)	Exit pupil dis. (mm.)	Entrance pupil dis. (mm.)	Design	Remarks
T.Z.F.2 and 2¹	Pz.Kpfw.I. Models A and B	7.92 mm. MG.13	None	2.5	28	19	19	5.2	13	Zeiss	It is not known with what gun the T.Z.F.2. was used, nor in which vehicle. Monocular.
T.Z.F.4	Pz.Kpfw.II. Models A to C	2 cm. Kw.K.30 7.92 mm. MG.34	1200	2.5	25	22.5	20	7	17.5	Leitz	First confirmed Leitz design. Monocular.
T.Z.F.4b/1	Turret MG.42 on Commander's Tanks	MG.42	1500	2.5	23°15'	22.5	26	6	15	Leitz	Monocular
T.Z.F.4/36 and 4/38	Pz.Kpfw.II. Model F.	2 cm. Kw.K.30 7.92 mm. MG.34	1200 800	2.5	25	22.5	21	7	17.5	Leitz	The range of 800 metres applies to T.Z.F.4/36 and that of 1200 metres to T.Z.F.4/38. Monocular.
T.Z.F.5a	Pz.Kpfw.III. Models A to D.	3.7 cm. Kw.K.(AP and HE) 7.92 mm. MG.34	2000 800	2.5	25	32.25	24	5	12.5	Leitz	Monocular.
T.Z.F.5a (Vorl) 5 cm.	Pz.Kpfw.III. Model E etc. (see Remarks)	5 cm. Kw.K.(AP and HE) 7.92 mm. MG.34	2000 1500	2.5	25	32.25	21.5	5	12.5	Leitz	Monocular. Modified T.Z.F.5a, superseded by T.Z.F.5e.
T.Z.F.5b	Pz.Kpfw.III with 7.5 cm. Kw.K. Models J to N. Pz.Kpfw.IV. Models B to F.	7.5 cm. Kw.K. 7.92 mm. MG.34	2000 800	2.4	23.5	32.25	21.5	5	12.5	Leitz	Monocular.
T.Z.F.5b/36	Pz.Kpfw.IV. Models B to F.	7.5 cm. Kw.K. 7.92 mm. MG.34	2000 800	2.4	23.5	32.25	23	6	14.4	Leitz	Monocular.
T.Z.F.5d	Pz.Kpfw.III. Models F and J.	5 cm. Kw.K.(APC and HE) 7.92 mm. MG.34	3000 1500	2.4	25	31.8	20.13	5.5	13.2	Leitz	Monocular.
T.Z.F.5e	Pz.Kpfw.III. Models L and M.	5 cm. Kw.K.39 A.P. or A.P.C. H.E. 7.92 mm. MG.34	1500 3000 1200	2.4	25	31.8	20.13	5.5	13.2	Leitz	Monocular.
T.Z.F.5f (Vorl)	Pz.Kpfw.IV. Models F2 to H.	7.5 cm. Kw.K.40 APCBC HE A.P.40 7.92 mm. MG.34	2500 3300 1500 (see Remarks)	2.4	25	31.8	20.13	5.5	13.2	Leitz	Monocular.
T.Z.F.5f.1. and f.2.	Pz.Kpfw.IV. Models G to J.	7.5 cm. Kw.K.40 APCBC HE A.P.40 Hollow charge 7.92 mm. MG.34	3000 4000 2000 3400 (see Remarks)	2.5	25	32	26	6	15	Leitz	Monocular. The Hollow Charge scale serves for the M.G. also.
T.Z.F.6 and 6/38.	Pz.Sp.Wg.II(Pz.Kpfw.II. Model L (Luchs) Sd.Kfz.123	2 cm. Kw.K.30 and 38) and 7.92 mm. MG.34)	1200	2.4	22	28.4	21	5	12	Leitz	Monocular.
T.Z.F.9b and b/1	Pz.Kpfw.Tiger Model E. (T.Z.F.96 and early models B) (T.Z.F.96/1)	8.8 cm. Kw.K.36(96) " " " 43 (96/1) 7.92 mm. MG.34	4000 1200	2.4	25	32.5	57	6	15	Leitz	Binocular. Adjustable interocular distance.
T.Z.F.9d	Pz.Kpfw.Tiger Model B.	8.8 cm.Kw.K.43 APCBC HE A.P.40 Hollow charge 7.92 mm. MG.34	4000 6000 2500 3000 (see Remarks)	2.5 5	27 13°30'	32.3	34	6.4 3.2	16	Leitz	Monocular. The H.E. scale is believed to serve for the M.G. also.

- 14 -

Type	Used on	Guns and ammunition	Range Scales (Metre)	Mag. (X)	Field (Deg.)	Overall length (less eye guard (ins)	Weight (lbs.)	Exit pupil dis. (mm.)	Entrance pupil dis. (mm.)	Design	Remarks
T.Z.F.12	Pz.Kpfw. Panther Model D.	7.5 cm. Kw.K.42 APCBC (L/70) HE A.P.40 7.92 mm. MG.34	3000 4000 2000 (see Remarks)	2.5	29	45.1	63.88	6.2	15	Leitz	Binocular. Light and dark filters fitted. The H.E. scale serves for the MG also.
T.Z.F.12a	Pz.Kpfw. Panther Models A and G.	As above	"	2.5 5	19 15	44.5	44	6.2 3.1		Leitz	Monocular, dual magnification

B.   HULL M.G. TELESCOPES

Type	Used on	Guns and ammunition	Range Scales (Metre)	Mag. (X)	Field (Deg.)	Overall length (less eye guard (ins)	Weight (lbs.)	Exit pupil dis. (mm.)	Entrance pupil dis. (mm.)	Design	Remarks
K.Z.F.1	Early models of most tanks.	7.92 mm. MG.34 (gimbal mountings)	200 (fixed)	1.8	18			5		-	Cranked, monocular, moving-eyepiece type.
K.Z.F.2	Pz.Kpfw.I, Commanders Pz.Kpfw.II, Flamethrower Pz.Kpfw.III, Commanders and Models F to J. Pz.Kpfw.IV, Tiger and Panther.	7.92 mm. MG.34 (gimbal and ball mountings)	200 (fixed)	1.75	18	14.13	7	5		-	Cranked, monocular, type. Also K.Z.F.2+

NOMENCLATURE:- T.Z.F. - Turret sighting telescope (Turmzielfernrohr)
K.Z.F. - Ball mounting sighting telescope (Kugelzielfernrohr)

TABLE III - GERMAN TANK ENGINES

Type	M.305	HL 38 TR	HL 57 TR	HL 62 TR	HL 66 P	HL 108 TR	HL 120 TR	HL 120 TRM	HL 210 P 30 & P 45	HL 230 P 30 & P 45
Maker	Krupp	Maybach	Maybach	Maybach	Maybach	Maybach	Maybach	Maybach	Maybach	Maybach
Mounted in	Pz.Kpfw.I Model A	Pz.Kpfw.I Model B	Pz.Kpfw.II Models a1, 2 & 3	Pz.Kpfw.II Models b to F	Pz.Kpfw.II Model L (Lynx)	Pz.Kpfw.III Models A to C Pz.Kpfw.IV Model A	Pz.Kpfw.III Models D & E Pz.Kpfw.IV Model B	Pz.Kpfw.III Models F to N Pz.Kpfw.IV Models C to J	Pz.Kpfw. Panther early Models D Pz.Kpfw. Tiger Early Models E	Pz.Kpfw. Panther late Models D,A & G Pz.Kpfw. Tiger late Models E and Model B
Output (BHP)	57	95	130	135	171	230	320	300	650	700
At r.p.m.	2,500	3,000	2,600	2,600	3,200	2,600	2,800	3,000	3,000	3,000
Bore (mm)	92	90	100	105	105	100	105	105	125	130
Stroke (mm)	130	100	120	120	130	115	115	115	145	145
Capacity (litres)	3.46	3.79	5.7	6.19	6.754	10.838	11.9	11.952	21.35	23
No. of cylinders	4	6	6	6	6	12	12	12	12	12
Arrangement of cylinders	Horizontally opposed	In line	In line	In line	In line	60° Vee	60° Vee	60° Vee	60° Vee	60° Vee
Piston speed (ft/min)	2133	1970	2045	2045	2734	1963	2114	2265	2854	2856
Max. torque (lb. ft.)		181	263	300	1,058	506	592	580 at 2150 rpm		
Weight (lbs)		948	1345	1345		2028 to 2205	2028	2028		2866
Weight/HP (1 lb./BHP)		9.98	10.35	9.98	6.18	8.82 to 9.62	6.31	6.76		4.09
H.P./Litre	16.4	25	22.8	21.8	25.3	21.3	26.9	25.2	30.9	30.4
Fuel consumption (lb/BHP/hr)		0.55	0.55	0.55		0.517 to 0.561	0.517 to 0.561	0.517 to 0.561		
Compression ratio	5.2:1	6.7:1	5.6:1	6.5:1		6.5:1	6.7:1	6.5:1	6.8:1	6.8:1
Cooling	Air	Water	Water	Water	Water	Water	Water	Water	Water	Water
Carburetor - No. Type	2 Solex JFP	1 Solex 40JFF2	1 Solex 40JFF2	1 Solex	2 Solex	2 Solex 40JFF2	2 Solex 40JFF2	2 Solex 40JFF2	4 Solex 40JFF2 2D	4 Solex 52FFJ
Oil capacity (pints)	21	21	25	25		35 to 44	44	44	44	44
Lubrication	Wet sump pressure circ.	Dry sump.	Dry sump.	Dry sump.	Dry sump.	Dry sump.	Dry sump.	Dry sump.	Dry sump.	Dry sump.
BMEP (lb/in^2)				110.48		100.49		106.5		129.2
Metric H.P. per cm2 of piston area				0.269	0.329	0.254		0.2887		0.4352
Litre capacity per cubic metre of engine space				6.66	12.75			11.28		14.81
Metric H.P. per cubic metre of engine space				148.6	323			283		448
Ignition	Bosch IR Magneto	Bosch SR6 Magneto	Bosch SR6 Magneto	Bosch SR6 Magneto		1 or 2 Bosch JO 12 L 14 or SR 6	2 Bosch SR 6 Magnetos	1 Bosch JO 12 114 Magnetos	2-6 cyl. Bosch Magnetos JGN6R18	2-6 cyl. Bosch Magnetos JGN6R18

Probably due to the Maybach monopoly in tank engines, later tanks such as the 56-ton Tiger Model E and the 67-ton Tiger Model B were seriously underpowered, the engine being the same as that used in the 45-ton Panther. At the end of the war, numerous firms (including BMW, Klockner - Humboldt - Deutz, Simmering, Daimler Benz and M.A.N. - Argus) were in the process of designing engines with an output of 1,000 H.P. or more, among the types projected being air cooled and water cooled C.I. and I.C. engines, of in-line, 'V', 'H' and 'X' form with from 8 to 24 cylinders. None of these designs was sufficiently advanced for employment in tanks, however, and the "Maus" was powered by a modified Daimler Benz MB 517 motor boat engine. Maybach were also in the process of boosting the HL 230 engine by petrol injection, to give 900 metric H.P., this boosted engine being known as the HL 234. Dr. Ing. h. c. F. Porsche K.G. was also working on a gas turbine power plant for AFVs, but this project had not progressed very far.

(d) <u>Transmission</u>

With the exception of the Porsche 'Leopard', 'Tiger' and 'Maus', referred to in Chapters 2 and 3, which had electric transmissions, all operational German tanks had conventional mechanical transmission, final drive and steering.

As in engines, Maybach enjoyed a monopoly in gearboxes, which were made by their subsidiary Zahnradfabrik, of Friedrichshafen. The Pz.Kpfw. I, II, IV and Panther, as well as certain Pz.Kpfw.III's were fitted with hand-operated crash (or synchromesh on Panther) gearboxes. The remaining Pz.Kpfw.III's were provided with a Maybach 'Variorex' multi-speed, pre-selective, vacuum-operated gearbox, which, however, was not a success owing to the limited power available with unassisted vacuum operation. Both models of the Pz.Kpfw. Tiger were provided with a development of the 'Variorex' gearbox, the Olvar, operated hydraulically instead of by vacuum.

Experiments were made on various vehicles with a torque-converter transmission by Voith of Heidenheim but this type of transmission was never taken into general use.

(e) <u>Suspension</u>

German designers appear to have used most kinds of springing media in their tank suspensions. Semi-elliptic leaf springs were employed on the Pz.Kpfw. I, II, early Pz.Kpfw. III's and Pz.Kpfw. IV, lateral torsion bars were fitted to the latest Pz.Kpfw. II (Lynx), later Pz.Kpfw. III (from Model E onwards), Tiger Models E and B, and the Pz.Kpfw. Panther, longitudinal torsion bars (springing two wheels) on the Porsche 'Leopard', 'Elefant' and early 'Maus', volute springs on the 'Einheitsfahrgestell' for the Pz.Kpfw. III/IV and the later 'Maus', helical springs on the 'E.100', and belleville washers on the E.10, 25, 50 and 75.

During the greater part of the War, the torsion bar was the most favoured springing medium. Helical and volute springs, and belleville washers were, however, being developed for incorporation in projected tanks.

Independent suspension with medium sized bogie wheels and return rollers was used on the Pz.Kpfw. I, II and III, 2-wheeled bogies were favoured for the Pz.Kpfw. IV, the Porsche tanks and the Pz.Kpfw. III/IV, and independent large disc wheels overlapped (Tiger Model B) or interleaved and overlapped (Tiger Model E and Panther), without return rollers, were incorporated in later designs.

Bogie wheels were, in all tanks up to the Pz.Kpfw. Tiger Model E, provided with rubber tyres. In subsequent tanks (including late Pz.Kpfw. IV and Tiger Model E), steel-tyres, resilient bogie wheels were used.

(f) **Tracks**

German designers favoured the cast manganese steel type of track link of skeleton (early) or recessed (later) form. Centre-guided tracks of single-link design were employed on all early tanks, - the Pz.Kpfw. Tiger Model B and 'Maus' however, employed an asymmetrical two-link track. Pin retention was either by S-pin, split pin or circlip and washer.

7. SPECIFICATIONS OF TANKS TAKEN INTO SERVICE

(i) Pz.Kpfw. I. (Sd.Kfz. 101)

Two models produced, Models A and B, also Commander's version with fixed turret, known as Kl.Pz.Bef.Wg. (Sd.Kfz. 265), based on the Model B chassis.

General Specification

	Model A	Model B	Commander's
Weight (in action)	5.3 tons	5.7 tons	5.65 tons
Crew	2	2	3
Armament	Two 7.92 mm. M.G's 34 in turret		One 7.92 mm. M.G. in turret ball mounting
Ammunition	61 Mags. of 25 rds. each (1525 rds.)		-
Armour			
Turret front	15 mm. at 10°		15 + 17 mm. at 23°
" sides	15 mm. at 22°		15 mm. at 20°, 23° & 18°
" rear	15 mm. at 22°		15 mm. at 20°
" roof	8 mm. at 72° and horizontal		8 mm. at horizontal
Hull and superstructure			
Front vertical plate	15 mm. at 22°		15 + 17 mm. at 23°
" glacis plate	8 mm. at 68° & 72°		8 + 12 mm. at 71° & 74°
Lower nose plate	15 mm. at 27°		15 + 17 mm. at 25°
Superstructure side	15 mm. at 8° & 17°		As for turret side
Hull side	15 mm. vertical		15 mm. vertical
Tail plate	15 mm. at 15° & 40°		15 mm. at 20° & 55°
Belly	6 mm. horizontal		6 mm. horizontal
Roof	6 mm. " & 32°		7 mm. at 85°
Engine			
Type	Krupp M.305 (4 cyl. petrol)	Maybach NL 38 TR (6 cyl. petrol)	
Output	60 B.H.P. at 2500 rpm.		100 B.H.P. at 2000 rpm.
Gearbox	5 speed crash type		
Steering gear	Clutch brake type		
Drive	Front sprocket		
Suspension	5 single rubber tyred bogie wheels, rear one acting as idler, rear 4 connected by girder and 3 return rollers each side.		As for Model A, except additional steel rear idler fitted, off ground, and 4 return rollers each side.

	Model A	Model B	Commander's

Tracks

Cast single link skeleton type with single central wheel path and two guide horns.

Dimensions

	Model A	Model B	Commander's
Overall length	13 ft. 0 in.	14 ft. 6 in.	14 ft. 0 in.
" width	6 ft. 9 in.	6 ft. 9 in.	6 ft. 9 in.
" height	5 ft. 7 in.	5 ft. 7 in.	6 ft. 5 in.
Track centres	5 ft. 6 in		5 ft. 6 in.
" width	$10\frac{1}{4}$ in.		11 in.
Ground clearance	$9\frac{3}{4}$ in.		$11\frac{1}{2}$ in.
Track on ground	8 ft. 5 in		8 ft. 0 in.

Performance

	Model A	Model B	Commander's
Max. speed (roads)	24 m.p.h.		25 m.p.h.
" " (cross country)	–		–
Radius of action			
(roads)	90 miles		95 miles
(cross country)	60 miles		70 miles
Gradient	30°		30°
Trench	4 ft. 7 in.		4 ft. 7 in.
Step	1 ft. 2 in.		1 ft. 2 in.
Fording depth	1 ft. 11 in.		1 ft. 11 in.

Observation

Sighting telescope T.Z.F.2. for turret armament, also vision ports in turret and hull some of which are provided with armour flaps and glass blocks.

Communication

W./T. set and flag in Models A and B. Two W./T. sets in Commander's Model.

(ii) Pz.Kpfw. II. (Sd.Kfz. 121)

Five early models, obsolete by 1939, Models a_1, a_2, a_3, b, and c. Characteristics briefly as follows:-

Model a_1. Crew of 3, 2 cm. Kw.K. 30 and M.G. 34 coaxial in turret. Weight $7\frac{1}{2}$ tons. 6 leaf-sprung bogie wheels in articulated pairs. Girder between hull pivots. 3 return rollers and cast rear idler. Maybach HL 57 TR (5.7 litre) engine. No final reduction. Clutch/brake steering.

Model a_2 As above, but modified engine compartment and welded rear idler.

Model a_3. As above, with minor modifications to suspension and cooling.

Model b. Maybach HL 62 TR (6.2 litres) engine. New track. Final reduction gear and other minor modifications. Weight just under 8 tons.

Model c. New suspension introduced, which was retained in later models, consisting of 5 independently leaf-sprung bogie wheels and 4 return rollers on each side. Improved steering mechanism. Weight increased to $8\frac{1}{2}$ tons.

Subsequent models were A to F (incl.) and L. Brief characteristics as follows:-

Model A, B and C. Armour originally 15 mm., but by June 1941 frontal armour increased by additional 15 and 20 mm. plates. No major differences between these models, or between these and Model c.

Model D and E. New suspension, consisting of 4 large diameter bogie wheels, and no return rollers, each side. Later converted to flame throwing tanks (Pz.Kpfw. II (F)) weighing 10 tons and with 30 mm. frontal armour (sd.Kfz. 122).

Model F. Homogeneous front armour increased to 35 mm. (nose) and 30 mm. (remainder). New design of front superstructure shortens vehicle by 5 in. Dummy aluminium visor on right of driver's visor. New type of conical idler fitted. A.R.V. Cupols with 7 episcopes.

Model L. Basic redesign, bearing little resemblance to previous Pz.Kpfw. 11 except for armament. Known also as Pz.Sp.Wg. 'Luchs', Sd.Kfz. 123 (Armoured Reconnaissance Vehicle 'Lynx').

General Specification	Early Models	Model F	Model L (Lynx)
Weight (in action)	10 tons approx.		11.8 tons
Crew	3		4
Armament	2 cm. Kw.K. 30 or 38 with coaxial 7.92 mm. M.G. 34 in turret.		2 cm. Kw.K. 38 with coaxial 7.92 mm. M.G. 34.
Ammunition	2 cm. - 180 rds. 7.92 mm. - 2550 rds.		2 cm. - 330 rds. 7.92 mm. - 2250 rds.
Armour			
Turret front	15 mm. curved	30 mm. curved	30 mm. at 10°.
" sides	15 mm. at 23° (+ 20 mm. later)	15 mm. at 22°	20 mm. at 20°.
" rear	15 mm. at 22°	15 mm. at 22°	20 mm. at 20°
" roof	10 mm. at 74° and horizontal	10 mm. at 77° and horizontal	13 mm. at 80° and horizontal
Superstructure front	15 mm. at 3° (+ 20 mm. later)	30 mm at 10°	20 mm. vertical
" sides	15 mm. vertical	20 mm. vertical	30 mm. at 5°
" rear	15 mm. at 7°	15 mm. at 7°	20 mm. at 30°
" roof	15 mm. horizontal	15 mm. horizontal	13 mm. horizontal
Hull glacis	15 mm. at 74° (+ 15 mm later)	20 mm. at 72°	20 mm. at 70°
" nose	15 mm. at 32° (+ 20 mm. later)	35 mm. at 13°	30 mm. at 25°
" sides	15 mm. vertical	20 mm. vertical	20 mm. vertical
" belly	5 mm. horizontal	5 horizontal	10 horizontal

	Early Models	Model F	Model L (Lynx)
Engine			
Type	See notes above	Maybach HL 62 TRM 6 cyl. Petrol	Maybach HL 66 P 6 cyl. Petrol 178 B.H.P.
Output		140 B.H.P. at 2600 r.p.m.	
Gearbox	Synchromesh 6 F. and 1 R speed gearbox, type SSG 48		
Steering	See notes above	Epicyclic clutch and brake type	
Drive	Front sprocket (single type)		Double-ringed front sprocket
Suspension	See notes above	See notes above	5 units/side each consisting of 2 large dia. wheels independently sprung on single torsion bars. No return rollers
Tracks	Single Link, single pin cast skeleton type, with single central wheel path and twin guide horns		Single link, single pim cast recessed type with 4 wheels paths and twin guide horns
Dimensions			
Overall length	15 ft. 2¾ in.	14 ft. 9 in.	14 ft. 6 in.
" width	7 ft. 4 in.	7 ft. 4 in.	8 ft. 2 in.
" height	6 ft. 5¾ in.	6 ft. 5¾ in.	7 ft. 0 in.
Ground clearance	1 ft. 1 in.	1 ft. 1 in.	1 ft. 2 in.
Track centres	6 ft. 2 in.	6 ft. 2 in.	6 ft. 9½ in.
" width	11.⅛ in.	11.⅛ in.	11.⅛ in.
" on ground	7 ft. 10 in.	7 ft. 10 in.	7 ft. 1½ in.
Performance			
Max. speed			
(roads)		30 m.p.h.	40 m.p.h. (est.)
(cross Country)		12 m.p.h.	-
Radius of action			
(roads)		-	155 miles
(cross country)		-	93 miles
Gradient		35°	30o
Trench		6 ft. 0 in.	-
Step		1 ft. 6 in.	-
Fording depth		3 ft. 0 in.	4 ft. 7 in.
Observation			
Sighting telescope	T.Z.F.4.	T.Z.F.4/36 or 38	T.Z.F. 6 or 6/38
		Commander's cupola with episcopes	1 episcope and 2 periscopes and turret roof

	Early Models	Model F	Model L (Lynx)
Observation		Driver's visor with glass block	Driver's and W/T operator's visors in superstructure front plate

Vision slits in hull and turret sides and turret rear with glass blocks.

Communication   W/T set and intercommunication

(iii) Pz. Kpfw. III.

MODEL	A	B	C	D	E	F	G	H	J	L	M	N
WEIGHT (in action) tons	18	18	18	19	20	20	20	20	22	22	22	22
CREW	5	5	5	5	5	5	5	5	5	5	5	5
ARMAMENT (Main)	3·7cm. Kw. K. (L/45)				5cm. Kw. K. (L/42)				5cm. KwK 39 (L/60)			7·5cm.Kwk (L/24)
7·92mm MG34 (Subsidy) no.	3	3	3	3	2	2	2	2	2	2	2	2
AMMUNITION (Main Armt.) Rds.					99	99	99	99	99-78	78	78	64
" (Subsidy) "					2000	2000	2000	2000	2000	4950	4950	3450
ARMOUR												
Turret front (15°) mm	14·5	14·5	14·5	30	30	30	30	30	30	57+20	57+20	57+20
" sides (25°) "	14·5	14·5	14·5	30	30	30	30	30	30	30	30	30
" rear (12°) "	14·5	14·5	14·5	30	30	30	30	30	30	30	30	30
" roof (83° & horiz) "	10	10	10	10	10	10	10	30	10	10	10	10
S'structure front (9°) "	14·5	14·5	14·5	30	30	30	30	30+32	50	50+20	50+20	50+20
" glacis (84°) "									25	25	25	25
" sides (vertical) "	14·5	14·5	14·5	30	30	30	30	30	30	30	30	30
" rear (13°) "	14·5	14·5	14·5	30	30	30	30	30+32	53	50	50	50
" roof (horiz.) "	18	18	18	18	18	18	18	18	18	18	18	18
Hull front (52° & 21°) "	14·5	14·5	14·5	30	30	30	30	30+32	50	50	50	50
" sides (vertical) "	14·5	14·5	14·5	30	30	30	30	30	30	30	30	30
" rear (10°) "	14·5	14·5	14·5	30	30	30	30	30+32	53	50	50	50
" belly (horiz.) "	14·5	14·5	14·5	30	30	30	30	30	30	30	30	30
ENGINE (Maybach) Type	HL108TR	HL108TR	HL108TR	HL120TR	HL120TRM	HL120TRM	HL120TRM	HL120TRM	HL120TRM	HL120TRM	HL120TRM	HL120TRM
Output B.H.P.	248	248	248	300	320	320	320	320	320	320	320	320
GEARBOX (Z-F) Type	SFG75	SFG75		Variorex	Variorex	Variorex	Variorex	Variorex	SSG77	SSG77	SSG77	SSG77
No. of speeds	5F.1R.	5F.1R.	5F.1R.	10F.4R.	10F.4R.	10F.4R.	10F.4R.	10F.4R.	6F.1R.	6F.1R.	6F.1R.	6F.1R.
DRIVE	FRONT SPROCKET											
SUSPENSION												
No. of bogie wheels/side	5	8	8	8	6	6	6	6	6	6	6	6
No. of return rollers "	2	3	3	3	3	3	3	3	3	3	3	3
Springs (type)	5 helical	2,leaf	3,leaf	3,leaf	Independant torsion bar							
TRACKS	Single link, single pin cast skeleton type, with single central guide horn.											
DIMENSIONS (feet & ins.)												
Overall length (incl. gun)	17'9"	17'9"	17'9"	17'9"	17'9"	17'9"	17'9"	17'9"	17'9" or 20'2½"	20'2½"	20'2½"	17'9"
width	9'7"	9'7"	9'7"	9'7"	9'7"	9'7"	9'7"	9'7"	9'7"	9'7"	9'7"	9'7"
height	8'6"	8'4"	8'4"	8'4"	8'4"	8'3"	8'3"	8'3"	8'3"	8'3"	8'3"	8'3"
Ground clearance	1'3"	1'3"	1'3"	1'3"	1'3"	1'3"	1'3"	1'3"	1'4"	1'4"	1'4"	1'4"
Track centres	6'8¾"	6'8¾"	6'8¾"	6'8¾"	6'8¾"	6'8¾"	6'9½"	6'9½"	6'9½"	6'9½"	6'9½"	6'9½"
" width	14¼"	14¼"	14¼"	14¼"	14¼"	14¼"	15"	15"	15"	15"	15"	15"
" on ground					9'4¼"	9'4¼"	9'4¼"	9'4¼"	9'4¼"	9'4¼"	9'4¼"	9'4¼"
PERFORMANCE												
Max speed (rds.) m.p.h.					24	24	24	24	28	28	28	28
" " (X country) "					11	11	11	11	12	12	12	12
Radius of action (rds) miles					108	108	108	108	108	108	108	108
" (X country)					60	60	60	60	60	60	60	60
Gradient degrees	35°	35°	35°	35°	35°	35°	35°	35°	35°	35°	35°	35°
Trench feet & ins.					8'6"	8'6"	8'6"	8'6"	8'6"	8'6"	8'6"	8'6"
Step " " "					2'0"	2'0"	2'0"	2'0"	2'0"	2'0"	2'0"	2'0"
Fording depth					2'7½"	2'7½"	2'7½"	2'9"	2'9"	2'9"	4'3"	2'9"
OBSERVATION												
Sighting Telescope (Main Armt.)	T.Z.F.5a	T.Z.F.5a	T.Z.F.5a	T.Z.F.5a	vorl T.Z.F.5d	T.Z.F.5d	T.Z.F.5d	T.Z.F.5d	T.Z.F.5d	T.Z.F.5e	T.Z.F.5e	T.Z.F.5e
" " (hull M.G.)	KZF2	KZF2	KZF2	KZF2	KZF2	KZF2	KZF2	KZF2	KZF2	KZF2	KZF2	KZF2
COMMUNICATION	W/T transmitter & receiver & internal communication system fitted to all tanks											

(iv) Pz. Kpfw. IV.

MODEL	A	B	C	D	E	F1	F2	G	H	J
WEIGHT (in action) Tons	17·1	17·5	17·5	19·7	21·5-22	22	23·25	23·25	24·6	24·6
CREW	5	5	5	5	5	5	5	5	5	5
MAIN ARMAMENT	7·5 cm. Kw. K (L/24)						7·5cm Kw K40 (L/43)		7·5cm Kw K40 (L/48)	
7·92mm. M-G. 34's No.	2	1	1	2	2	2	2	2	2	2
AMMUNITION - 7·5cm rds.	80	80	80	80	80	80	87	87	87	87
" - 7·92mm rds.				2800		3150	3150	3150	3150	3150
ARMOUR										
Turret front (11°) mm.	20	20	30	30	30	50	50	50	50	50
" sides (26°) "	20	20	20	20	20	30	30	30	30	30
rear (16°)	20	20	20	20	20	30	30	30	30	30
" roof (84° & horizontal)	10	10	10	10	10	10	10	10	16-30	16-30
S'structure front (10°)	14·5	30	30	30	30+30	50	50	50	85	85
" sides (Vertical)	14·5	14·5	14·5	20	20+20	30	30	30	30	30
glacis (73°)	14·5	14·5	14·5	20	20	25	25	25	20	20
rear (12°)	15	15	14·5	20	20	20	20	20	20	20
roof (horizontal)	11	11	11	11	11	11	11	11	11	16
Hull front (12°)	14·5	30	30	30	50	50	50	50	85	85
" sides (Vertical)	14·5	14·5	14·5	20	20+20	30	30	30	30	30
rear (90°)	15	15	14·5	20	20	20	20	20	20	20
belly (horizontal)	8	8	8	10	10	10	10	10	10	10
ENGINE (Maybach) Type	HL108TR	HL120TR	HL120TRM	HL120TRM	HL120TRM	HL120TRM	HL120TRM	HL120TRM	HL120TRM	HL120TRM
Output (at 2,800 r.p.m.) B.H.P.	295 (at 2,600 rpm)	268	268	268	268	268	268	268	268	268
GEARBOX (Z.F.) Type	SFG75	SSG76	SSG76	SSG76	SSG76	SSG76	SSG76	SSG77	SSG77	SSG77
No. of speeds	5	6	6	6	6	6	6	6	6	6
STEERING	Wilson type - Epicyclic clutch and brake									
DRIVE	TWO RING FRONT SPROCKET									
SUSPENSION										
No. of wheels/side	8	8	8	8	8	8	8	8	8	8
" " return rollers/ "	4	4	4	4	4	4	4	4	4	3
Springing	4 articulated pairs per side, each pair sprung on ¼ elliptic springs.									
TRACKS	Single link, single pin, cast skeleton type. Central guide horn.									
DIMENSIONS (feet & inches)										
Overall length (incl. gun)	19'3"	19'3"	19'3"	19'4⅝"	19'4⅝"	19'5½"	22'11⅝"	22'11⅝"	24'2"	24'2"
" width	9'4¼"	9'4¼"	9'4¼"	9'4⅝"	9'4⅝"	9'5⅜"	9'5⅜"	9'5⅜"	10'9½"	10'9½"
" height	8'6"	8'6"	8'6"	8'6"	8'6"	8'6⅜"	8'6⅜"	8'6⅜"	8'6⅜"	8'6⅜"
Ground clearance	1'3¾"	1'3¾"	1'3¾"	1'3¾"	1'3¾"	1'3¾"	1'3¾"	1'3¾"	1'3¾"	1'3¾"
Track centres	7'10⅛"	7'10⅛"	7'10⅛"	7'10½"	7'10½"	8'0⅝"	8'0⅝"	8'0⅝"	8'0⅝"	8'0⅝"
" width	1'3"	1'3"	1'3"	1'3"	1'3¾"	1'3¾"	1'3¾"	1'3¾"	1'3¾"	1'3¾"
on ground	11'6½"	11'6½"	11'6½"	11'6½"	11'6½"	11'6½"	11'6½"	11'6½"	11'6½"	11'6½"
PERFORMANCE										
Max. speed (roads) m.p.h.	20	26	26	26	26	26	25	25	25	28
" " (X country) "	7-14	7-18	7-18	7-18	7-18	7-18	10	10	10	15
Radius of action (rds.) miles.	93	125	125	125	125	125	125	125	125	187
" " " (X country) "	62	80	80	80	80	80	80	80	80	111
Gradient degrees	35	30	30	30	30	30	30	30	30	30
Trench feet & inches	7'6½"	7'6½"	7'6½"	7'6½"	7'2⅝"	7'2⅝"	7'2⅝"	7'2⅝"	7'8½"	7'8½"
Step "	2'0"	2'0"	2'0"	2'0"	2'0"	2'0"	2'0"	2'0"	2'0"	2'0"
Fording depth "	2'7½"	2'7½"	2'7½"	2'7½"	3'3⅜"	3'3⅜"	3'3⅜"	3'3⅜"	3'11¼"	3'11¼"
OBSERVATION										
Sighting telescope (Main Armt.)		T.Z.F.5b or 5b/36	T.Z.F.5b or 5b/36	T.Z.F.5b or 5b/36	T.Z.F.5b or 5b/36	T.Z.F.5b or 5b/36	T.Z.F.5f(Verl)	T.Z.F.5f(Verl) or T.Z.F.5f/1	T.Z.F.5f(Verl) or T.Z.F.5f/1	T.Z.F.5f/1 or T.Z.F.5f/2
" " Subsidy. Armt.	K.Z.F.1	—	—	K.Z.F.2.	K.Z.F.2	K.Z.F.2	K.Z.F.2	K.Z.F.2	K.Z.F.2	K.Z.F.2
COMMUNICATION	W/T TRANSMITTER AND RECEIVER with intercommn. on all tanks.									

V. Pz.Kpfw. Panther (Sd.Kfz.171)

Three Models (D, A & G) of fighting tank taken into service, also 2 types of Commander's tank (Sd.Kfz.267 & 268) differing from fighting tank and each other only in wireless equipment. 2 types of armoured recovery vehicle, Pz. Berge.WG. Panther (Sd.Kfz.179) (one with winch and spade and one without) also produced, based on Panther chassis Models D & A, together with an O.P. vehicle fitted with special observation instruments and dummy main armament based on Model D.

Data Model	D	A	G	A.R.V.	O.P.Tank
Weight (in action) tons	44 tons 15½ cwt.			42	
Crew	5	5	5	4	4
Armament (main)	7.5 cm. Kw.K.42 (L/70)			2 cm. Kw.K.38	-
7.92 mm.M.G.34 (no.)	1	3	3	1	2
Ammunition (Main armt) rds.	79	79	79		-
" (7.92 mm.) rds.	2500	4500	4500		4500
Armour.					
Turret front mm.	110 at 10°	110 at 10°	110 at 10°	-	
" sides "	45 at 25°	45 at 25°	45 at 25°	-	
" rear "	45 at 28°	45 at 28°	45 at 28°	-	
" roof "	15 at 83° & 88°	15 at 83° & 88°	15 at 83° & 88°	-	
Superstructure front "	80 at 55°	80 at 55°	80 at 55°	80 at 50°	80 at 55°
" sides "	40 at 40°	40 at 40°	50 at 30°	40 at 40°	40 at 40°
" rear "	40 at 30°	40 at 30°	40 at 30°	40 at 30°	40 at 30°
" roof "	15 horizontal	15 horizontal	40 horizontal	15 horizontal	15 horizontal
Hull front "	80 at 55°	80 at 55°	80 at 55°	80 at 55°	80 at 55°
" sides "	40 vertical	40 vertical	40 vertical	40 vertical	40 vertical
" rear "	40 at 30°	40 at 30°	40 at 30°	40 at 30°	40 at 30°
" belly "	20 + 13 horizontal	20 + 13 horizontal	20 + 13 horizontal	20 + 13 horizontal	20 + 13 horizontal
Engine (Maybach) Type	HL210 P.30	HL230 P.30		HL210 P.30 or HL230 P.30	HL210 P.30
Output at 3000 rpm. B.H.P.	642	690		642 or 690	642
Gearbox (Z.F.) Type	AK 7 - 200			AK 7 - 200	AK 7 - 200
No. of speeds	7 forward 1 reverse			7 F. 1 R.	7 F. 1 R.
Steering	Discontinuous regenerative type giving 1 radius of turn for each gear engaged.				
Drive	FRONT SPROCKET				
Suspension	8 stations per side, each consisting of 2 large bogie wheels, and independently sprung on 2 torsion bars connected in series. Wheels overlapped and interleaved. One small return roller behind sprocket.				
Tracks	Single link single pin type, recessed construction 4 wheel paths and twin guide horns.				
Dimensions					
Overall length Ft.& in. (incl.Gun)	29' 1"	29' 1"	29' 1"	26' 9"	22' 7"
" width " "	11' 3"	11' 3"	11' 3"	10' 9"	11' 3"
" height " "	9' 9"	9' 9"	9' 9"	9' 0"	
Ground clearance " "	1' 10"	1' 10"	1' 10"	1' 10"	1' 10"
Track centres " "	8' 7½"	8' 7½"	8' 7½"	8' 7½"	8' 7½"
" width " "	2' 1¾"	2' 1¾"	2' 1¾"	2' 1¾"	2' 1¾"
Track on ground " "	12' 10"	12' 10"	12' 10"	12' 10"	12' 10"
Performance					
Max speed (roads) m.p.h.	34	34	34	20	34
" " (X country) "	15	15	15	10-15	15
Radius of action miles (roads)	105	110	110	105	105
" " (X country) "	53	55	55	53	53
Gradient Degrees	35°	35°	35°	35°	35°
Trench ft. & in.	6' 3"	6' 3"	6' 3"	6' 3"	6' 3"
Step " "	3'	3'	3'	3'	3'
Fording depth " "	4' 7"	4' 7"	4' 7"	4' 7"	4' 7"

Data　　　　Model	D	A	G	A.R.V.	O.P. Tank
Observation					
Sight - main armament	T.Z.F. 12	T.Z.F. 12a	T.Z.F. 12a	-	-
" subsidiary "	-	K.Z.F.2	K.Z.F.2	K.Z.F.2 (Mod.A)	K.Z.F.2 (in turret)
R/F	-	-	-	-	Em. 1.25 m. R (Pz).
Observation periscopes	-?	?-	T.S.R.1	-	T.B.F.2 & T.S.R.1 or S.F14Z.
Odometer	-	-	-	-	Blockstelle 'O'.
Cupola	6 slits with glass blocks	7 episcopes		-	7 episcopes
Driver		2 episcopes	1 periscope		2 episcopes
Loader		-	Episcope		-
W/T operator	2 episcopes & rectangular port.		1 periscope		2 episcopes and 1 rectangular port.
Communication	Fu.5 and Fu. 2 OR Fu.2 only.				Fu.Sprech. 'f' and re-receiver M.W.E. 'c'.

Note.   **Commander's tanks (Pz.Bef.Wg.Panther. Sd.Kfz.267 and 268)**

    Sd.Kfz.267 had Fu.5 and Fu.8 W/T equipment
    Sd.Kfz.268 " Fu.5 " Fu.7 "   "
    7.5 cm. Ammunition (both types)   64 rds.
    7.92 mm.   "   ("   "   )   4800 rds. (mods. D & A)
                                                 5100 rds. (mod. G.)

    Other details as for fighting tanks.

vi)   **Pz.Kpfw. Tiger Model E (Sd.Kfz.181) and Model B (Sd.Kfz.182)**

		Model E	Model B	
			Original turret.	Production turret.
Weight (in action)	tons	56	67 tons 7 cwt.	68 tons 13 cwt.
Crew		5	5	5
Armament (Main)		8.8 cm. Kw. K.36 (L/56)	8.8 cm. Kw.K.43 (L/71)	
7.92 mm. M.G.'s	No.	2	3 (1 for A.A.)	3 (1 for A.A.)
Ammunition (8.8 cm.)	rds.	92	78	84
" (7.92 mm)	"	5700	5850	5850
Armour				
Turret front	mm.	100 at 10°	100 rounded	185 at 10°
" sides	"	82 vertical	80 at 30°	80 at 21°
" rear	"	82 vertical	80 at 30°	80 at 20°
" roof	"	26 at 81° and 90°	40 at 78°, 90° and 20°	44 at 80°, 90° and 80°
Superstructure front	"	102 at 10°	150 at 50°	150 at 50°
" sides	"	80 vertical	80 at 25°	80 at 25°
" rear	"	82 at 8°	80 at 30°	80 at 30°
" roof	"	26 horizontal	40 horizontal	40 horizontal
Hull front	"	102 at 24°	100 at 50°	100 at 50°
" glacis	"	61 at 80o	-	-
" sides	"	63 vertical	80 vertical	80 vertical
" rear	"	82 at 8°	80 at 30°	80 at 30°
" belly	"	26 horizontal	40 and 25 horizontal	40 and 25 horizontal
Engine (Maybach)				
Type		HL 230 P45	HL 230 P30	HL 230 P30
Output at 3000 r.p.m. BHP		700	700	700

	Model E	Model B	
		Original turret.	Production turret.
Gearbox (Maybach)			
Type	Olvargetriebe 40 1216	Olvargetriebe 40 1216 B.	
No. of speeds	8 F. 4 R.	8 F. 4 R.	8 F. 4 R.
Steering	Henschel L 600 C regenerative type (2 radii).	Henschel L 801 (regenerative controlled differential - 2 radii of turn).	
Drive	FRONT SPROCKET		
Suspension	8 stations/side, each having triple overlapping and interleaved large dia. bogi wheels independently sprung on torsion bars. Outer wheels may be removed for use with transport tracks. No return rollers.	9 stations/side, each having 2 large dia. resilient bogi wheels independently sprung on torsion bars. Wheels overlapped only. No return rollers.	
Tracks	Single link, single pin type. Wide tracks for operation and narrow tracks for transportation. 6 wheel paths on wide and 4 on narrow tracks. 2 guide horns.	2 link recessed type track with asymmetrical guide horns and 4 wheel paths. Connecting link has no driving lugs or guide horns.	
Dimensions			
Overall length (incl. gun)	27 ft. 9 in.	33 ft. 8 in.	33 ft. 8 in.
" width (wide tracks)	12 ft. 3 in.	12 ft. 3 5/8 in.	12 ft. 3 5/8 in.
(narrow tracks)	10 ft. 4 in.	10 ft. 8 3/4 in.	10 ft. 8 3/4 in.
Overall height	9 ft. 4 3/4 in.	10 ft. 1 5/8 in.	10 ft. 1 5/8 in.
Ground clearance	1 ft. 5 in.	1 ft. 7½ in.	1 ft. 7½ in.
Track centres (wide tracks)	9 ft. 3½ in.	9 ft. 1 7/8 in.	9 ft. 1 7/8 in.
" (narrow tracks)	8 ft. 11½ in.	8 ft. 6 3/4 in.	8 ft. 6 3/4 in.
" width (wide tracks)	2 ft. 4½ in.	2 ft. 7 in.	2 ft. 7 in.
" " (narrow tracks)	1 ft. 8½ in.	2 ft. 2 in.	2 ft. 2 in.
Track on ground	12 ft. 6 in.	13 ft. 6½ in.	13 ft. 6½ in.
Performance			
Max speed (roads) m.p.h.	23	25.7	25.7
" " (X country) "	12.4	9 - 12	9 - 12
Radius of action miles (roads)	73	106	106
Radius of action " (X country)	42	75	75
Gradient	35°	35°	35°
Trench		8 ft. 2 3/8 in.	8 ft. 2 3/8 in.
Step	2 ft. 7 in.	2 ft. 9½ in.	2 ft. 9½ in.
Fording depth	13 ft. (first 495 tanks). 4 ft. (subsequent tanks).	5 ft. 3 in.	5 ft. 3 in.
Observation			
Main armament sight	T.Z.F.9(b)	T.Z.F.9(b) 1	T.Z.F.9(d)
Hull M.G. sight	K.Z.F.2	K.Z.F.2	K.Z.F.2
Cupola	5 vision slits w/glass blocks	7 episcopes	7 episcopes
Driver	1 visor in front vert. plate. 1 episcope in hatch cover.	1 periscope in hatch cover.	1 periscope in hatch cover

	Model E	Model B	
		Original turret.	Production turret.
Hull gunner	1 episope in hatch cover.	1 episcope in hatch cover.	1 episcope in hatch cover.
Loader	1 vision port in turret wall. S.F. 14Z	1 episcope in turret roof. S.F.14Z?	1 episcope in turret roof. T.S.R.1
Communication	W/T set (transmitter and receiver with intercommn.) on all tanks.		

Note.

Commander's tanks (Sd.Kfz.267 and 268, Tiger Model E only) have following W/T equipment:

    Pz.Bef.Wg. Tiger (Sd.Kfz.267)   Fu. 5 and Fu. 8
    " " " " (Sd.Kfz.268)   Fu. 5 and Fu. 7

8. TABLE OF LEADING DATA OF GERMAN TANKS TAKEN INTO SERVICE

Name and Model	Weight	Crew	Dimensions	Armour thicknesses and angles to vertical	Armament	Ammunition carried	Engine	Suspension and tracks	Performance	Remarks
	A = Unladen B = In action		A = Length (excl gun) B = Width overall C = Height overall D = Belly clearance E = Track on ground F = Track centres G = Track width H = Track pitch	A = Turret front B = Turret sides C = Superstructure front D = Glacis plate E = Lower nose plate F = Hull sides G = Superstructure sides H = Superstructure roof I = Tail plate J = Belly plate	A = Turret B = Hull				A = Max speed roads B = Max speed cross country C = Radius of action roads D = Radius of action cross country E = Trench crossing F = Stop G = Water forded H = Max gradient	
Pz.Kpfw.I (Sd.Kfz.101)	A. 5 tons B. 5.5 tons	2-Commander/gunner and Driver/WT operator	A. 13 ft. 0 in. (Model A) 14 ft. 6 in. (Model B) B. 6 ft. 9 in. C. 5 ft. 7 in. (Model A) 9¾ in. (Model B) 11½ in. D. (Model A) E. 8 ft. 5 in. (Model A) 8 ft. 0 in. (Model B) F. 5 ft. 6 in. G. 10¼ in. (Model A) 11 in. (Model B) H. 3 11/16 in.	A. 15 mm. at 10° B. 15 mm. at 22° C. 15 mm. at 22° D. 8 mm. at 72° (upper) 69° (lower) E. 15 mm. at 27° F. 15 mm. vertical G. 15 mm. at 17° (front) 8° (rear) H. 6 mm. at 32° horizontal (centre) I. 15 mm. at 15° (upper) 40° (lower) J. 6 mm. horizontal	A. Two 7.92 mm.MGs13K (Dreyse) B. None.	7.92 mm. = 1525 rds in sixty-one 25 rd. mags.	Krupp M-305 4 cyl. air-cooled petrol. 60 BHP at 2500 rpm. (Model A) Maybach NL 38 TR 6 cyl. water cooled 100 BHP at 3000 rpm. (Model B)	Model A – 5 rubber tyred road wheels, front independent, rear 4 in 2 bogie pairs on ½ elliptic leaf springs. Rear wheel larger and serves as idler. Wheels connected by a girder. Model B – as above except separate rear idler fitted, off ground. Tracks, single pin cast, skeleton type, with twin guide horns and central wheel path.	A. 24 m.p.h. B. C. 95 miles D. 70 miles E. 4ft. 7 in. F. 1ft. 2 in. G. 1 ft. 11 in. H. 30°	Commander's model of this tank, with fixed turret, known as "Kl.Pz. Bef.Wg. (Sd.Kfz.265)"
Pz.Kpfw.II Model F (Sd.Kfz.121)	A. 8 tons 15 cwt B. 10 tons (approx)	Three. Commander gunner Driver/ W.T.op.	A. 14 ft. 9 in. B. 7 ft. 4 in. C. 6 ft. 1 in. D. 1 ft. 3 in. E. 7 ft. 10 in. F. 6 ft. 2 in. G. 11¼ in. H. 3 5/8 in.	A. 30 mm. curved. B. 15 mm. at 23° C. 30 mm. at 3° D. 20 mm. at 72° E. 35 mm. at 13° F. 15 mm. vertical G. 20 mm. vertical H. 15 mm. horizontal I. 15 mm. at 6° (upper) 10 mm. at 62° (lower) J. 6 mm. horizontal	A. One 2 cm. Kw.K.30, or Kw.K.38, One 1.92 mm. MG.34 (coaxial) B. None	2 cm. – 180 rds. in eight-con 10 rd. mags. 7.92 mm. 2550 rds.	Maybach HL 62 TR 6 cyl. water cooled petrol giving 140 BHP at 2600 rpm.	5 rubber tyred bogie wheels each side, independently sprung on ¼ elliptic leaf springs. Front sprocket, rear idler. Single-pin cast skeleton tracks with twin skeleton guide horns and central wheel path.	A. 30 m.p.h. B. 12 m.p.h. C. – D. – E. 6 ft. 0 in. F. 1 ft. 6 in. G. 3 ft. 0 in. H. 35°	Models – a1, a2, a3, b, c, A, B, C, D and E. All models have same crew and armament but differ in suspension. (Models a1, a2, a3, b, c, D and E) armour thicknesses, hull design and engine. All approximately same weight, dimensions and performance. Models D and E later converted to F/T tanks known as Pz.Kpfw. II(F) – Sd.Kfz.122.

Name and Model	Weight	Crew	Dimensions	Armour thicknesses and angles to vertical	Armament	Ammunition carried	Engine	Suspension and tracks	Performance	Remarks
				See Sheet 1 for explanation of symbols						
Light Recce tank "Lynx" (Sd.Kfz.123) (Pz.Kpfw.II, Model L)	A. 9 tons (approx) B. 11.8 tons	Four Commander Gunner Driver W.T. operator	A. 14 ft. 6 in. B. 8 ft. 2 in. C. 7 ft. 0 in. D. 1 ft. 2 in. E. 7 ft. 1½ in. F. 6 ft. 9½ in. G. 1 ft. 2 in. H. 3¾ in.	A. 20 mm. @ 15° B. 20 mm. @ 20° C. 30 mm. @ 5° D. 20 mm. @ 70° E. 20 mm. @ 70° F. 20 mm. vertical G. 20 mm. vertical H. 13 mm. horizontal I. 20 mm. @ 30°(upper) 70°(lower) J.	A. One 2 cm.Kw.K. 38 with 7.92 mm. MG.34 coaxial B. None	2 cm. = 33 rds. 7.92 mm. = 13 bags (1950 rds)	Maybach 178 HP. 6 cyl. OHV.	5 units each side each with twin torsion bars (20 in all). Two large disc type interleaved bogie wheels on each unit.	A. 40 m.p.h. B. - C. 155 miles D. 93 miles E. - F. - G. 4 ft. 7 in. H. 30°	Pz.Kpfw.I. Model "L" (modified armour and suspension). Also known as Pz.Sp.Wg."Luchs" (Lynx)
Pz.Kpfw.III Model L(Sd.Kfz. 141)	A. 20 tons B. 22 tons	Five Commander Gunner Loader Hull gunner/ W.T. op. Driver	A. 17 ft. 9 in. B. 9 ft. 8 in. C. 8 ft. 3 in. D. 1 ft. 3 in. E. 9 ft. 4½ in. F. 8 ft. 2½ in. G. 1 ft. 3 in. H. 4¾ in.	A. 57 mm. @ 15° B. 30 mm. @ 25° C. 50 mm. + 20 mm.@ 9° D. 25 mm. @ 84° E. 50 mm. @ 20° F. 30 mm. vertical G. 30 mm. vertical H. 18 mm. horizontal I. 50 mm. @ 17°(upper) 9°(lower) J. 16 mm. horizontal	A. 5 cm.Kw.K.39 (L/60) coaxial 7.92 mm. MG.34 (See "Remarks") B. 7.92 mm. MG.34 in offside of glacis plate.	5 cm. = 78 rds. 7.92 mm. = 4950 rds.	Maybach OHV Petrol HL 120 TRM.V.-12. Output = 300 HP.	6 twin rubber tyred bogie wheels independently sprung on tersion bars, and three twin rubber tyred return rollers each side. Front sprocket rear idler. Single pin skeleton track links with central guide horn.	A. 28 m.p.h. B. 12 m.p.h. C. 100 miles D. 60 miles E. 8 ft. 6 in. F. 2 ft. 0 in. G. 2 ft. 9 in. H. 35°	Models = A,B,C,D,E,F, G,H,J,L,M and N. Models A,B,C and D have experimental suspensions. 3.7 cm. Kw.K. and coaxial 7.92 mm. MG.34 (2 MG.34 coaxial in Models A, B and C) with internal mantlet. External mantlet on all subsequent models. 5 cm.Kw.K(L/42) and one coaxial MG.34 in models E,F,G and H and early J, replaced in later models J and models L and M by 5 cm.Kw.K.39(L/60). Model N mounted 7.5 cm.Kw.K.(L/24), surplus from Pz.Kpfw.IV requirements.
Pz.Kpfw.IV Models H and J. (Sd.Kfz.161)	A. 20 tons B. 23 tons	Five Commander Gunner Loader Driver Hull gunner/ W.T. op.	A. 19 ft. 4 in. B. 9 ft. 7 in. C. 8 ft. 6 in. D. 1 ft. 2½ in. E. 11 ft. 6 in. F. 7 ft. 11 in. G. 1 ft. 3 in. H. 4¾ in.	A. 50 mm. @ 10° B. 30 mm. @ 26° C. 85 mm. @ 10° D. 20 mm. @ 72° E. 30 mm. @ 64° F. 30 mm. vertical G. 30 mm. vertical H. 12 mm. horizontal I. 20 mm. @ 11°(upper) 8°(lower) J. 10-15 mm. horizontal	A. 7.5 cm. Kw.K.40 (L/38), 92 mm. MG.34 coaxial. B. 7.92 mm. MG.34 (In R.H. side of front vertical plate)	7.5 cm. = 87 rds. 7.92 mm. = 30 bags (4500 rds)	Maybach OHV HL 120 TRM V-12, 300 HP.	4 bogie assemblies each side, each with two twin 18.5 in. diameter bogie wheels sprung on ¼ olliptic springs. Four return rollers.	A. 30 m.p.h. B. 15 m.p.h. C. 125 miles D. 80 miles E. 9 ft. 0 in. F. 2 ft. 0 in. G. 2 ft. 9 in. H. 30°	Wire mesh skirting fitted as from Model J. No power traverse on Model J - extra 44 gall. fuel tank in place of generator. Only three return rollers (Model J) Spaced shield round turret (both models). Models A,B,C,D,E,F,F2, G,H and J. Early Models had thinner armour. Models A, B,C,D,E and F = 7.5 cm. Kw.K(L/24) F2 and G = 7.5 cm. Kw.K.40 (L/43)
Pz.Kpfw.Panther Models D,A and G. (Sd.Kfz.171)	A. 42 tons (approx) B. 45 tons	Five Commander Gunner Loader Driver Hull gunner/ W.T. op.	A. 22 ft. 7 in. B. 10 ft. 8¾ in. C. 9 ft. 9 in. D. 1 ft. 7 in. E. 12 ft. 10 in. F. 8 ft. 7⅛ in. G. 2 ft. 2 in. H. 6 in.	A. 110 mm. @ 11° B. 45 mm. @ 25° C. 80 mm. @ 55° D. 80 mm. @ 55° E. 60 mm. @ 55° F. 40 mm. vertical G. 40 mm. @ 40° (Mods. D and A) 50 mm. @ 30° (Mod. G) H. 15 mm. horizontal (40 mm. front 12 in.) (Model G) I. 40 mm. @ 30° J. 15-33 mm. horizontal (see Remarks)	A. 7.5 cm.Kw.K. 42(L/70) 7.92 mm. MG.34 coaxial B. None in Model D. 7.92 mm. MG. 34 Mods A and G. 360° traverse smoke generator dischargers in turret roof.	7.5 cm. = 79 rds. 7.92 mm. = 4500 rds.	Maybach OHV HL 230 P30 V-12. 690 HP.	Large overlapping, interleaved bogie wheels, mounted in 8 units of 2 wheels each side. Each unit sprung on twin tersion bars in series. 1 return roller between sprocket and front bogie wheel.	A. 34 m.p.h. B. 20 m.p.h. C. 124 miles D. 62 miles E. 6 ft. 3 in. F. 2 ft. 11 in. G. 6 ft. 2 in. H. 35°	Part of belly reinforced by additional plate. 5 mm. H.S. skirting plates to top of track. 7.5 cm. Kw.K.42 (L/70) is 18 ft. 2 in. long overall.

Name and Model	Weight	Crew	Dimensions	Armour thicknesses and angles to vertical	Armament	Ammunition carried	Engine	Suspension and tracks	Performance	Remarks
Pz.Kpfw.Tiger Model E. (Sd.Kfz.181)	A. — B. 56 tons.	Five Commander Gunner Loader Driver Hull gunner/ W.T. op.	A. 20 ft. 8¼ in. B. 12 ft. 3 in. C. 9 ft. 4½ in. D. 1 ft. 5 in. E. 12 ft. 6 in. F. 9 ft. 3½ in. G. 2 ft. 4½ in. H. 5⅝ in.	See Sheet 1 for explanation of symbols A. 100-110 mm. (mantlet) B. 82 mm. vertical C. 102 mm. @ 10° D. 61 mm. @ 80° E. 63 mm. @ 65° F. 63 mm. vertical G. 80 mm. vertical H. 26 mm. horizontal I. 82 mm. @ 8° (undercut) J. 26 mm. horizontal	A. 8.8 cm.Kw.K. 36(L/56) 7.92 mm.MG.34 coaxial 6 smoke generator dischargers in turret sides. B. 7.92 mm. MG.34 (offside of superstructure frontplate)	8.8 cm. = 92 rds. 7.92 mm. = 5700 rds.	Maybach OHV HL 230 P45 V-12 592 HP (at 2500 governed r.p.m.)	Large overlapping, interleaved bogie wheels, mounted in 8 units of 3 wheels each side. Each unit sprung on single torsion bars. With wide tracks, each unit consists of one twin and one single bogie wheel. With narrow tracks, outer wheel removed from each unit.	A. 23 m.p.h. B. 12.4 m.p.h. C. 73 miles. D. 42 miles. E. — F. 2 ft. 7 in. G. 13 ft. (first 495 tanks produced) 4 ft. (tanks 496 onwards) H. 35°	With narrow (transportation) tracks: Width: 10 ft. 4 in. Track centres: 8 ft. 7½ in. Track width: 1 ft. 8½ in. Early tanks fitted with 5 S-mine dischargers on superstructure roof.
Pz.Kpfw. Tiger Model B. (Sd.Kfz.182)	A. 64 tons (old turret) 65 tons 4 cwt. (production turret) B. 67 tons 7 cwt. (old turret) 68 tons 13 cwt. (production turret)	Five Commander Gunner Loader Driver Hull gunner/ W.T. op.	A. 23 ft. 10 in. B. 11 ft. 11½ in. C. 10 ft. 2 in. D. 1 ft. 8 in. E. 13 ft. 6½ in. F. 9 ft. 1 7/8 in. G. 2 ft. 8½ in. H. 5.9 in. (All dimensions for vehicle fitted with wide (operational) tracks)	A. 180 mm. @ 10° B. 80 mm. @ 20° C. 150 mm. @ 50° D. 150 mm. @ 50° E. 100 mm. @ 50° F. 80 mm. vertical G. 80 mm. @ 25° H. 40 mm. horizontal I. 80 mm. @ 25° (undercut) J. 25-40 mm. horizontal.	A. 8.8 cm.Kw.K. 43(L/71) 7.92 mm. MG.34 coaxial 360° traverse smoke generator discharger on roof. B. 7.92 mm. MG.34 (offside of glacis plate)	8.8 cm. = 84 rds. 7.92 mm. = 5850 rds.	Maybach OHV HL 230 P45 V-12 592 HP (at 2500 governed r.p.m.)	Large overlapping bogie wheels mounted in 9 units of 2 wheels each side. Each unit sprung on single torsion bars.	A. 21.5 m.p.h. B. 15 m.p.h. (approx) C. 106 miles D. 75 miles E. 5 ft. 11 in. F. 2 ft. 9½ in. G. 5 ft. 9 in. H. 35°	Apron plates to top of tracks. Transportation (narrow) tracks may be fitted for loading purposes.

9. PHOTOS OF PROTOTYPES, PROJECTS AND TANKS TAKEN INTO SERVICE

Fig. 1. Pz.Kpfw.I, Model 'A'. (Originally 'L.&.S.', or Krupp 'L.K.B.I').

Fig. 2. Pz.Kpfw.I, Model 'B'.

Fig. 3. Pz.Kpfw.I, Commander's Model. (kl.Pz.Bef.Wg.).

Fig. 4. Pz.Kpfw.II, Models 'a1' 'a2' 'a3' and 'b'.

Fig. 5. Pz.Kpfw.II, Model 'c'.

Fig. 6. Pz.Kpfw.II. Models A, B and C.

Fig. 7. Pz.Kpfw.II, Models D and E.

Fig. 8. Pz.Kpfw.II, Model F.

Fig. 9. Pz.Kpfw.II, Model L 'Lynx' (Pz.Sp.Wg 'Luchs').

Fig. 10. Pz.Kpfw.III, Model A.

Fig. 11. Pz.Kpfw, Models B and C.

Fig. 12. Pz.Kpfw.III, Model D.

Fig. 13. Pz.Kpfw.III, Model E.

Fig. 14. Pz.Kpfw.III, Models F, G and H.

Fig. 15. Pz.Kpfw.III, Model J.

Fig. 16. Pz.Kpfw.III, Model L.

Fig. 17. Pz.Kpfw.III, Model M.

Fig. 18. Pz.Kpfw.III, Model N.

Fig. 19. Pz.Kpfw.IV. Model A.

Fig. 20. Pz.Kpfw.IV, Models B and C.

Fig. 21. Pz.Kpfw.IV. Model D.

Fig. 22. Pz.Kpfw.IV, Model E.

Fig. 23. Pz.Kpfw.IV, Model F1.

Fig. 24. Pz.Kpfw.IV, Model F2.

Fig. 25. Pz.Kpfw.IV, Model G.

Fig. 26. Pz.Kpfw.IV, Model H

Fig. 27. Pz.Kpfw.IV, Model J.

Fig. 28. Pz.Kpfw.Panther, Model D.

Fig. 29. Pz.Kpfw.Panther, Model A.

Fig. 30. Pz.Kpfw.Panther, Model G.

Fig. 31. Pz.Kpfw.Panther, Commander's Model (Pz.Bef.Wg.Panther).

Fig. 32. Panther 'OP' Tank. (Pz.Beob.Wg.Panther)

Fig. 33. Panther armoured recovery vehicle. (Pz.Berge.Wg.Panther)

Fig. 34. Pz.Kpfw.Tiger, Model E.

Fig. 35. Pz.Kpfw. Tiger, Model B (early turret design)

Fig. 36. Pz.Kpfw.Tiger, Model B (production turret).

Fig. 37. Krupp 'L.K.A.I' (first prototype of design to Pz.Kpfw.I specification)

Fig. 38. Krupp 'L.K.B.3' - third prototype of Pz.Kpfw.I. (Model B) as agricultural Tractor.

Fig. 39. La.S. (Krupptracktor) - tractor version of Pz.Kpfw.I.Model A.

Fig. 40. Pz.Kpfw.I.n.a.(V.K.601).

Fig. 41. Pz.Kpfw.I.n.A. verst.(V.K.1801).

Fig. 42. Krupp 'L.K.A.2' - design to Pz.Kpfw.II or La.S.100 specification.

Fig. 43. La.S.100 (designer unknown).

Fig. 44. La.S.100 (MAN).

Fig. 45. V.K.1301.

Fig. 46. V.K.901 mit neuer waffen.

Fig. 47. Pz.Kpfw.II n.A. verst. (V.K.1601).

Fig. 48. Pz.Kpfw.III experimental prototype with FAMO suspension.

Fig. 49. Rheinmetall 'Nb.Fz.' ('Pz.Kpfw.V').

Fig. 50. Rheinmetall 'Nb.Fz' ('Pz.Kpfw.VI').

Fig. 51. Krupp 'M.K.A.' - design to Pz.Kpfw.III or 'ZW' specification.

Fig. 52. Rheinmetall Borsig 'BW' (Pz.Kpfw.IV) prototype.

Fig. 53. V.K. 2002(MAN).

Fig. 54. V.K.2001(D).

Fig. 55. V.K.2001(K).

Fig. 56. V.K.3001(H).

Fig. 57. V.K.6501.

Fig. 58. Henschel 'DW 2'.

Fig. 59. V.K.3601(H).

Fig. 60. V.K.3601 as finally constructed.

Fig. 61. V.K.4501 (H).

Fig. 62. V.K.4501 (P).

Fig. 63. Daimler Benz Panther prototype V.K. 3002(D).

Fig. 64. V.K.4502(P).

Fig. 65. Panther Schmal Turm.

Fig. 67. E.100.

Fig. 68. Pz. Kpfw. 'Maus'.

Fig. 69. Pz. Kpfw. 38(t) with turret of Pz. Kpfw. IV. and 7.5 cm. (L/48) gun.

Fig. 70. Pz. Kpfw. IV mounting 7.5 cm. Kw. K. 42 in redesigned turret.

Fig. 71. Mockup of Pz. Kpfw. IV mounting 7.5 cm (L/70) gun.

Fig. 72. Pz. Kpfw. Panther with 8.8cm. Kw. K. 43(L/71).

Fig. 73. Pz. Kpfw. Tiger Model B mounting 10.5 cm. (L/68) gun.

Fig. 74. Model of Krupp V.K. 7001 (LÖWE or TIGER-MAUS).

10. Bibliography

    (i)   Early History -

Drawings and Documents
Files from Krupp, Henschel, M.A.N., Daimler Benz, M.N.H., Porsche K.G., and Rheinmetall Borsig held by B.I.O.S. Group V at F.V. Wing M.C. of S.

Minutes of conferences (Hitler - Speer) held at Foreign Documents Library, G.E.D., Foreign Office.

    (ii)   General Information

War Office (M.I.10) Technical Intelligence Summaries.
M.I.10., M.E. Intelligence Summaries.
G.S.I. (tech), B.A.O.R. Technical Intelligence Reports.
G.S.I. (tech), 21 A.Gp. Technical Intelligence Summaries.
G2 Tech Int. A.F.H.Q. Technical Intelligence Summaries.
German descriptive handbooks (D-Vorschrupten and H.Dv's) held by F.V. Wing M.C. of S.

    (iii)   Technical Examination Reports by Department of Tank Design, Ministry of Supply and M.C. of S., S.T.T. on:-

        Pz. Kpfw. I
        Pz. Kpfw. II
        Pz. Kpfw. III
        Pz. Kpfw. IV
        Pz. Kpfw. Panther
        Pz. Kpfw. Tiger
        Pz. Berge. Wg. Panther
        Pz. Kpfw. 38 (t)

    (iv)   Projected Developments

B.I.O.S. and C.I.O.S. Group V reports.
War Office Technical Intelligence Summaries.
B.A.O.R. Technical Intelligence Reports.
A.F.H.Q. Technical Intelligence Reports.
Files, drawings and documents from Krupp, Henschel, M.A.N., Daimler Benz, M.N.H., Porsche K.G., and Rheinmetall - Borsig held by B.I.O.S. Group V at F.V. Wing M.C. of S.

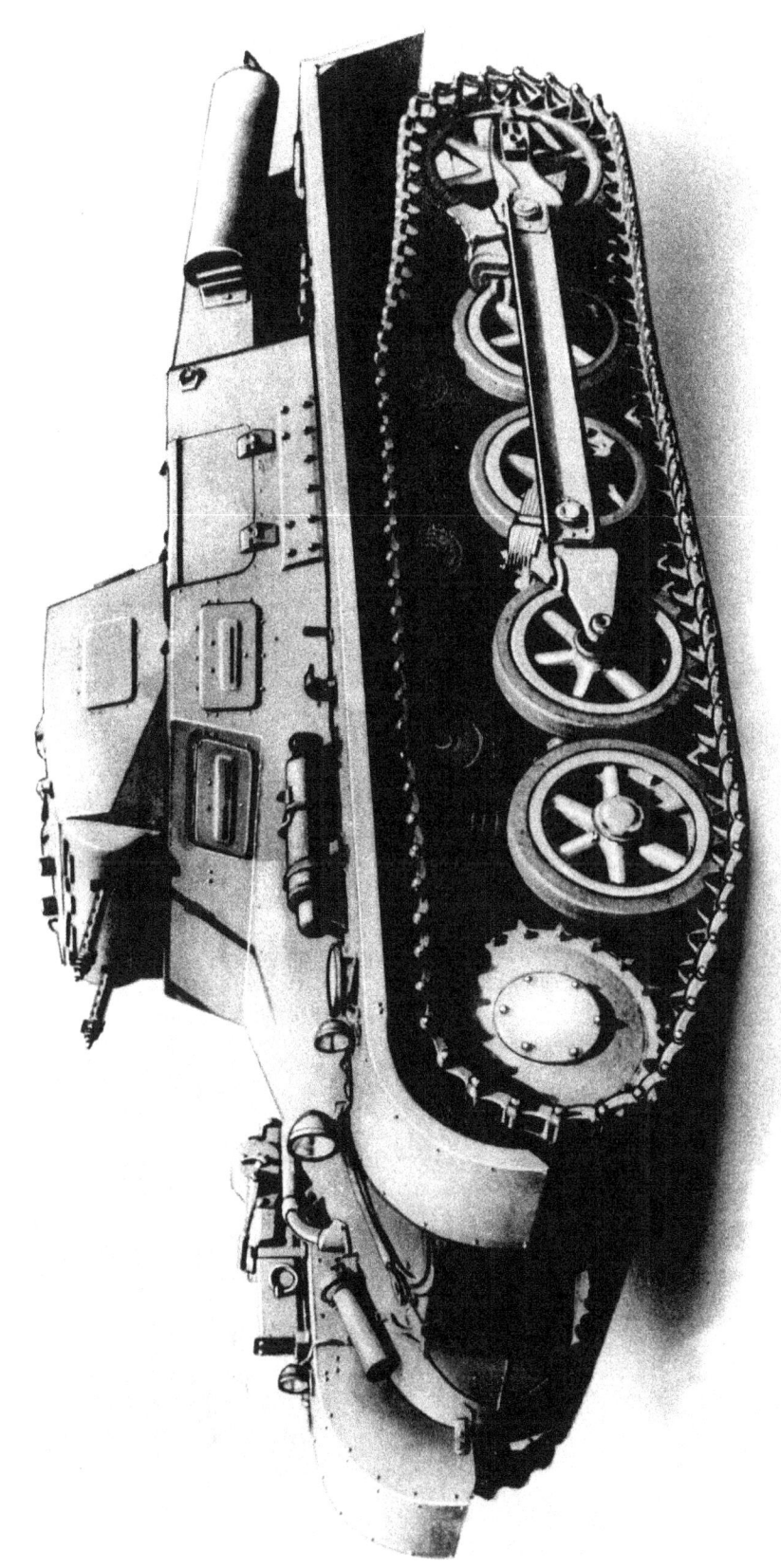

Fig. 1. Pz. Kpfw. 1 Model 'A' (Originally 'La.S.', or Krupp 'L.K.B.I.')

Fig.2. Pz.Kpfw.I, Model 'B'.

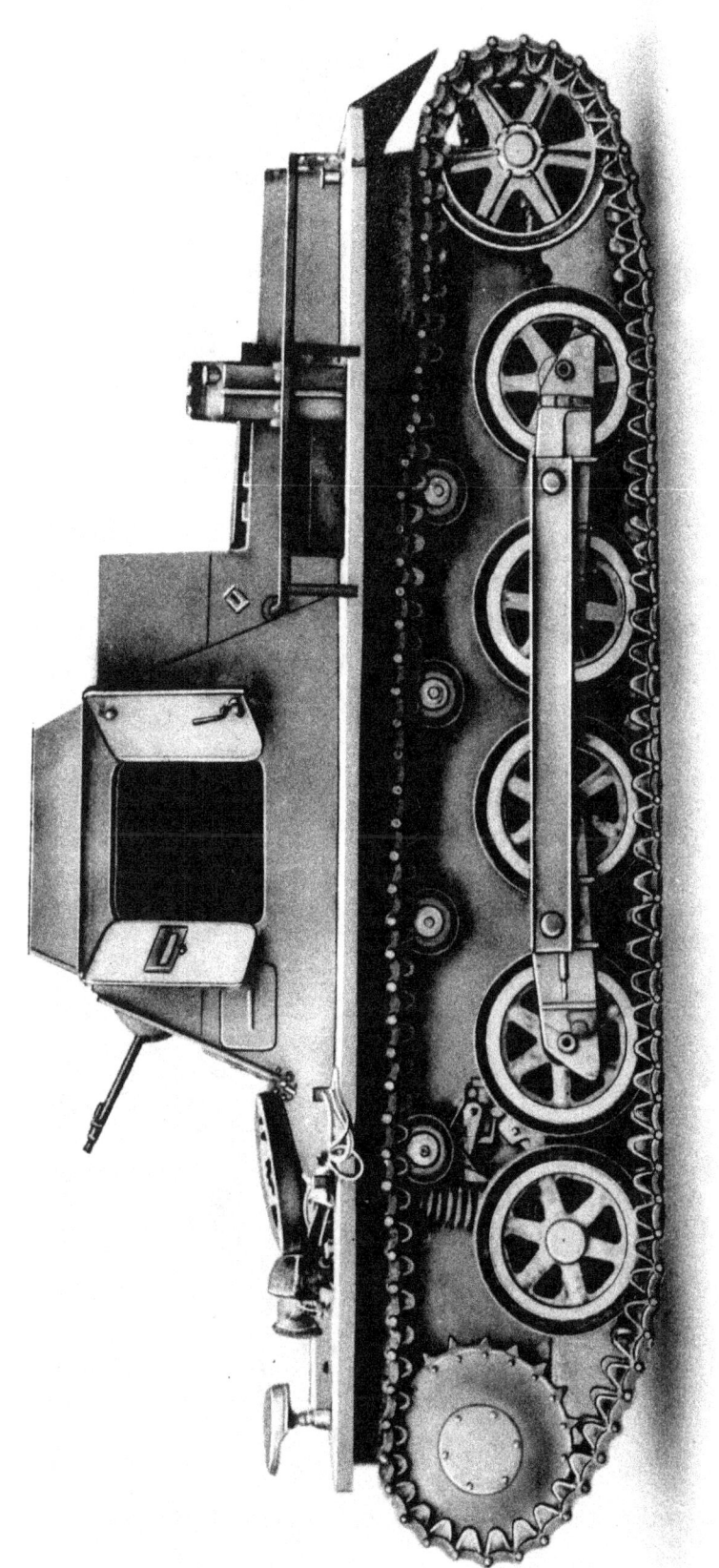

Fig.3.Pz.Kpfw.I, Commander's Model. (kl.Pz.Bef.Wg.).

Fig.4. Pz.Kpfw.II, Models 'a1' 'a2' 'a3' and 'b'.

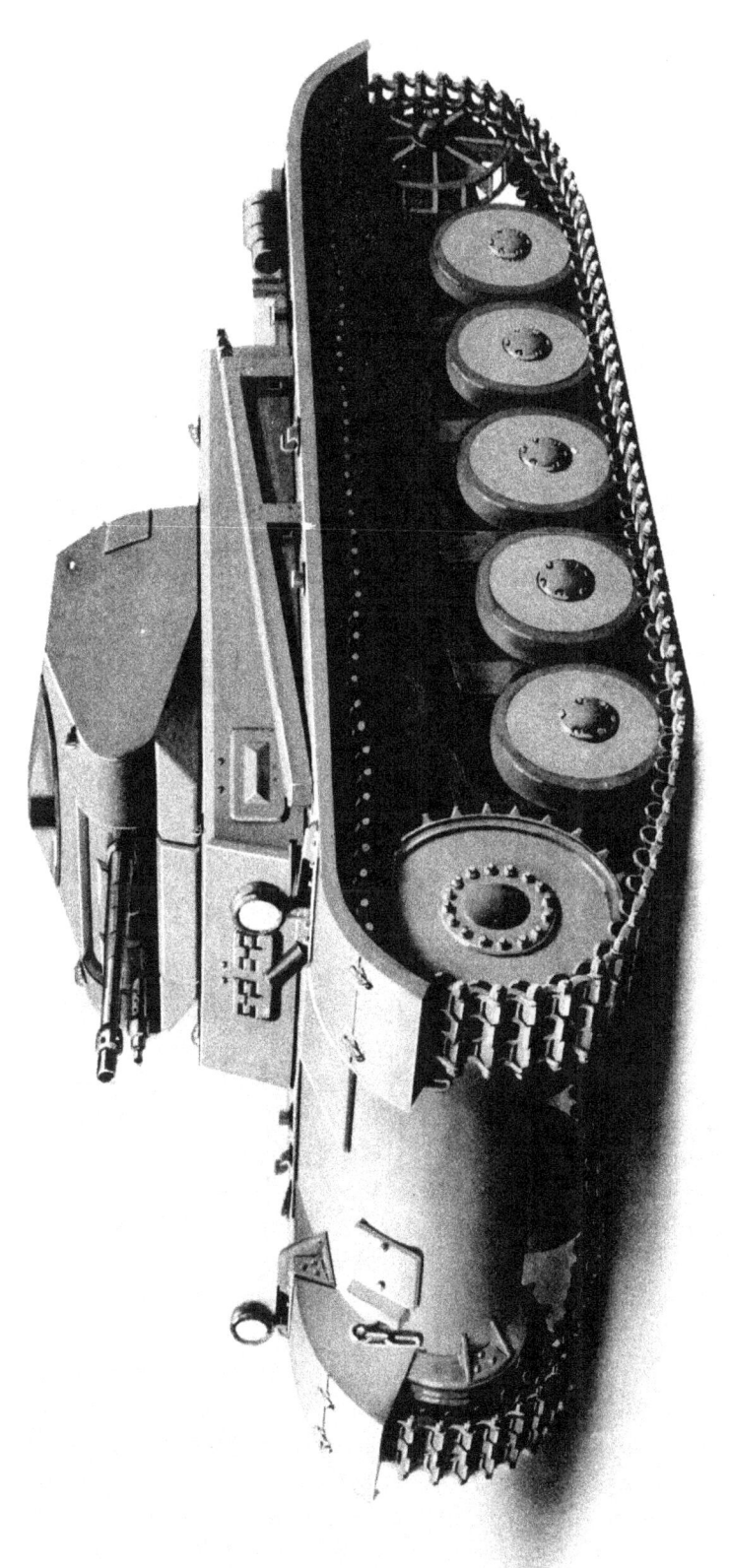

Fig. 5 Pz.Kpfw.II, Model 'c'.

Fig. 6. Pz.Kpfw.II Models A, B, and C.

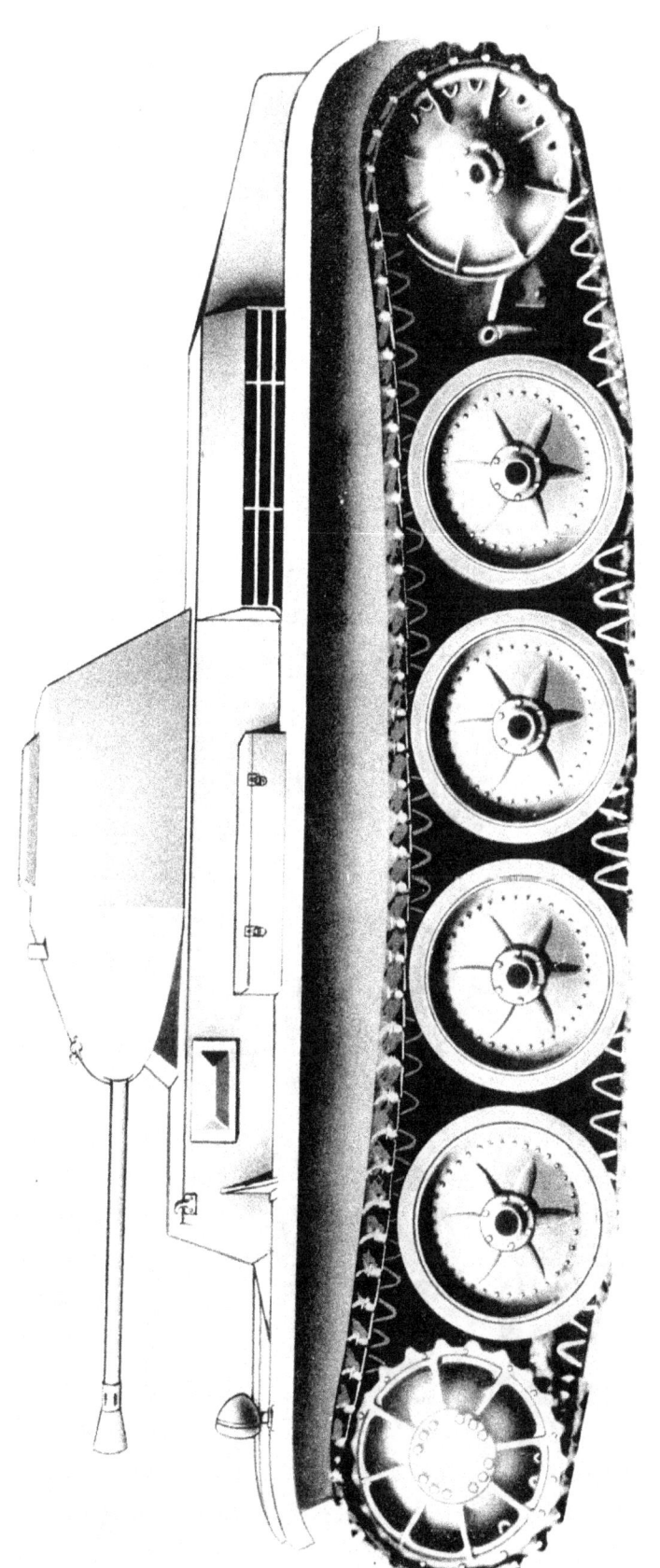

Fig. 7. Pz.Kpfw.II, Models D and E.

Fig. 8. Pz.Kpfw.II, Model F.

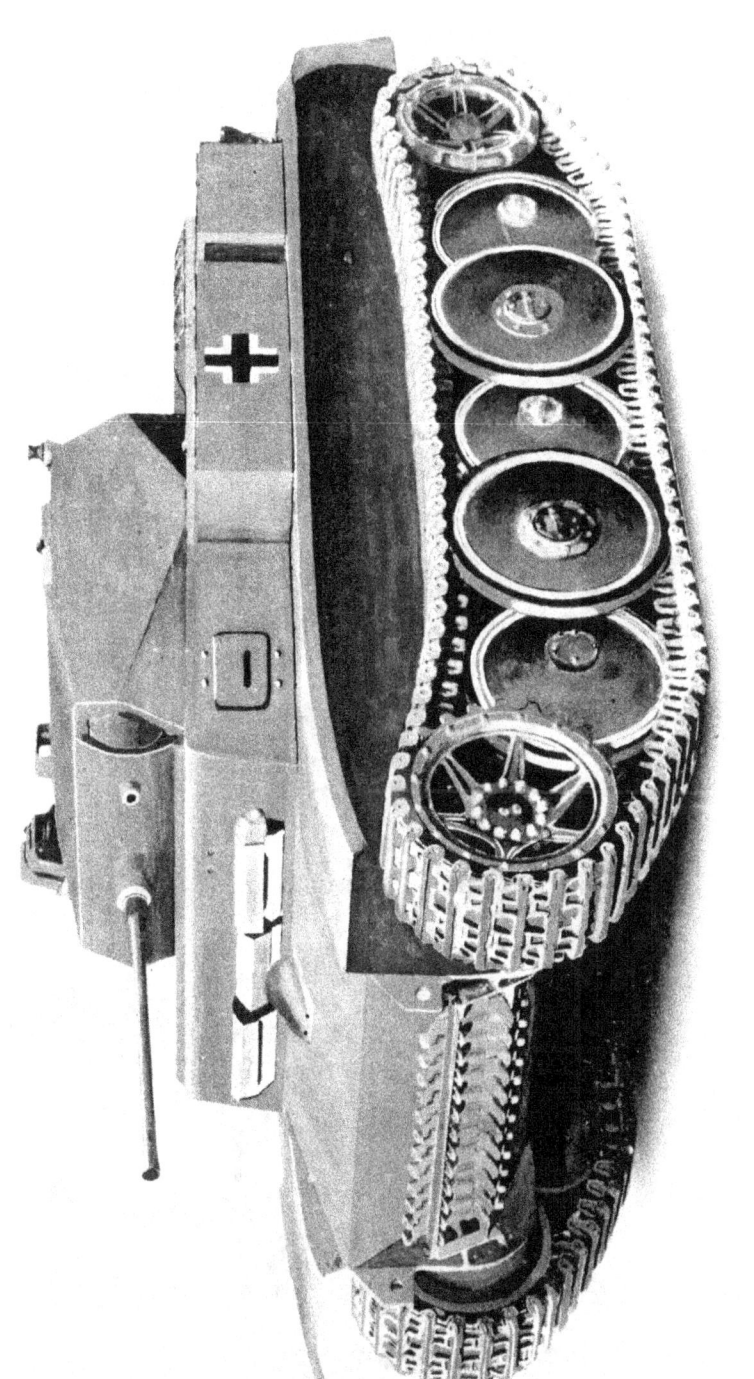

Fig. 9. Pz.Kpfw.II, Model L 'Lynx' (Pz.Sp.Wg. 'Luchs').

Fig. 10. Pz.Kpfw.III, Model A.

Fig.11. Pz.Kpfw.III, Models B and C.

Fig. 12. Pz.Kpfw.III, Model D.

Fig.13. Pz.Kpfw.III, Model E.

Fig. 14. Pz.Kpfw.III, Models F, G and H.

Fig. 15. Pz.Kpfw.III, Model J.

Fig. 16. Pz.Kpfw.III, Model L.

Fig. 17. Pz.Kpfw.III, Model H.

Fig. 18. Pz.Kpfw.III, Model N.

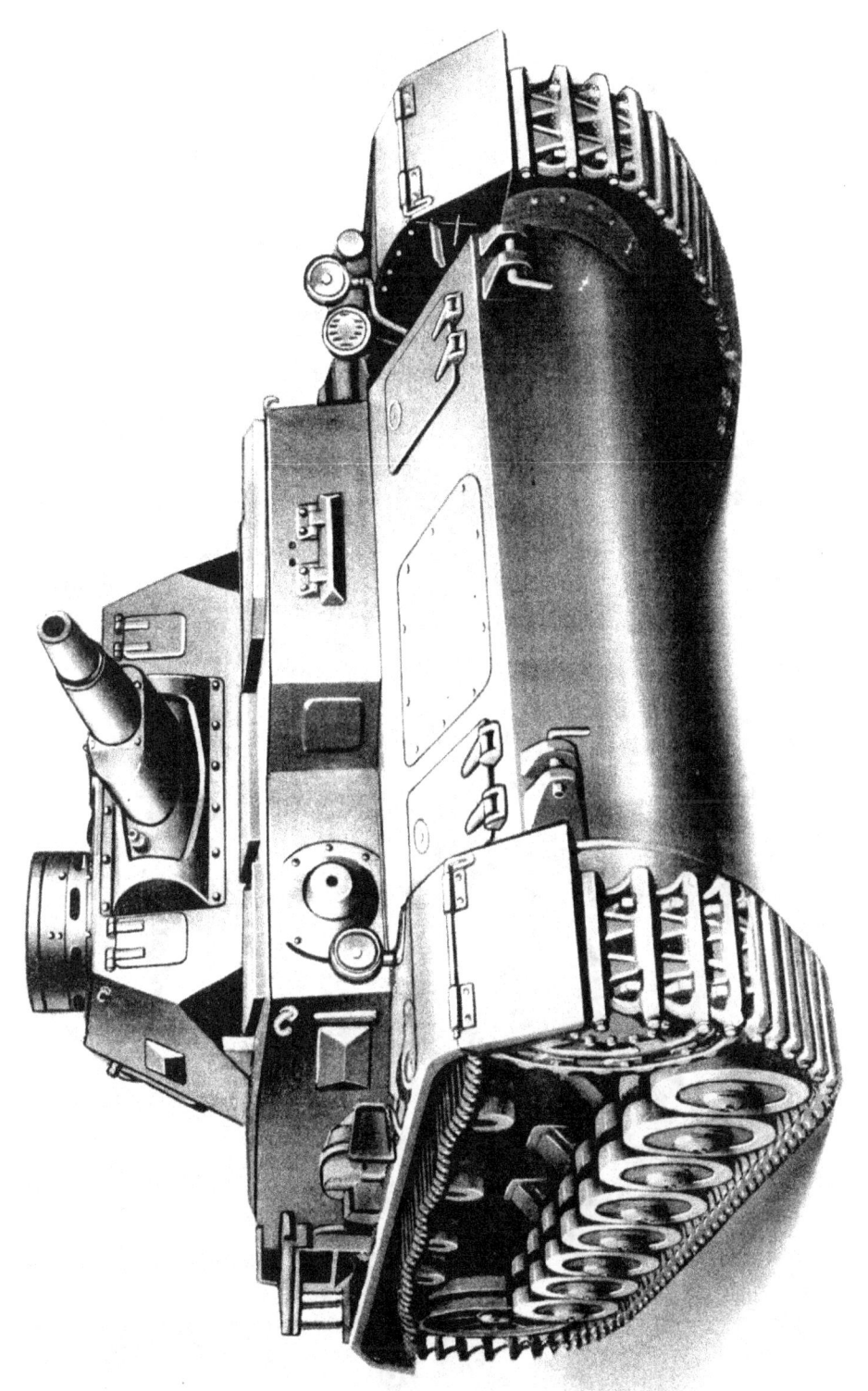

Fig. 19. Pz.Kpfw.IV, Model A.

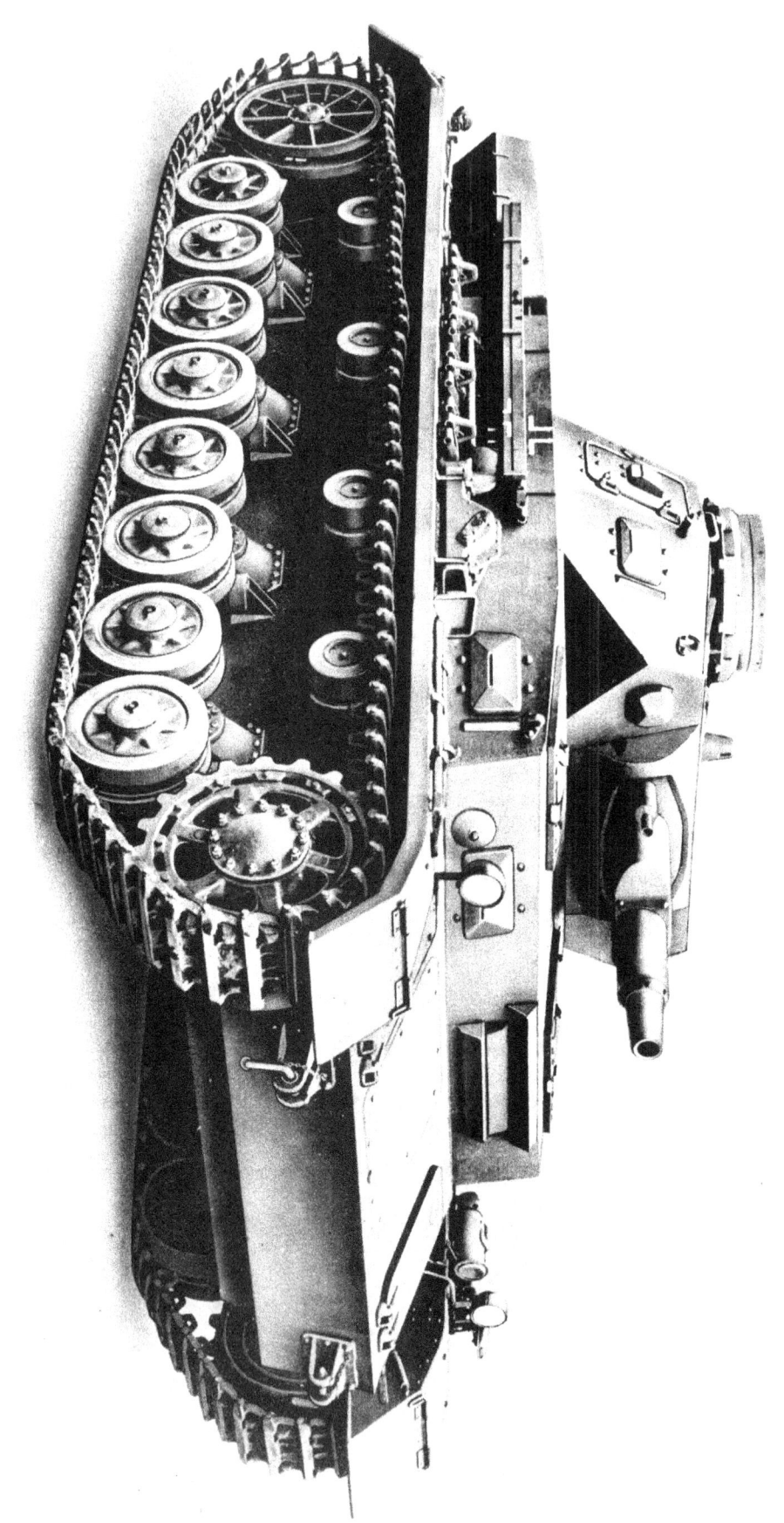

Fig. 20. Pz.Kpfw.IV, Models B and C.

Fig.21. Pz.Kpfw.IV.Model D.

Fig.22. Pz.Kpfw.IV, Model E.

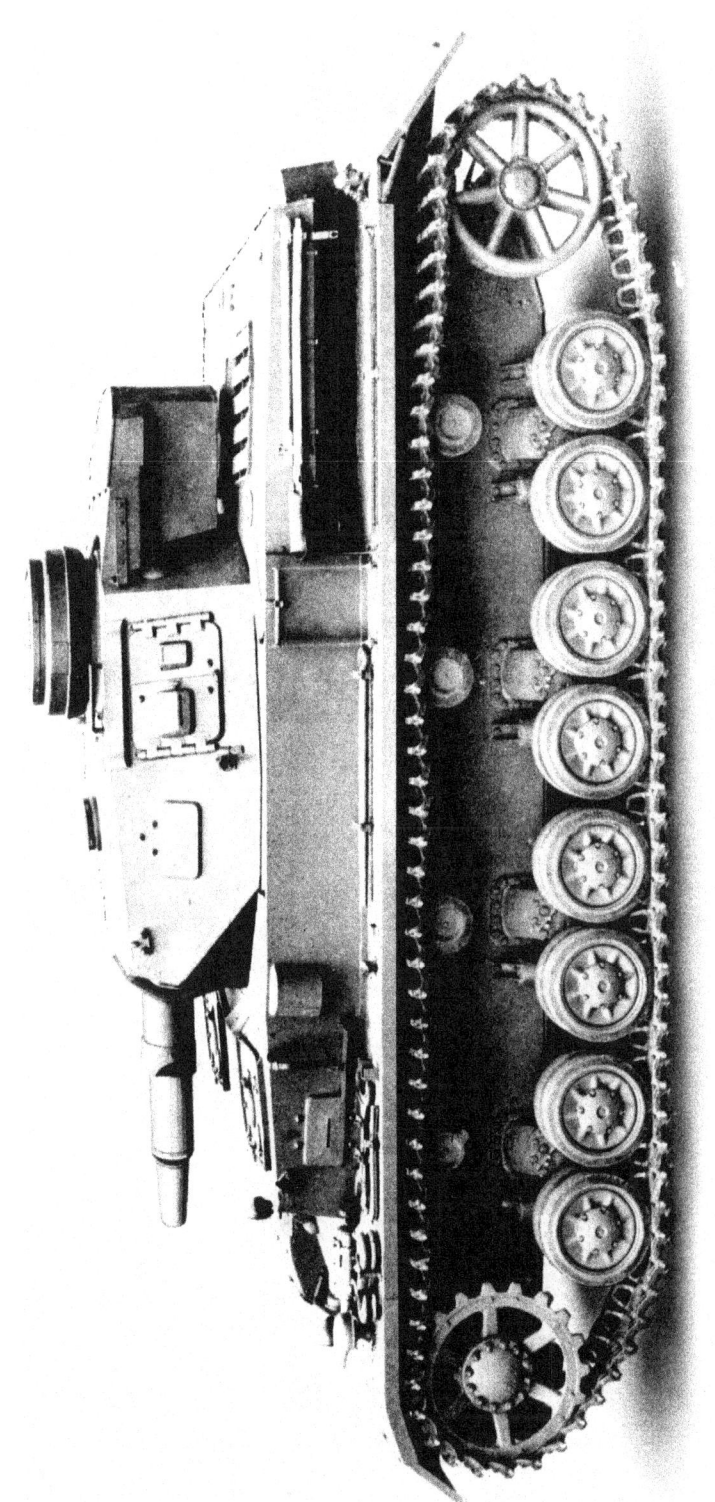

Fig. 23. Pz.Kpfw.IV, Model Fl.

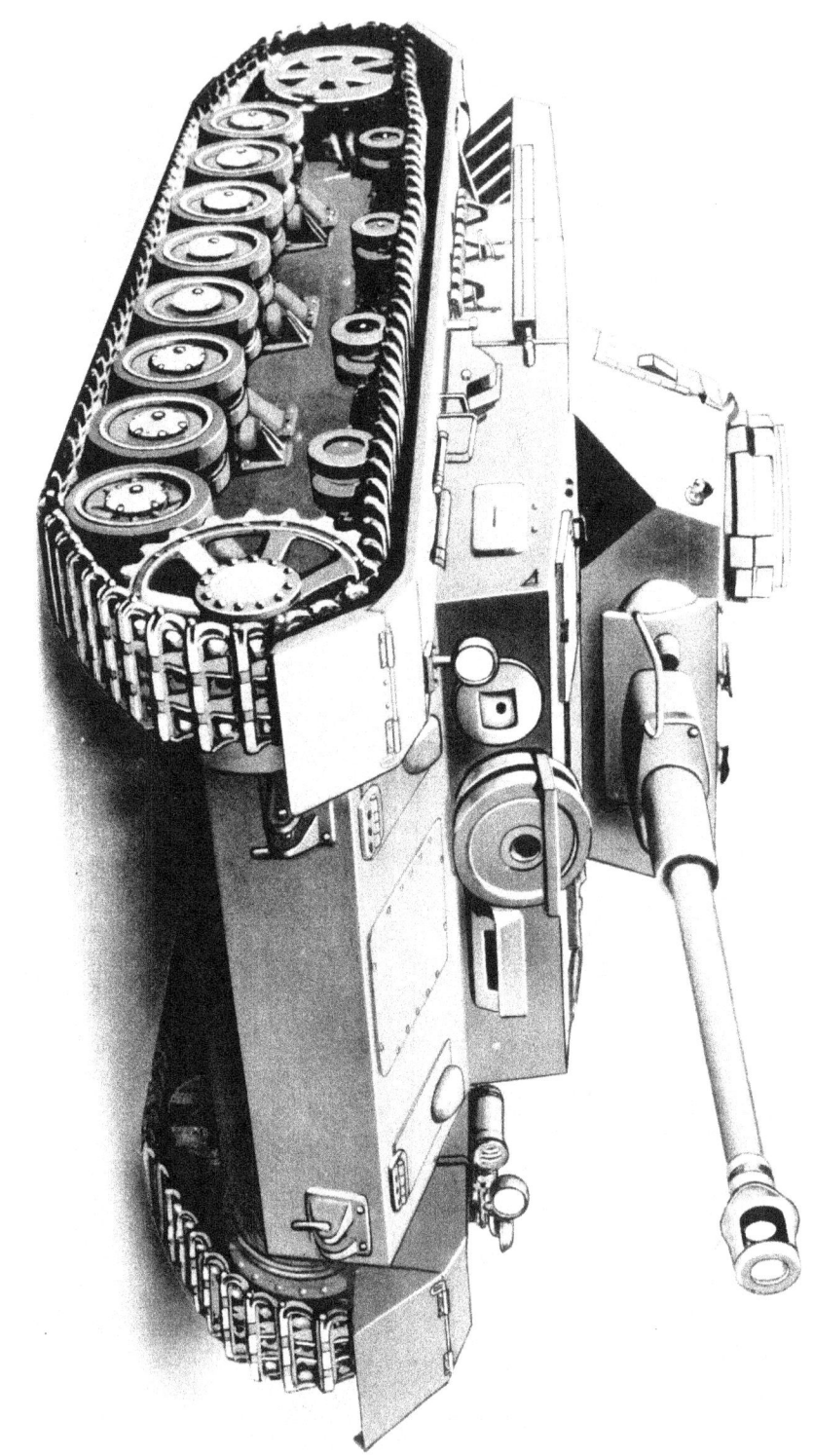

Fig.24 Pz.Kpfw.IV, Model F2.

Fig. 25. Pz.Kpfw.IV, Model G.

Fig. 26. Pz.Kpfw.IV, Model H.

Fig. 27. Pz.Kpfw.IV, Model J.

Fig. 28. Pz.Kpfw.Panther, Model D.

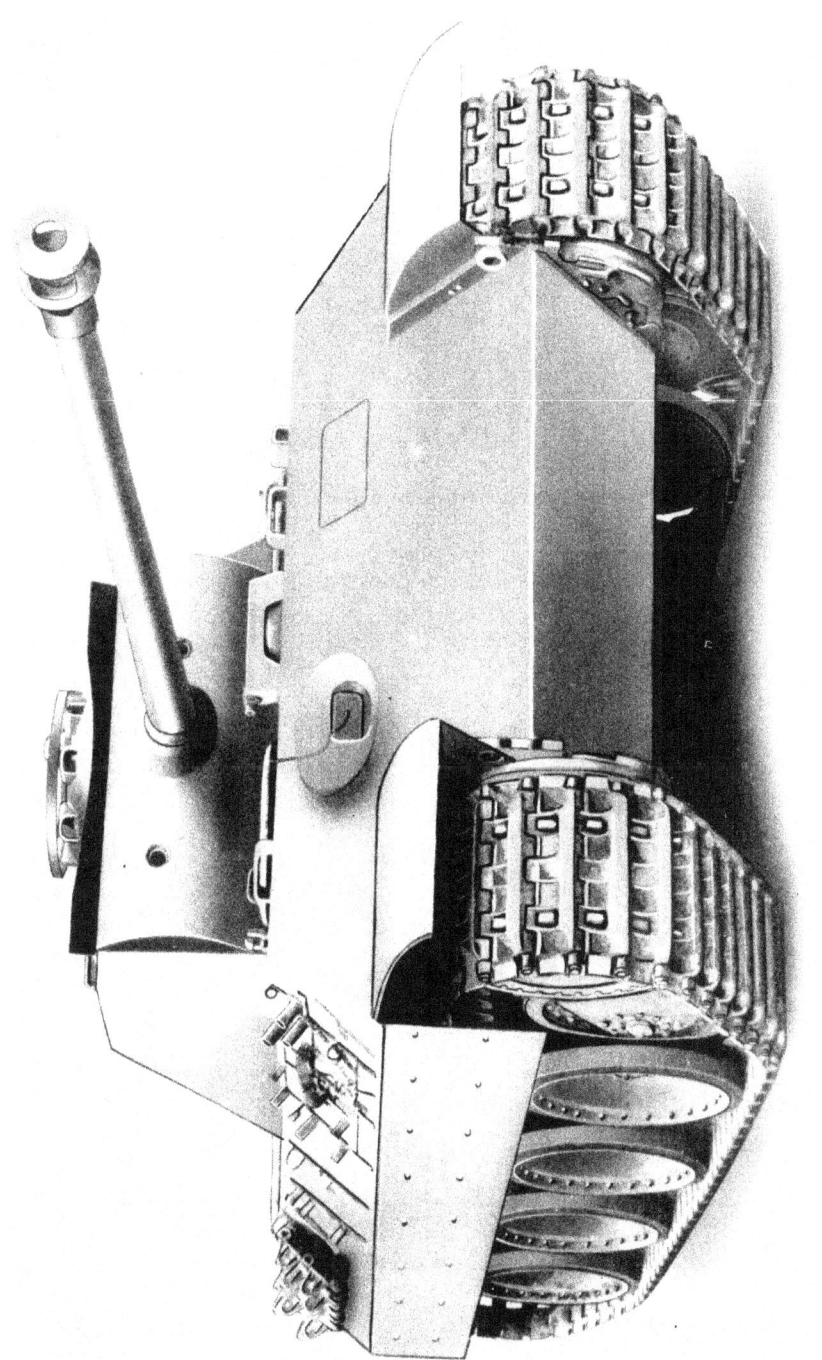

Fig. 29. Pz.Kpfw.Panther, Model A.

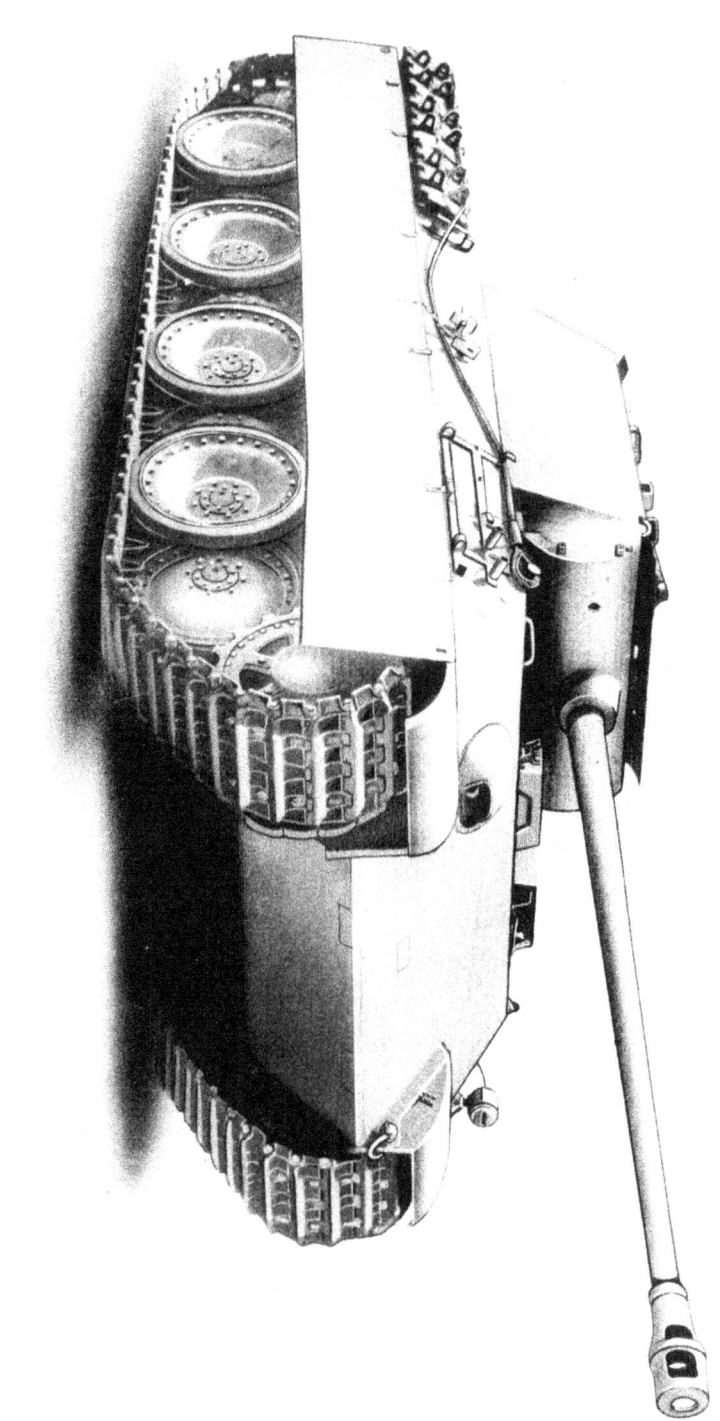

Fig. 30. Pz.Kpfw.Panther, Model G.

Fig. 31 Pz.Kpfw.Panther, Commander's Model (Pz.Bef.Wg.Panther).

Fig.32. Panther 'OP' Tank. (Pz.Beob.Wg.Panther).

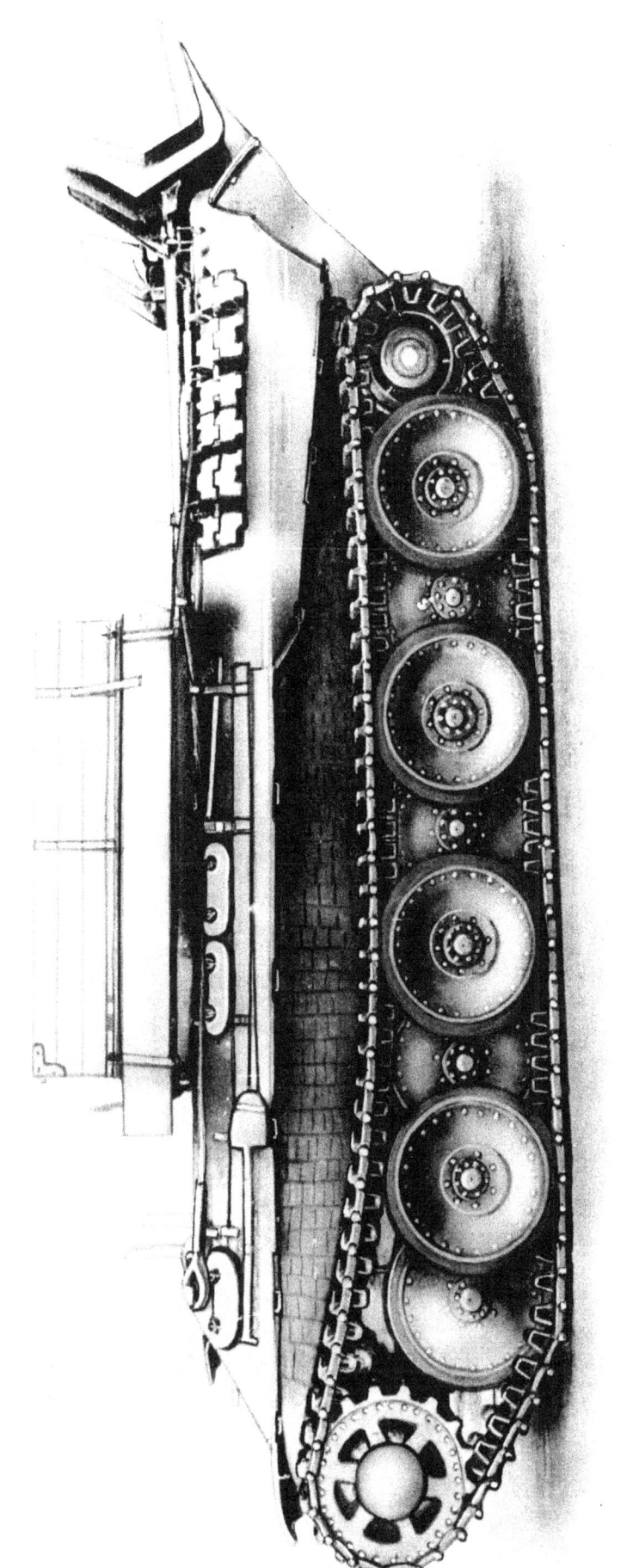

Fig.33. Panther armoured recovery vehicle. (Pz.Berge.Wg.Panther).

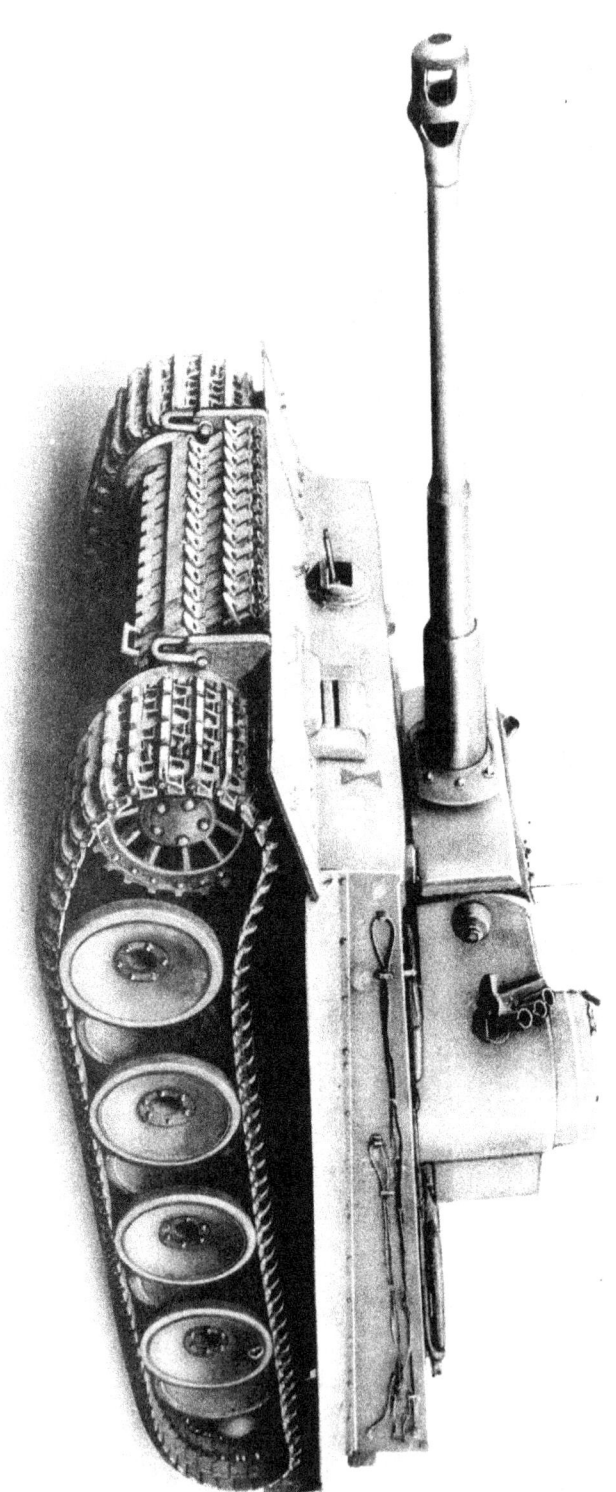

Fig. 34. Pz.Kpfw.Tiger, Model E.

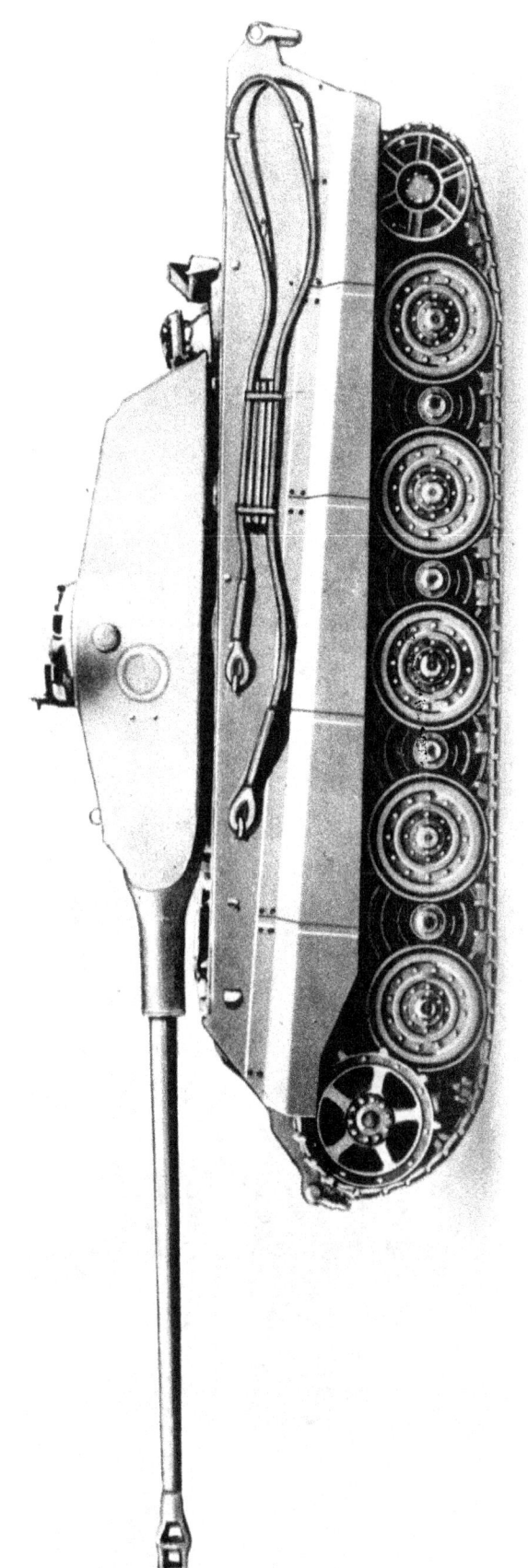

Fig. 35 Pz.Kpfw. Tiger, Model B (early turret design).

Fig. 36 Pz.Kpfw. Tiger, Model B (production turret).

Fig.37 Krupp "L.K.A.I." (first prototype of design to Pz.Kpfw.I. specification.

Fig.38 Krupp 'L.K.B.3 — third prototype of Pz.Kpfw.I (Model B) as agricultural tractor.

Fig. 39 La.S (KruppTractor) - tractor version of Pz.Kpfw.I Model A.

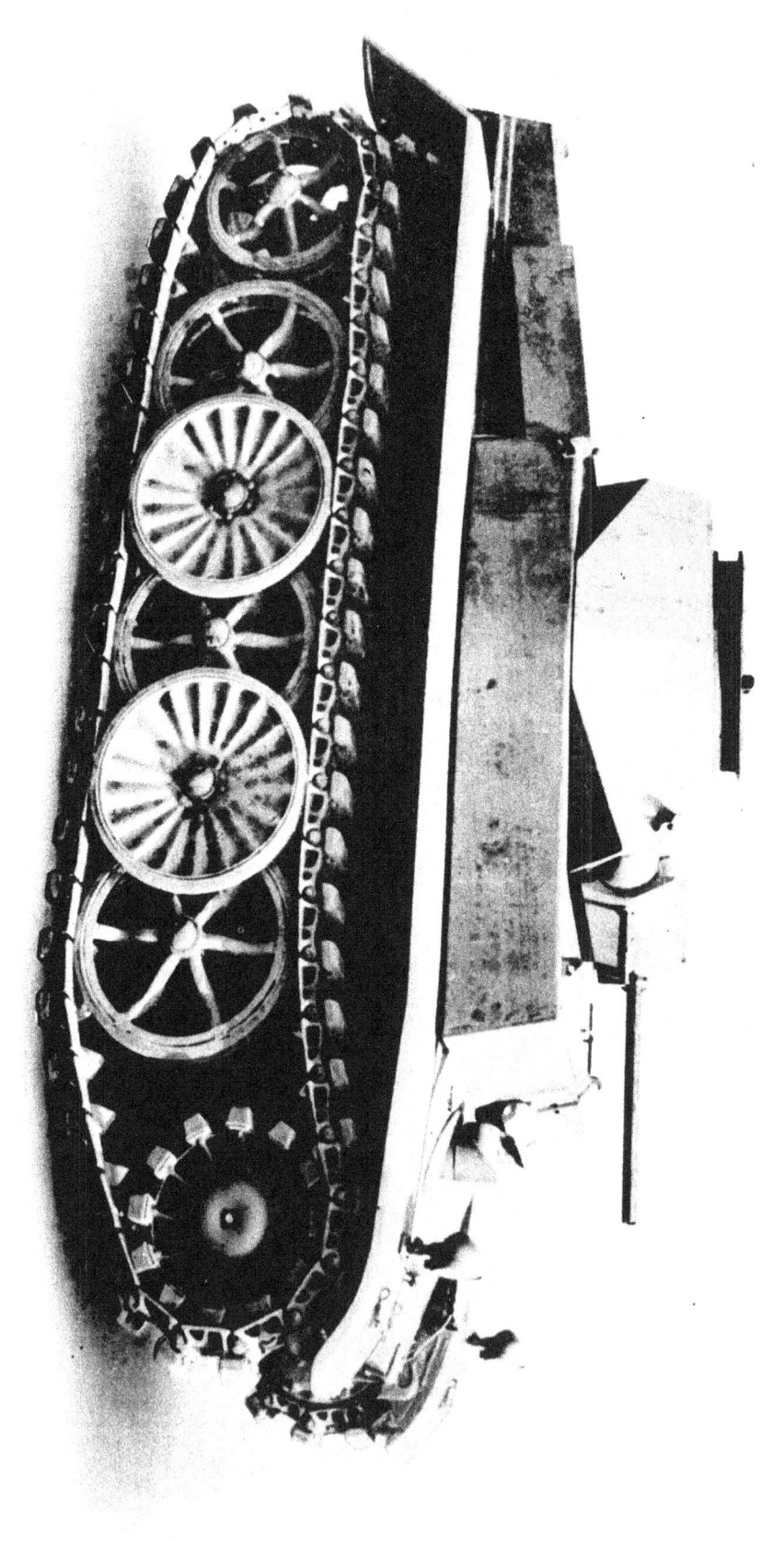

Fig. 40 Pz.Kpfw.I n.A.(V.K.601).

Fig. 41 Pz.Kpfw. I n.A verst. (V.K.1801).

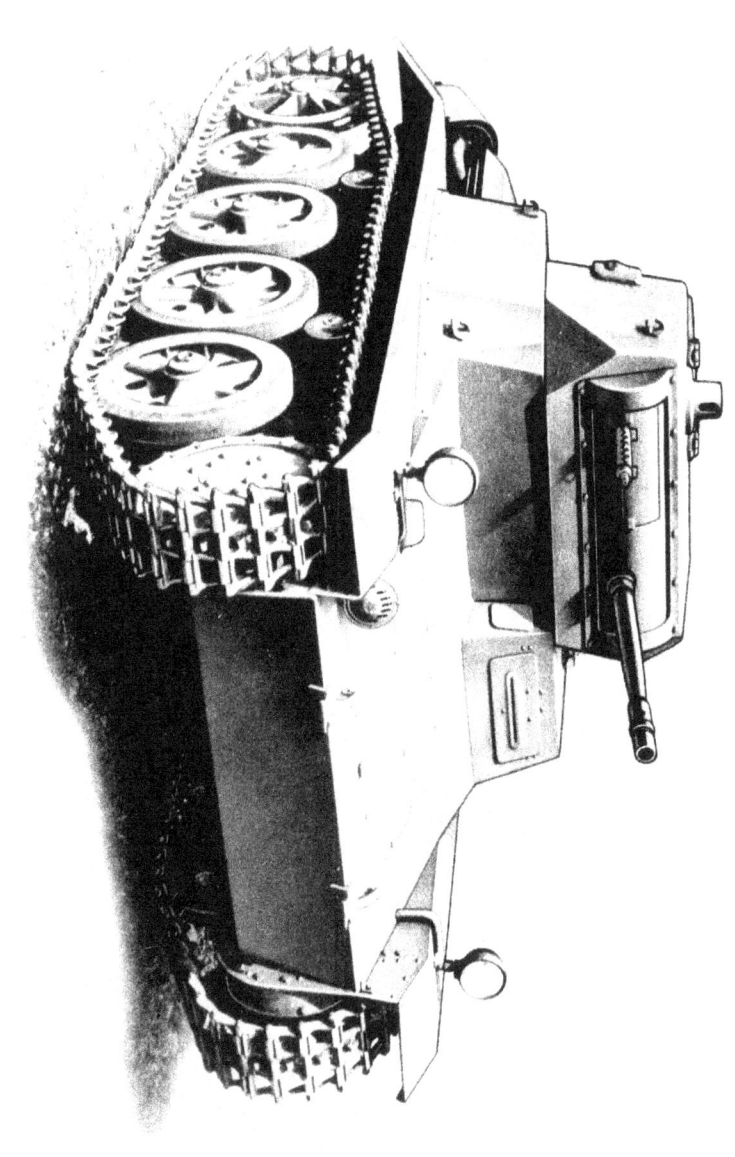

Fig.42 Krupp "L.K.A.2" - design to Pz.Kpfw.II or La.S.100 specification.

Fig. 43 La.S.100 (designers unknown).

Fig. 44 La.S.100 (MAN).

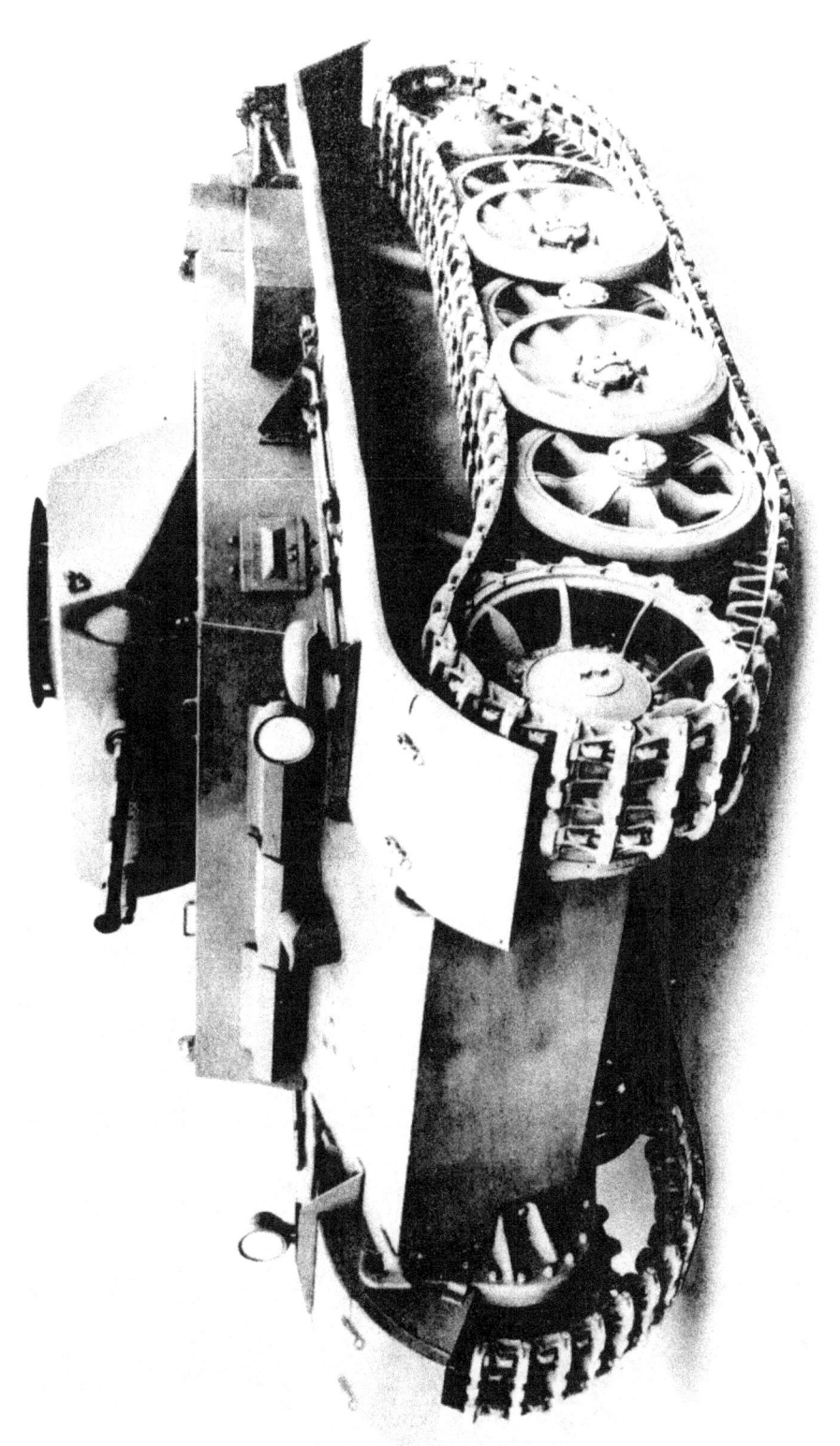

Fig. 45 V.K.1301

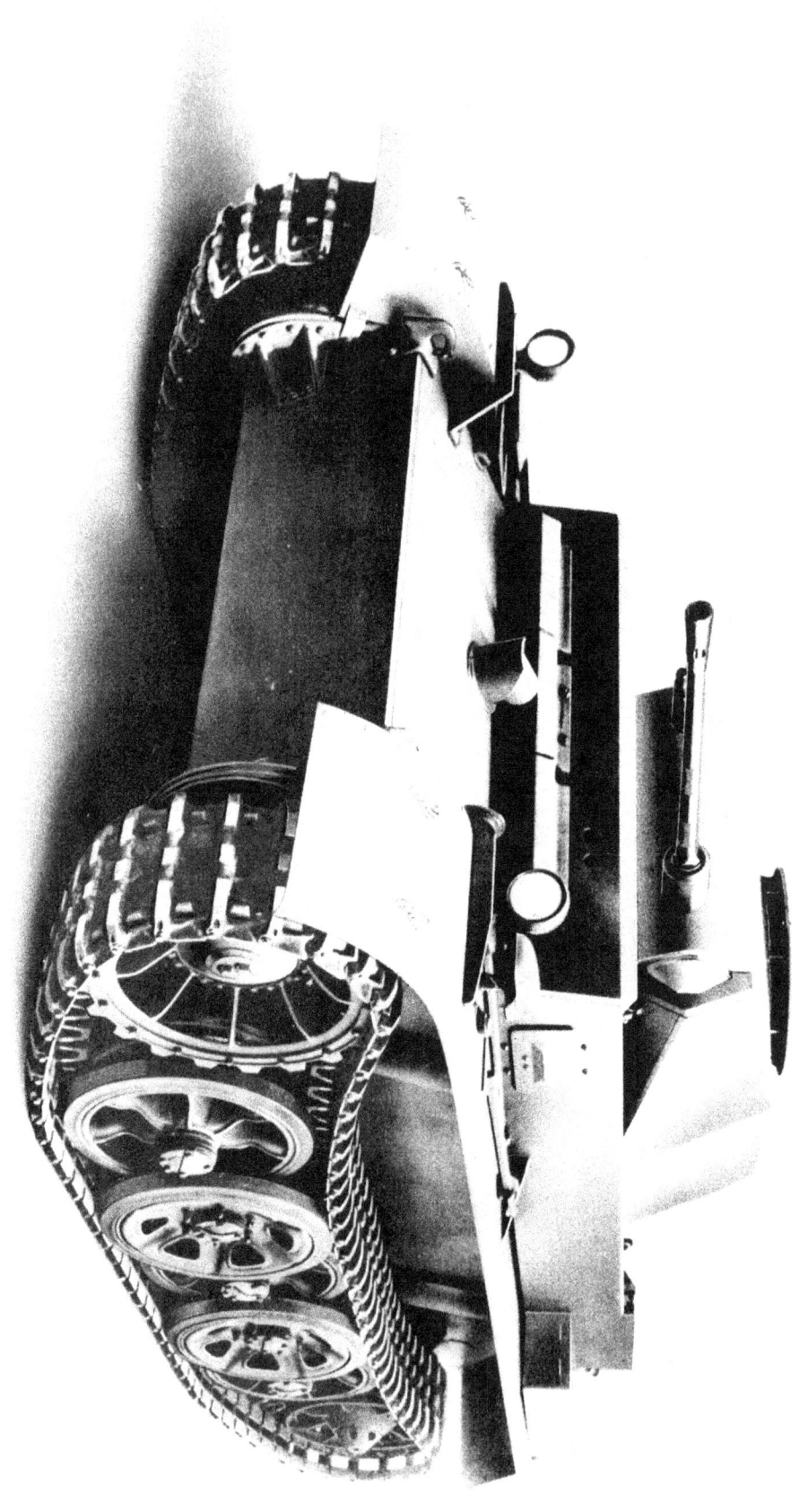

Fig. 46. V.K. 901 mit neuer waffen.

Fig. 47 Pz.Kpfw.II n.A.verst (V.K.1601).

Fig.48 Pz.Kpfw.III experimental prototype with FAMO suspension.

Fig. 49 Rheinmetall "Nb.Fz." ("Pz.Kpfw.V")

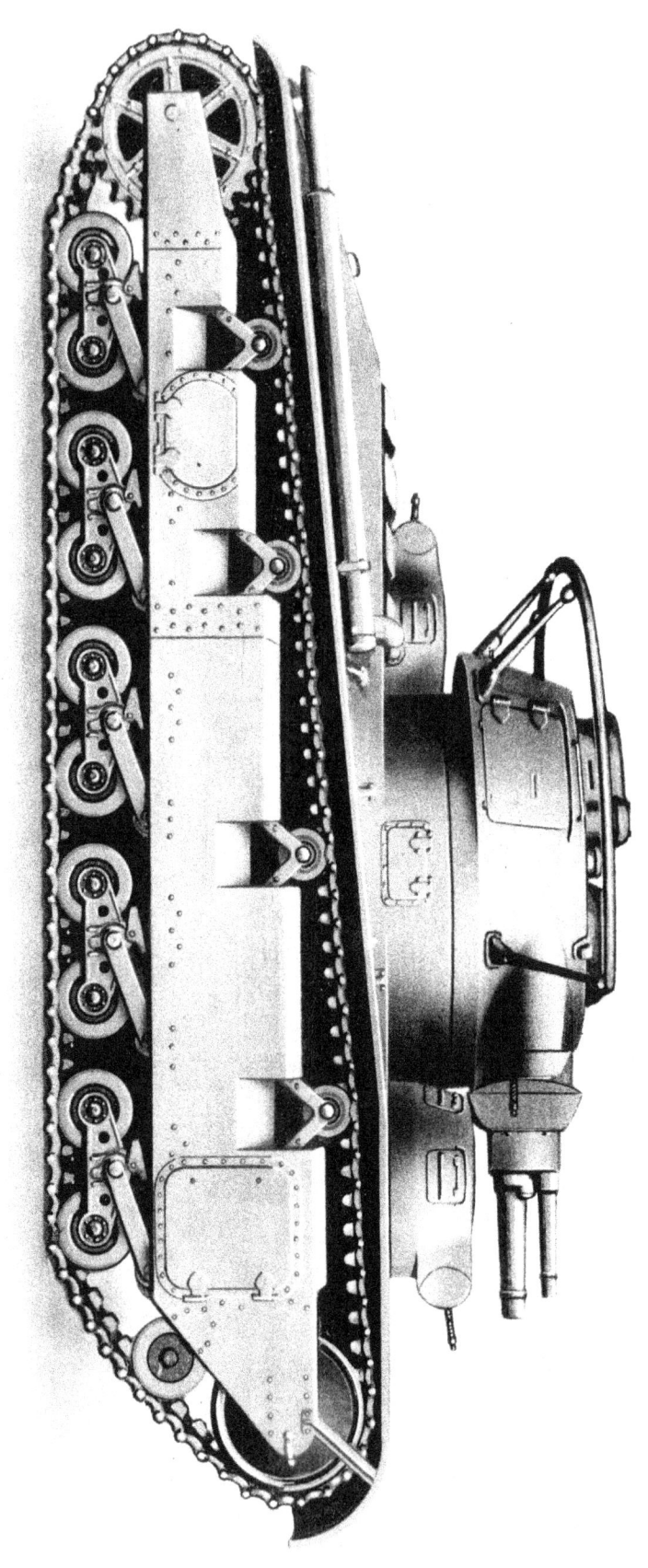

Fig.50 Rheinmetall "Nb.Fz" ("Pz.Kpfw.VI")

Fig.51 Krupp 'M.K.A' - design to Pz.Kpfw.III or 'ZW' specification.

Fig.52 Rheinmetall Borsig "bw" (Pz.kpfw.IV) prototype.

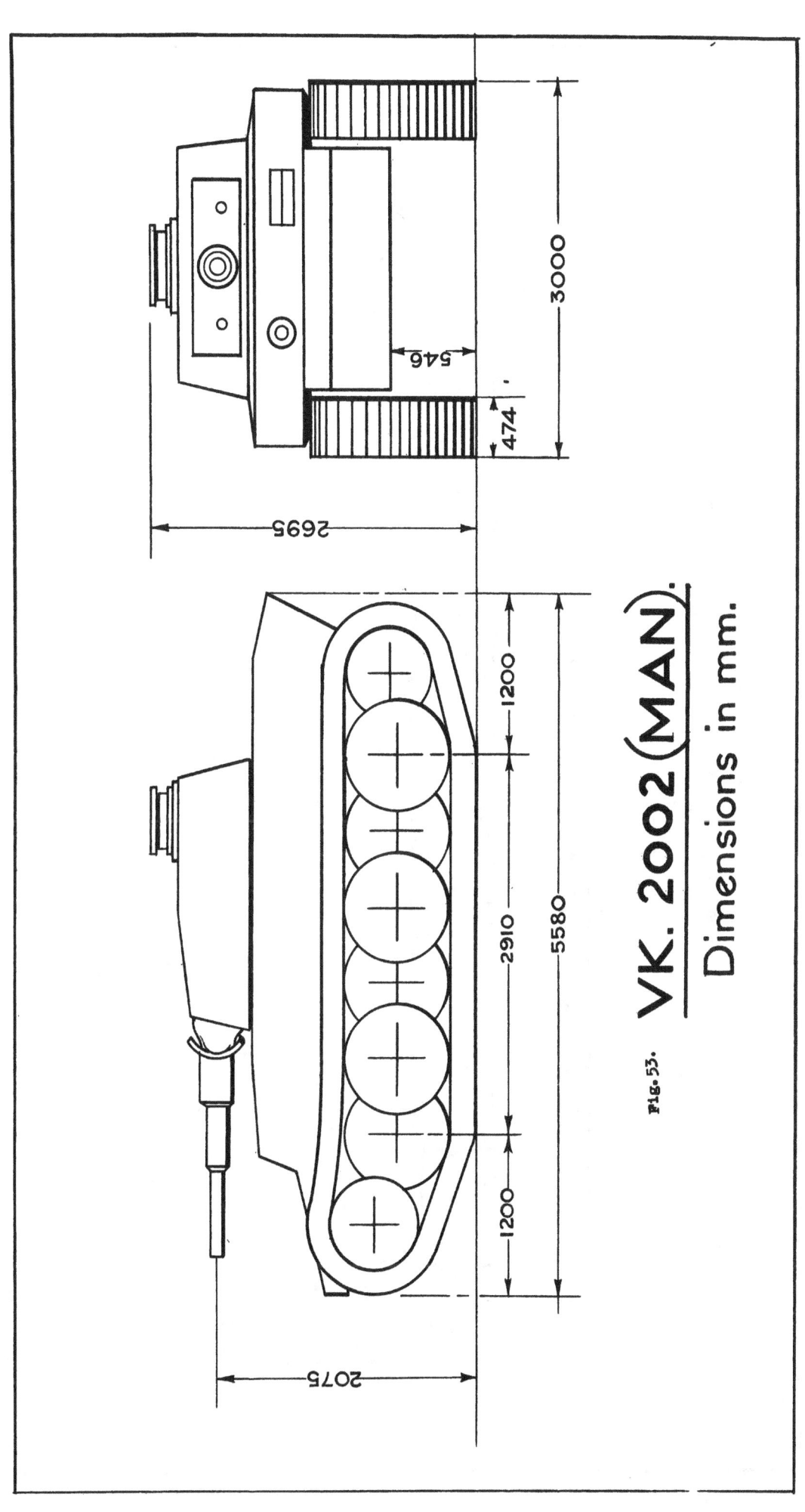

Fig. 53. **VK. 2002 (MAN).** Dimensions in mm.

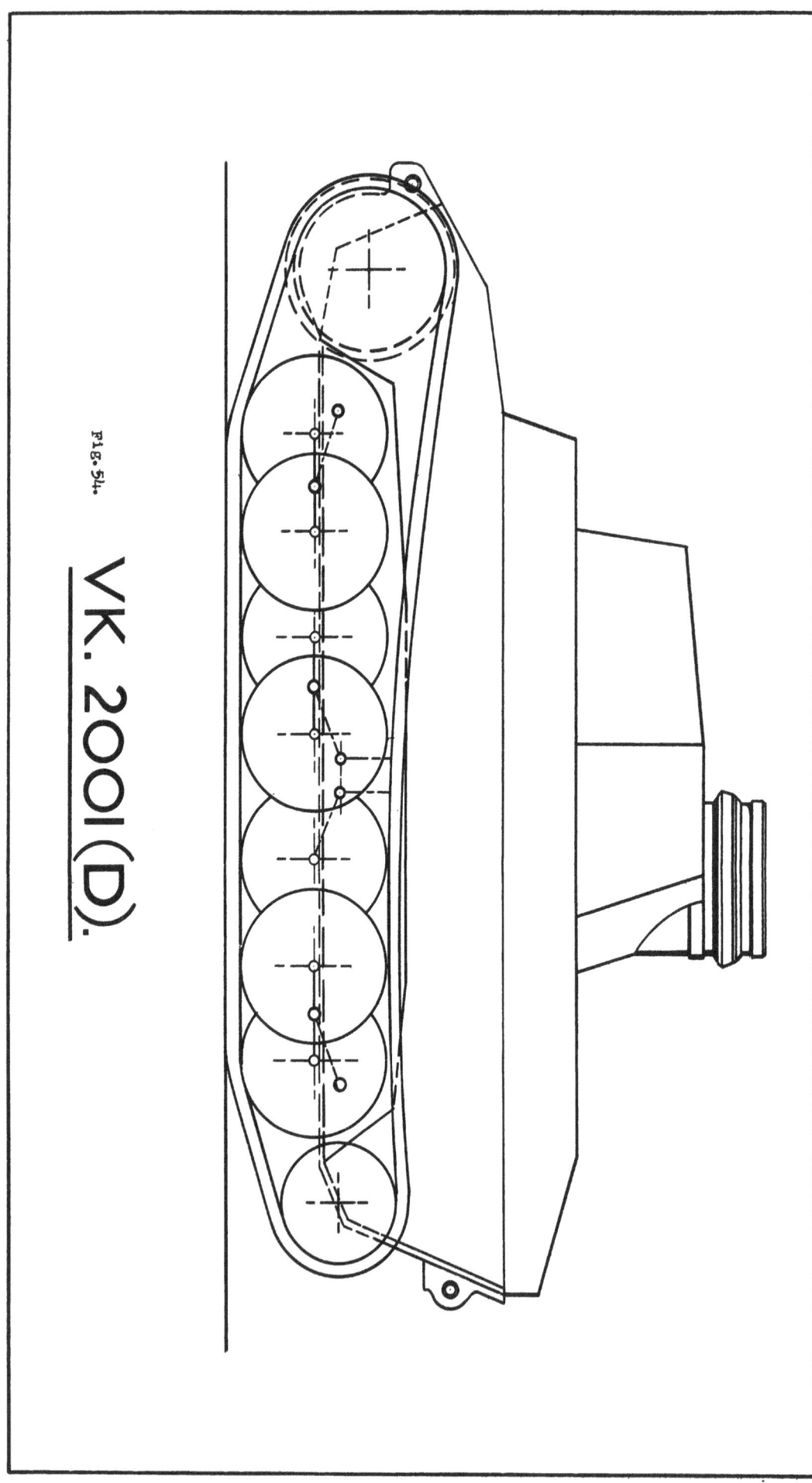

Fig. 54. VK. 2001(D).

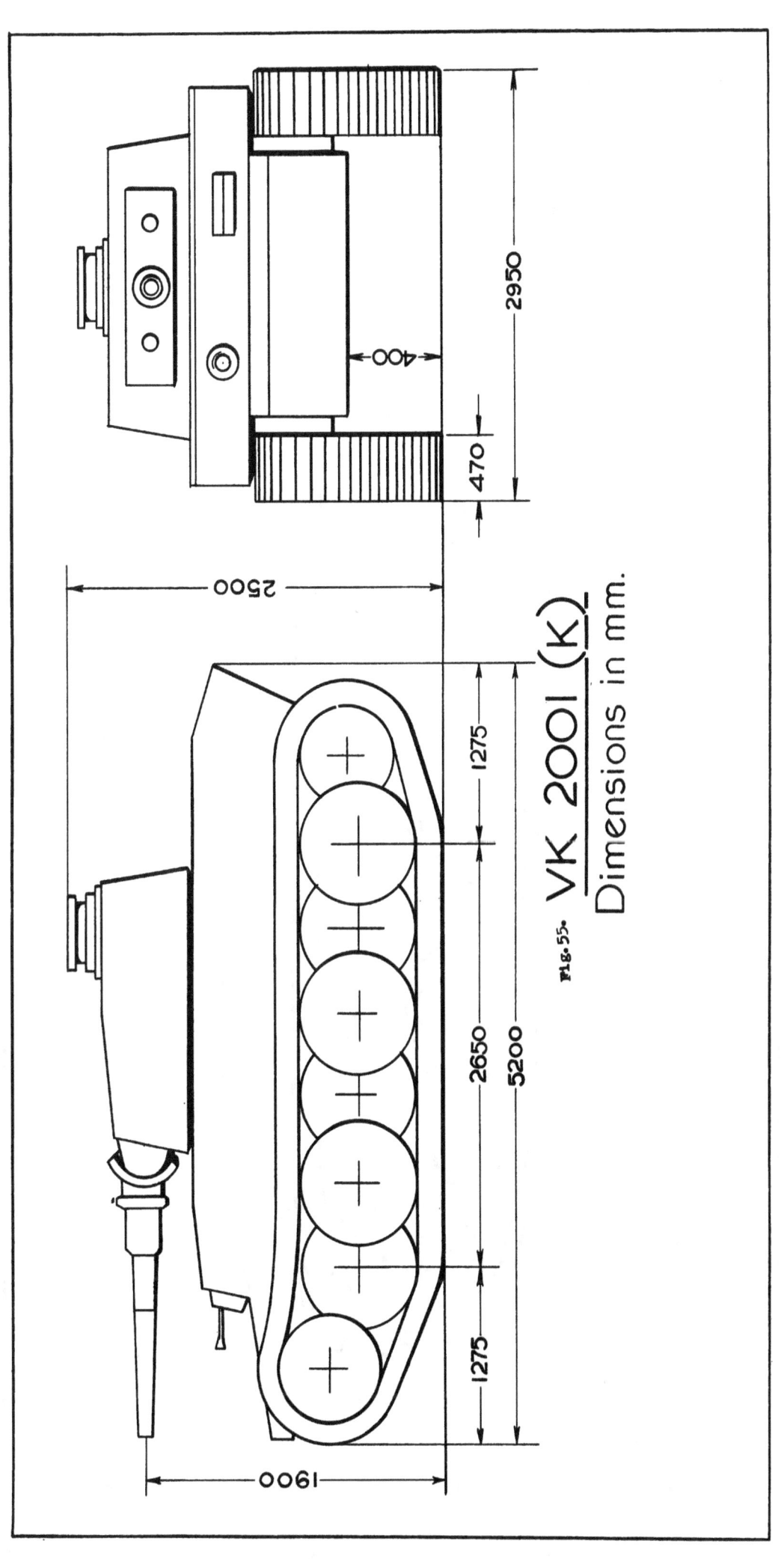

Fig. 55. VK 2001 (K) Dimensions in mm.

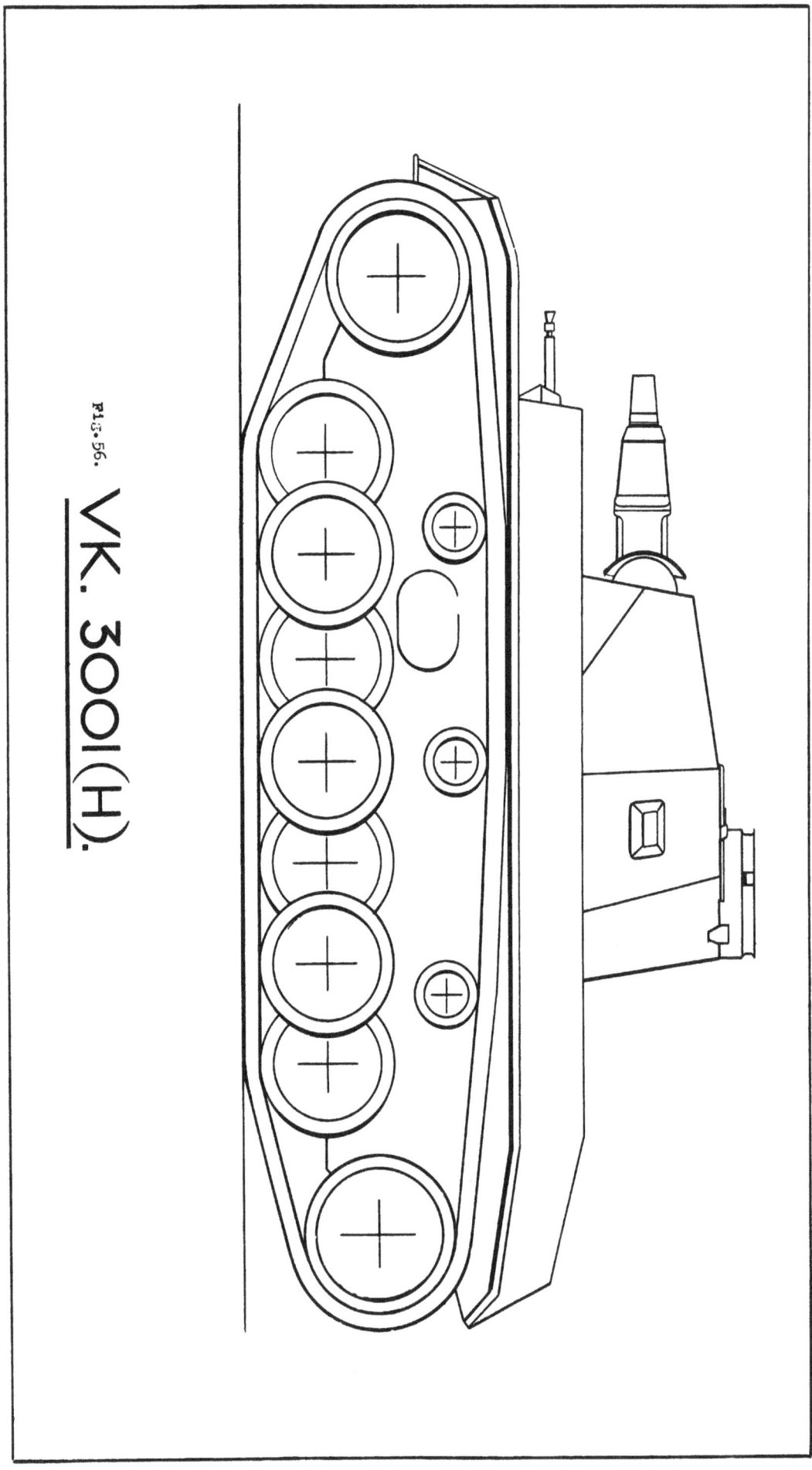

Fig. 56. VK. 3001(H).

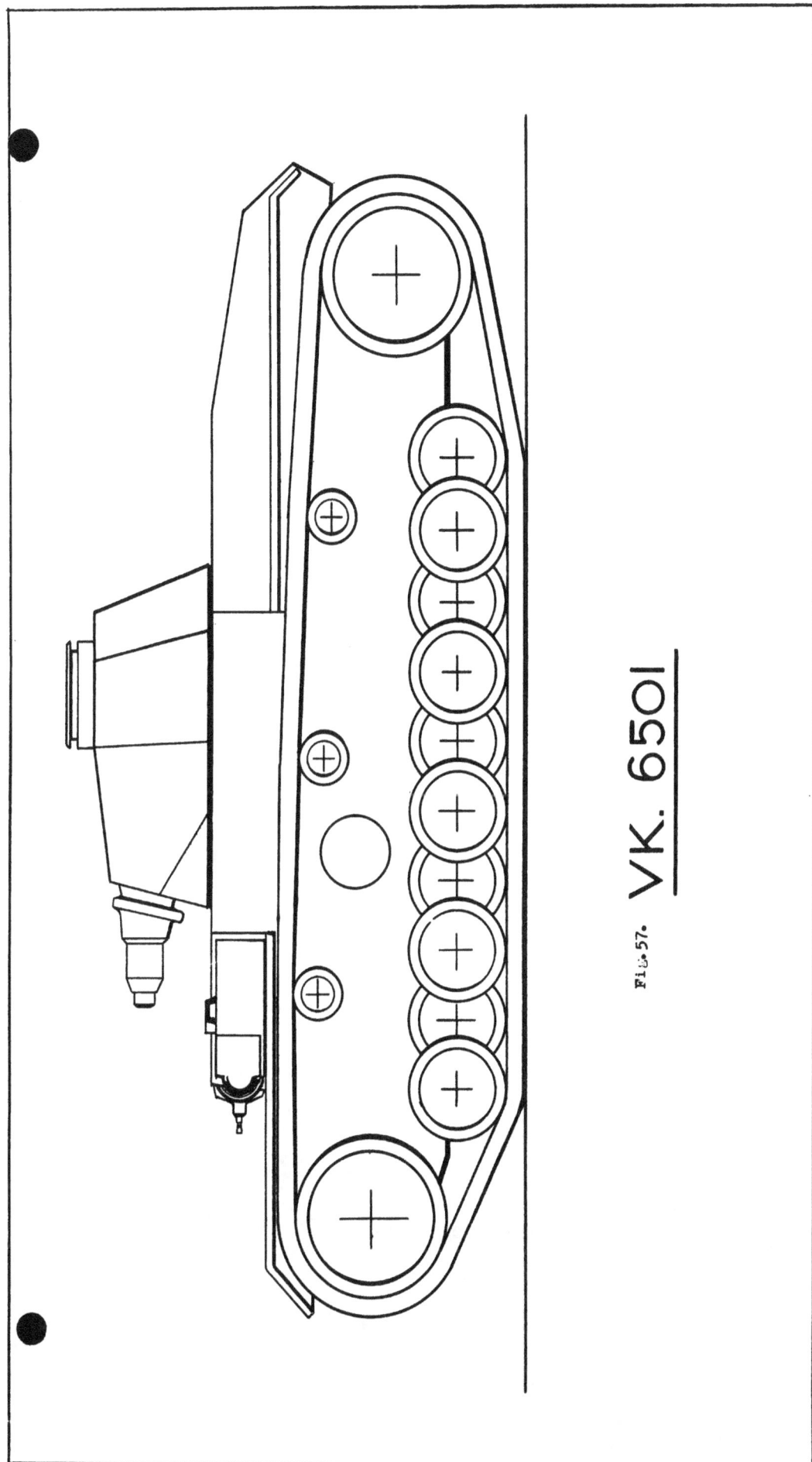

Fig.57. VK. 6501

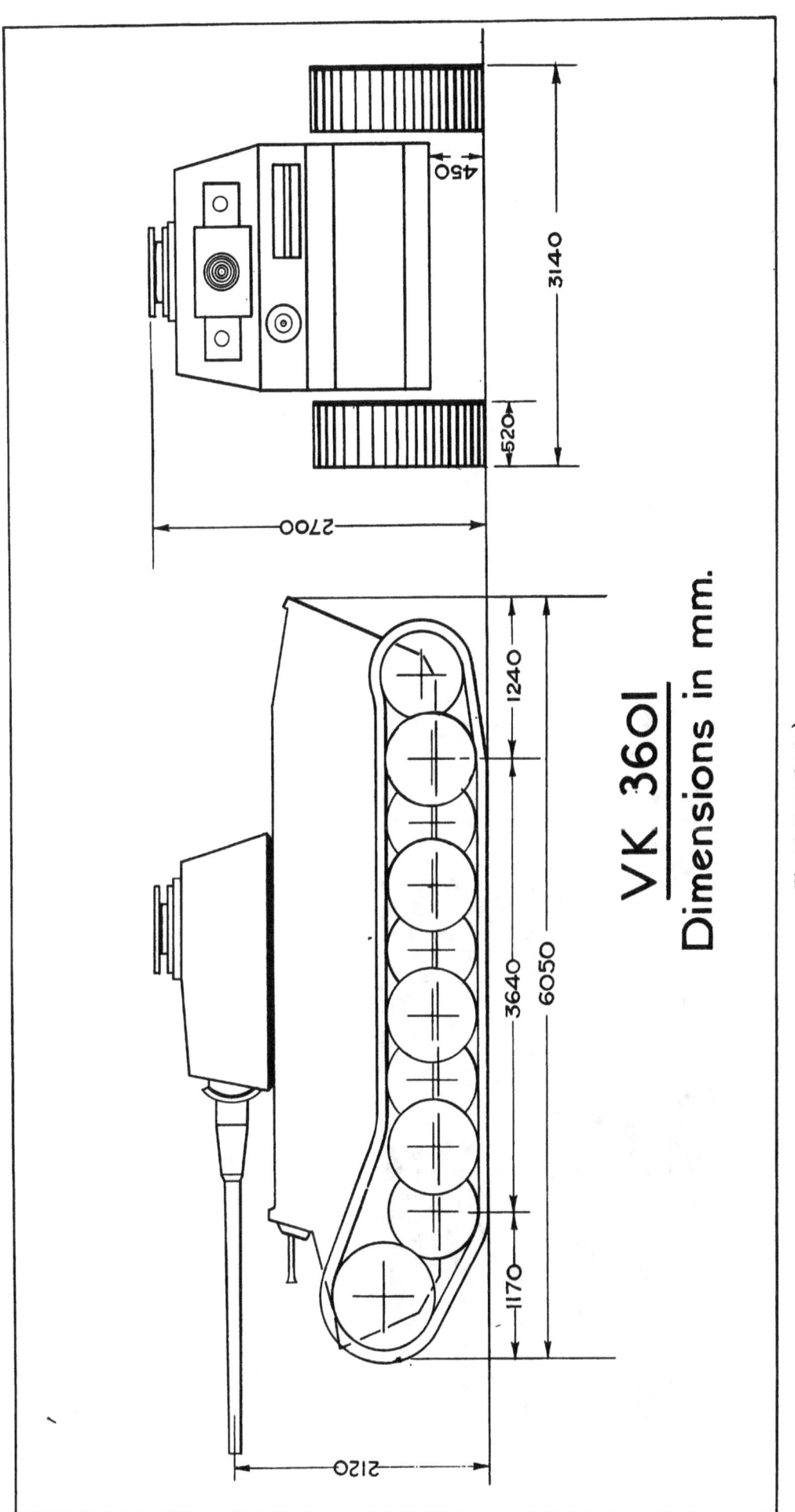

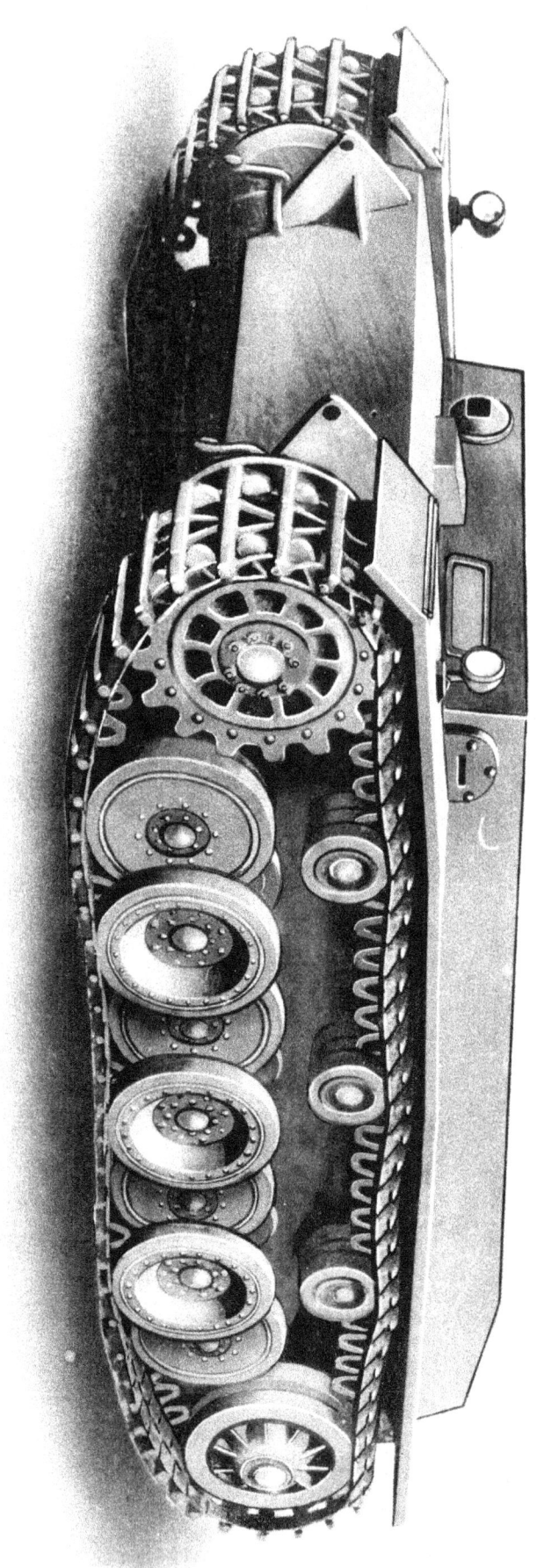

Fig. 60. V.K.3601 as finally constructed.

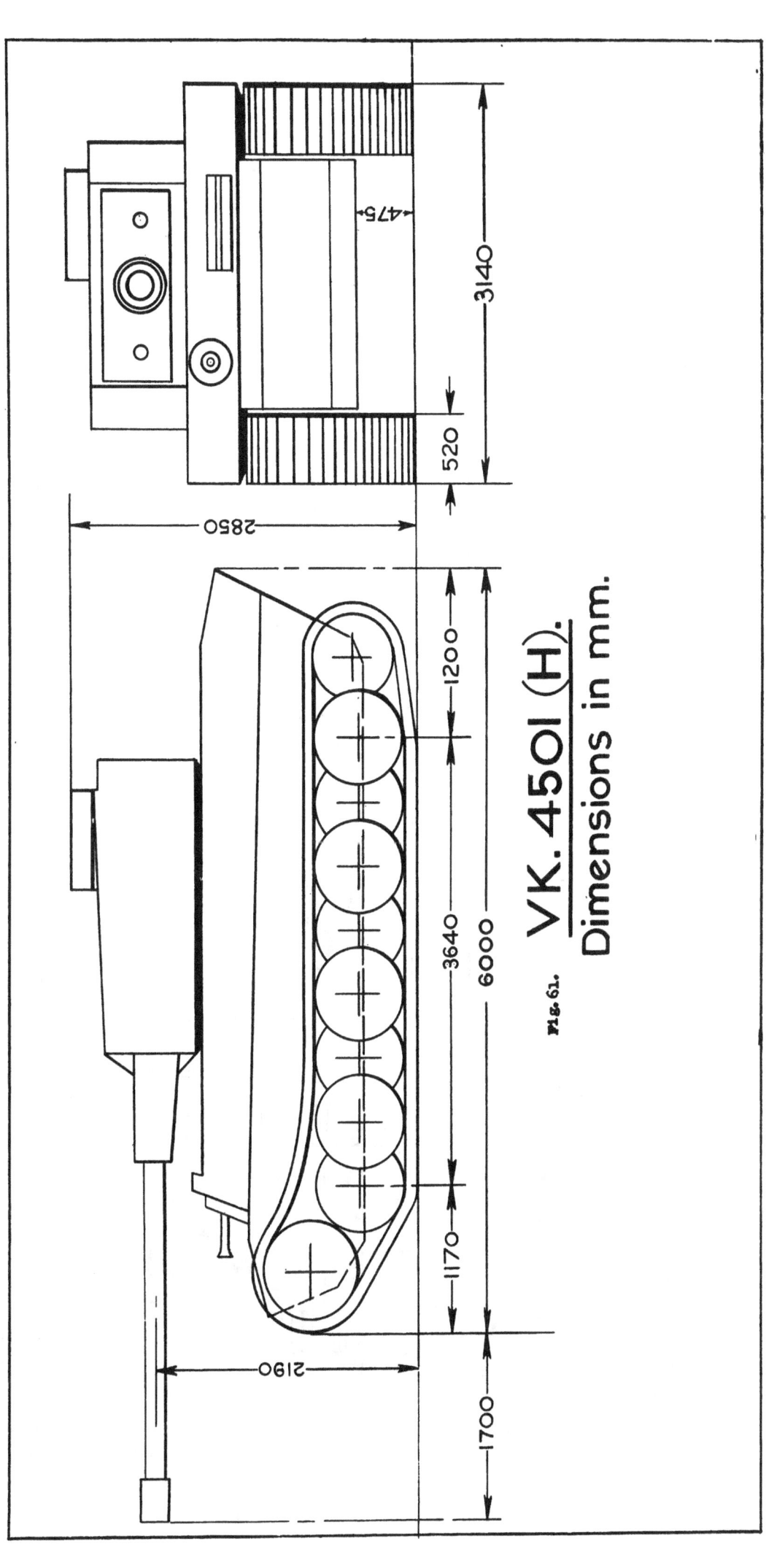

Fig. 61. **VK. 4501 (H).** Dimensions in mm.

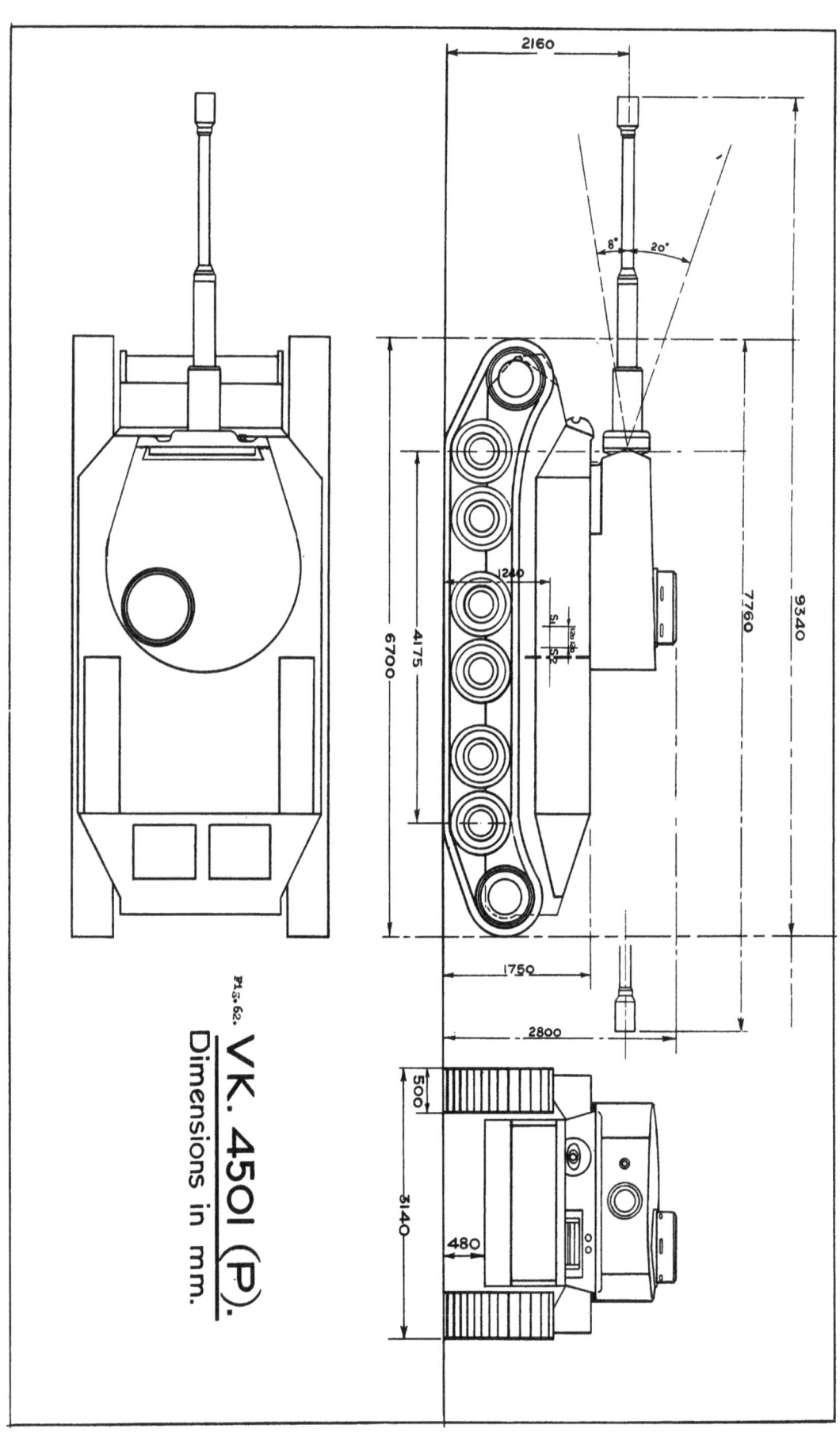

Fig. 62. VK. 4501 (P). Dimensions in mm.

Fig. 63 Daimler Benz Panther prototype V.K.3002(D)

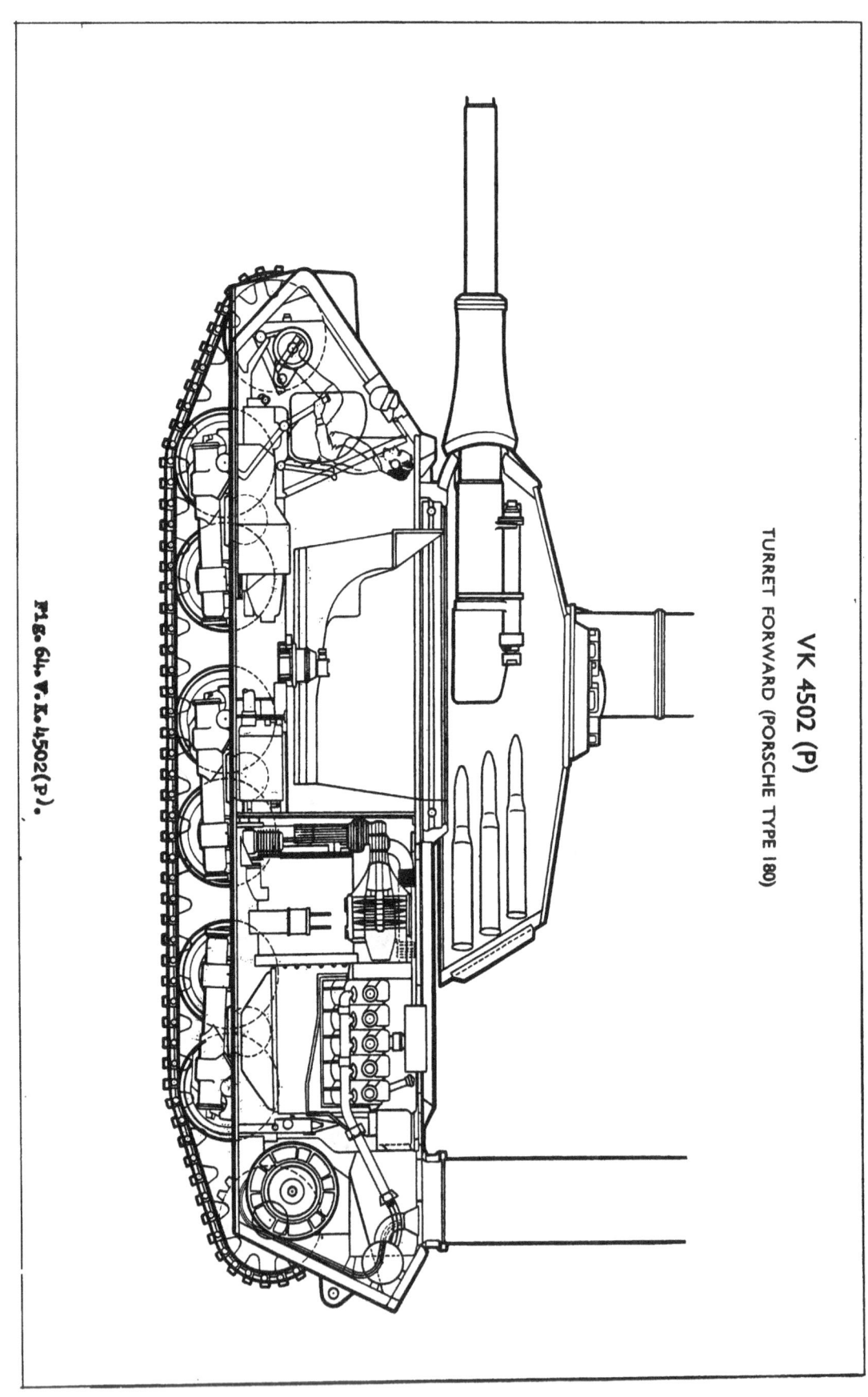

VK 4502 (P)
TURRET FORWARD (PORSCHE TYPE 180)

Fig. 64. V.K. 4502(P).

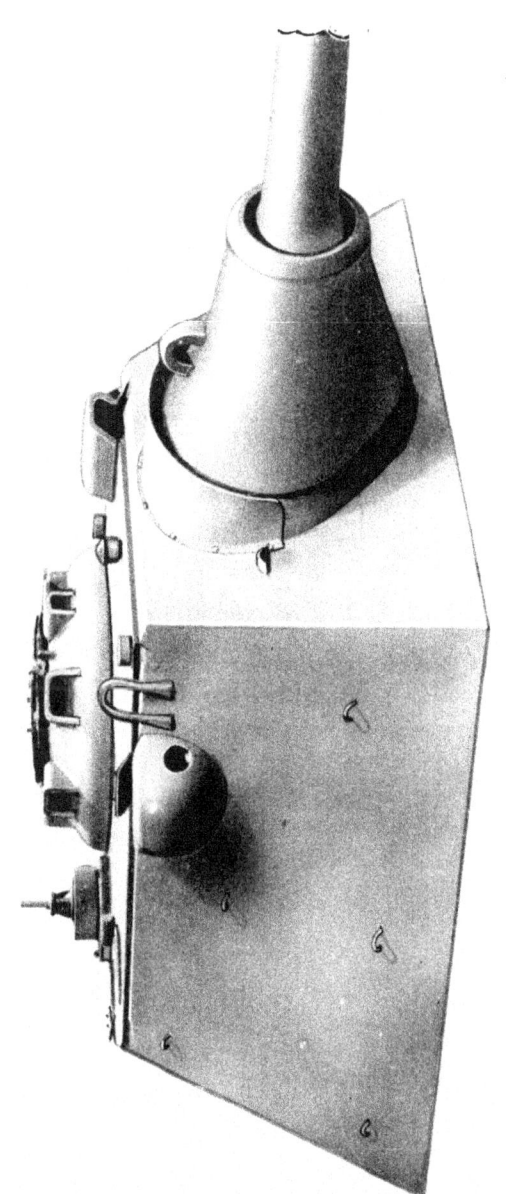

Fig. 65. Panther Schmal Turm

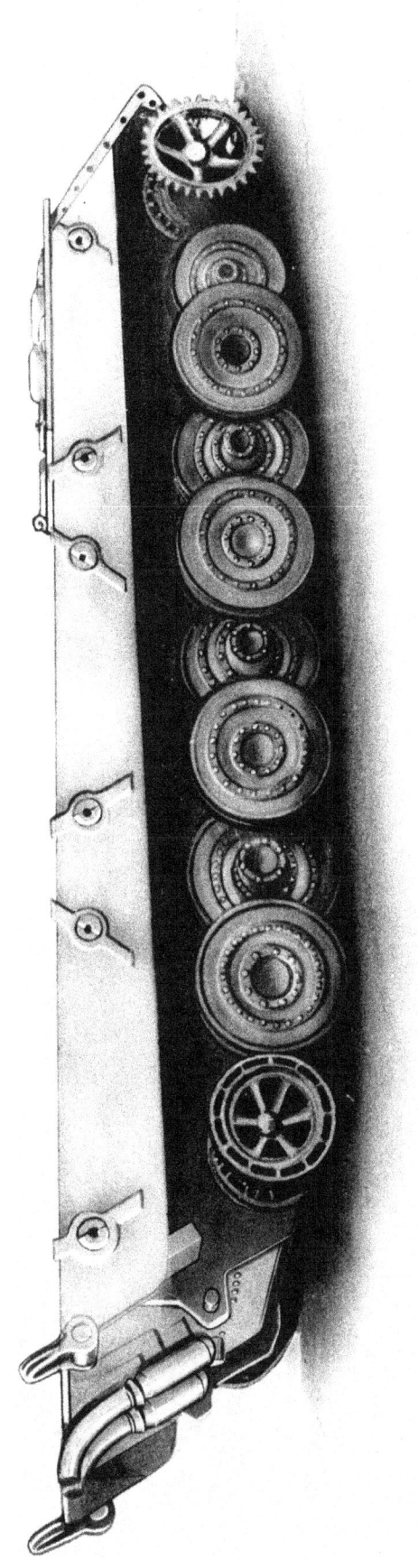

Fig. 67 E.100

Fig. 68 Pz.Kpfw. 'Maus'.

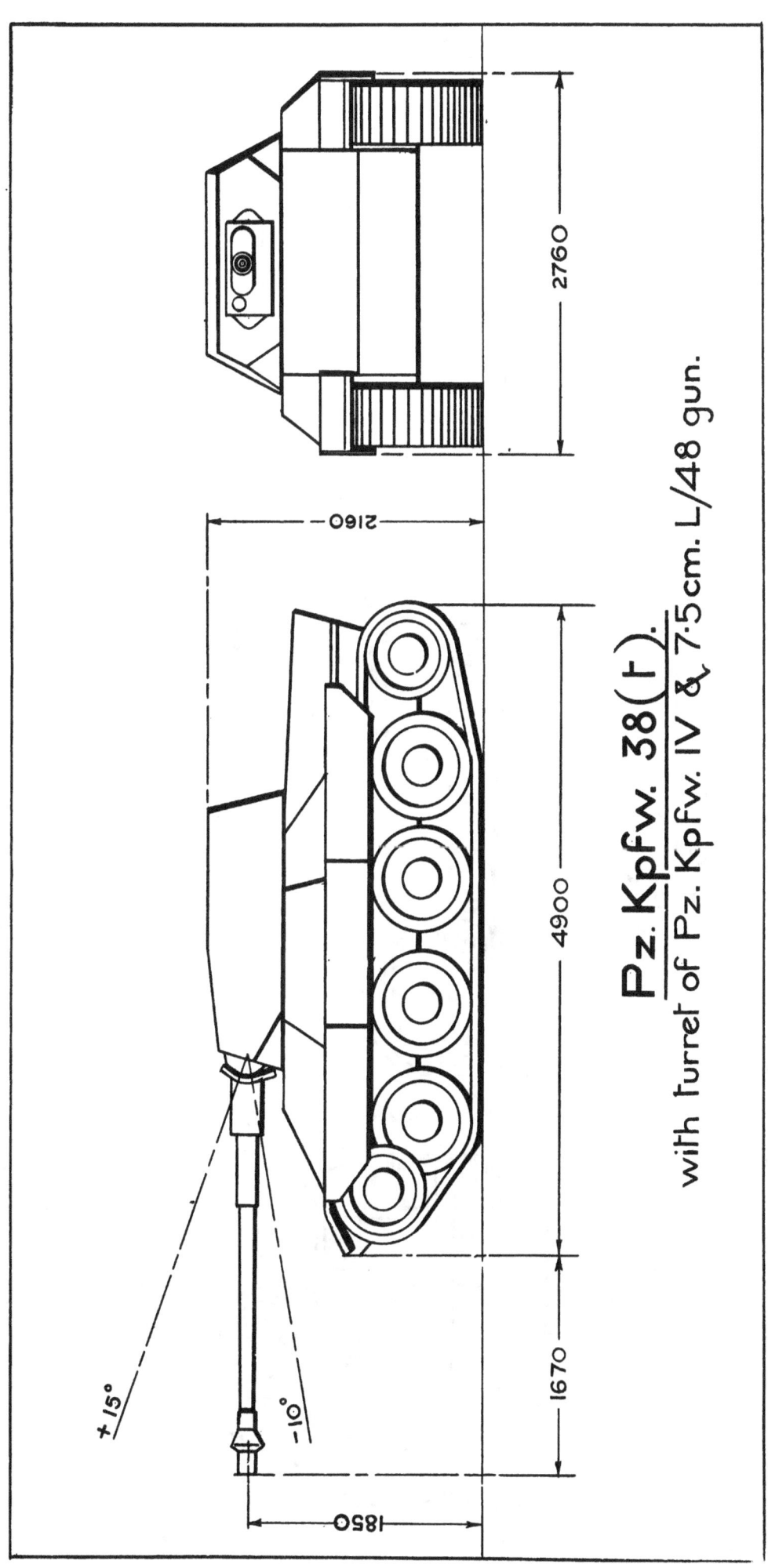

Fig. 69. Pz.Kpfw.38(t) with turret of Pz.Kpfw.IV and 7.5 cm. (L/48) gun.

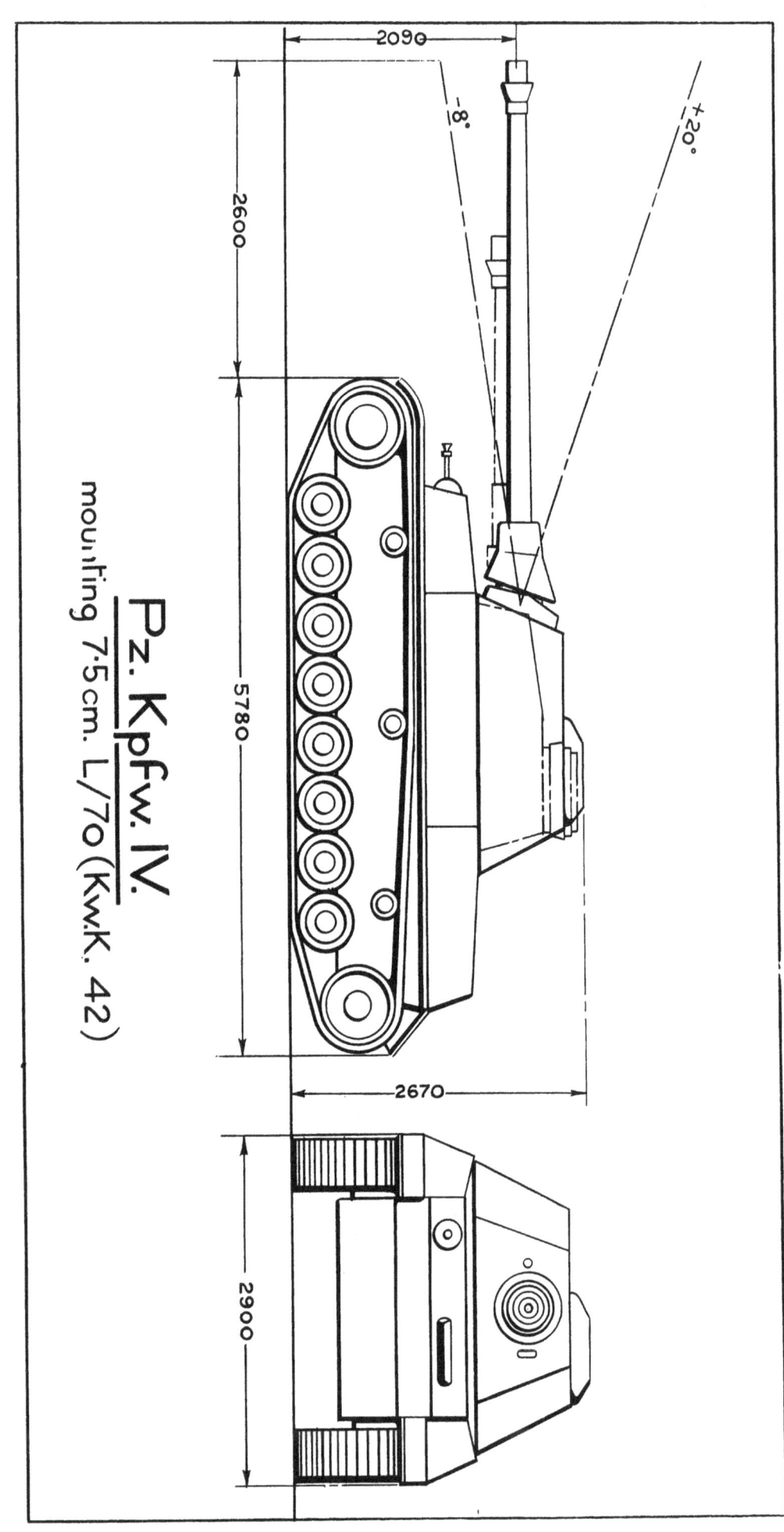

Fig. 70. Pz.Kpfw. IV mounting 7.5 cm. Kw.K.42 in redesigned turret.

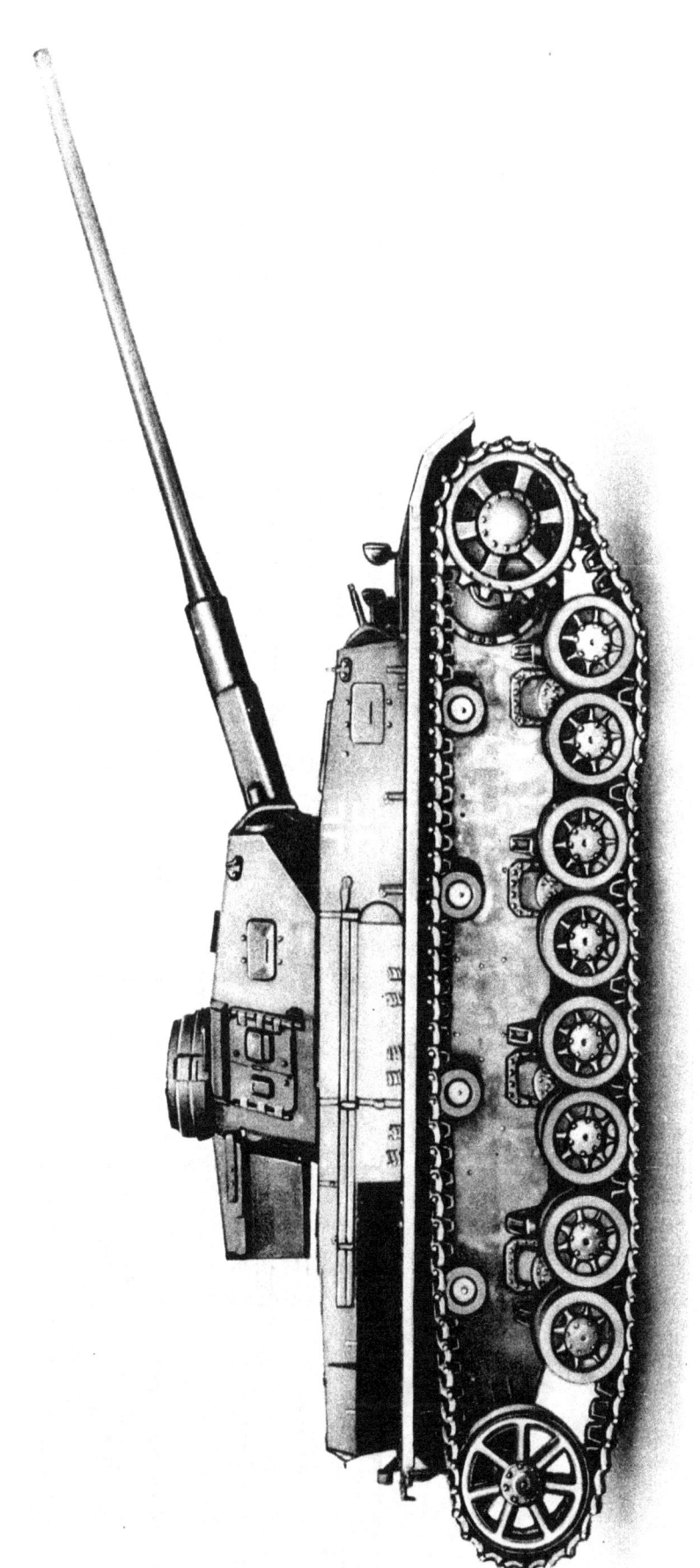

Fig.71 Mock-up of Pz Kpfw.IV mounting 7.5 cm. (L/70) gun.

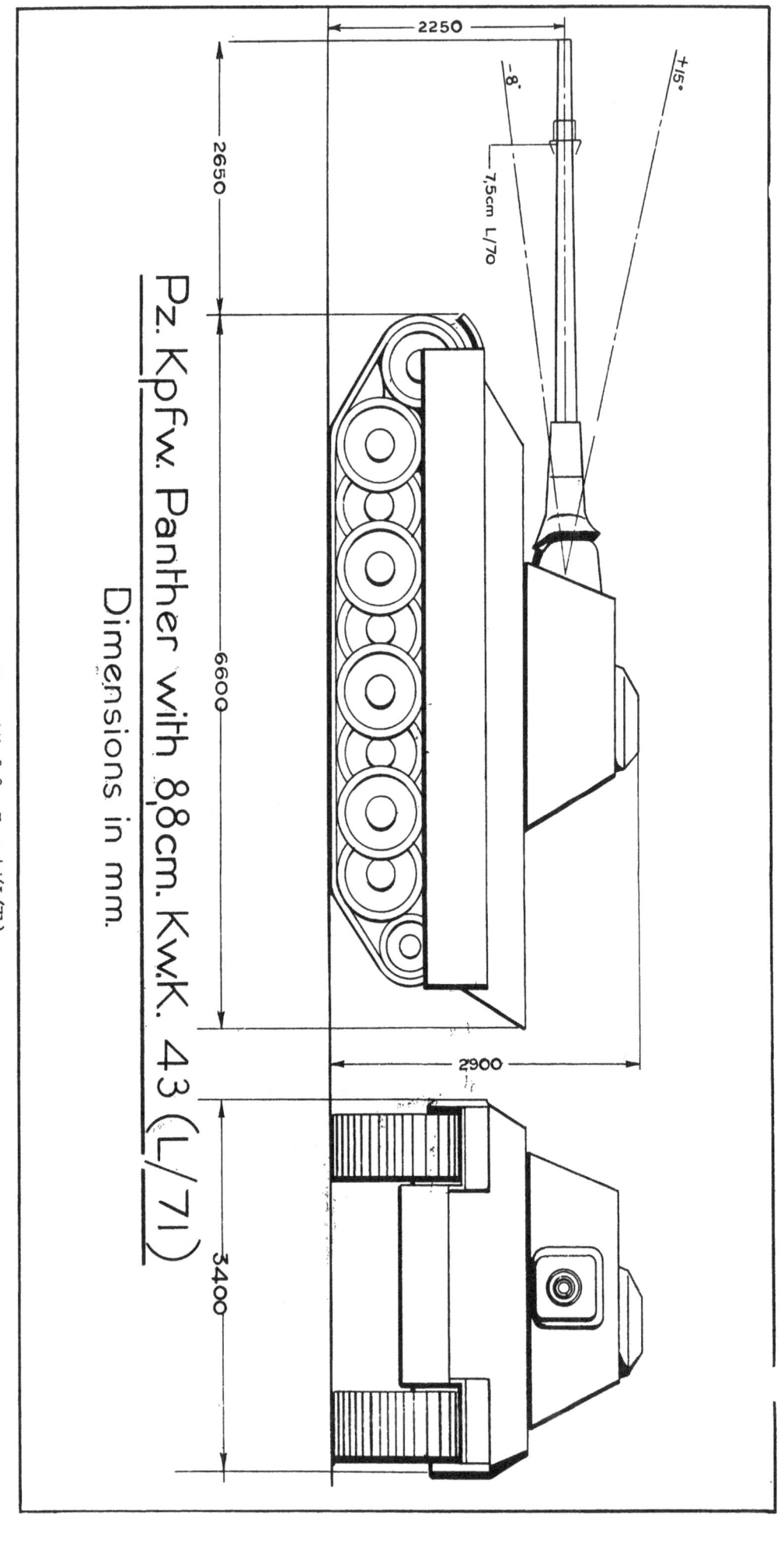

Fig. 72. Pz.Kpfw.Panther with 8.8cm.K.w.K. 43 (L/71)

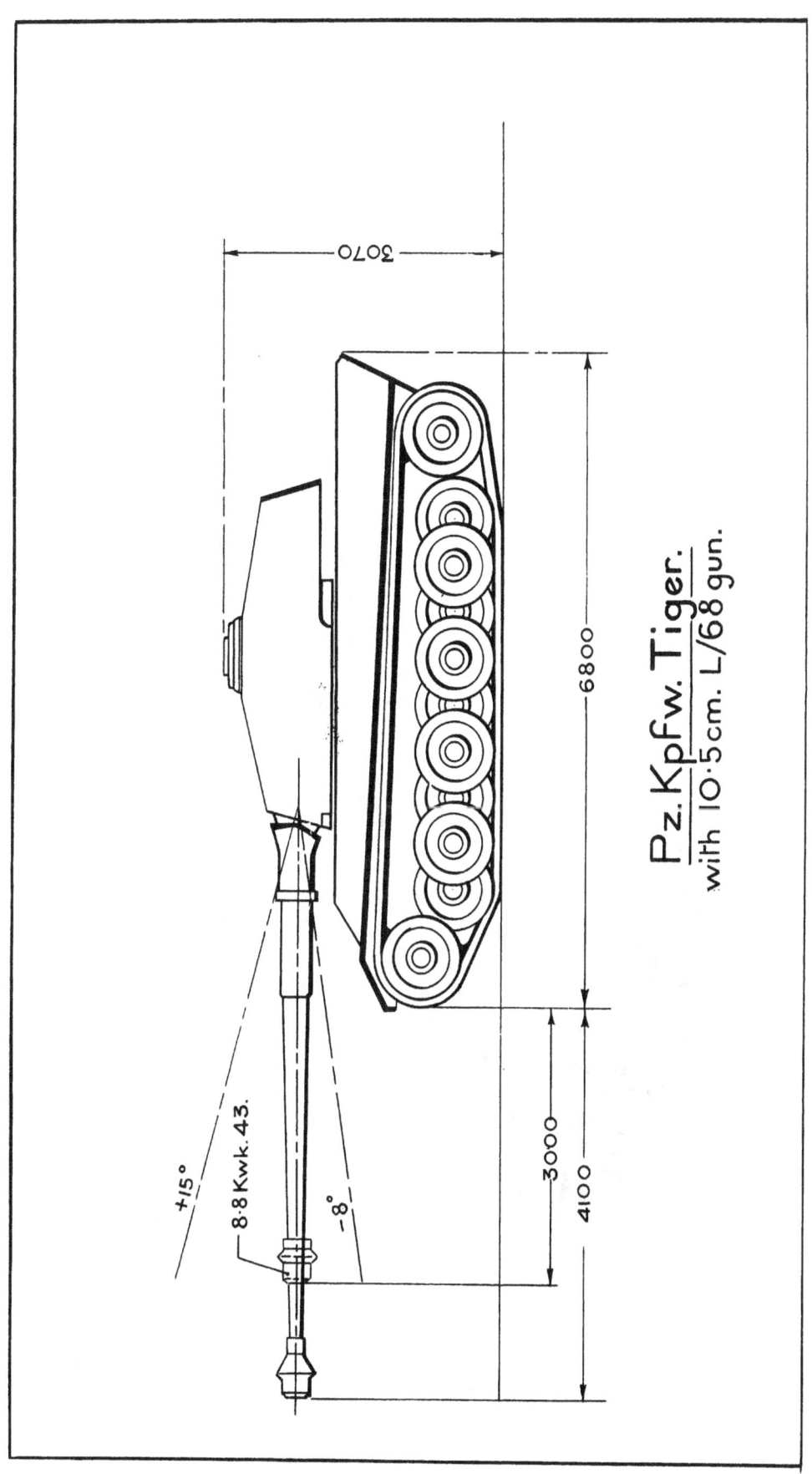

Fig. 73. Pz.Kpfw. Tiger Model B mounting 10.5cm. (L/68) gun.

Fig.74 Model of Krupp V.K.7001 (Löwe or Tiger-Maus).

SECTION TWO - SELF-PROPELLED ARTILLERY

Index to Section Two

1. Introduction.
2. Development of operational equipments.
3. Unsuccessful and unfinished projects.
4. Outline specifications of operational equipments.
5. Photos of operational and non-operational equipments.
6. Bibliography.

SECTION II - SELF-PROPELLED EQUIPMENTS

Part I

1. **Introduction.**

Before discussing the development of German self-propelled artillery during the war, it is necessary to explain their German nomenclature, as this is a guide to the class and role of the equipment referred to.

To begin with, as the Germans mounted most of their standard guns on S.P. carriages in addition to their normal field or tank mountings, it was found necessary to give such guns a special distinguishing nomenclature for ease of reference. Thus, all guns modified for mounting in a self-propelled role were distinguished by the abbreviation ('Sf.') or ('Sfl.') (Selbstfahrlafette, meaning 'self-propelled mounting') in brackets after the ordinary nomenclature, e.g. 7.5 cm. Pak 39 (L/48)(Sf).

In addition, in certain cases the nomenclature of the gun in its field (e.g. Pak) or tank (e.g. Kw.K) rôle was modified to indicate its rôle when self-propelled. Thus the Pak (Panzerabwekrkanone or anti-tank gun) was changed to Pjk (Panzerjagerkanone) when mounted on a tank destroyer, or Stu.K (Sturmkanone) when mounted as an assault gun. Other abbreviations used in self-propelled gun nomenclature were 'Stu.H.' and 'Stu.Mrs.' (Assault howitzer).

Although chassis consisted almost entirely of standard tank and semi-tracked vehicle hulls and chassis, certain distinctive names were needed for modified chassis. Thus we have a complete series of tank destroyer equipments all of which are based on modified tank chassis, known by the abbreviation ' Pz.Jag.' (Panzerjäger-tank hunter, in place of 'Pz.Kpfw.'(tank). Another abbreviation, used for certain earlier S.P. carriages for large calibre guns is 'Gw.' or 'Geschutzwagen' (gun carriage), again in place of 'Pz.Kpfw.'

In the case of certain assault equipments, the gun nomenclature was frequently used to cover the complete equipment (i.e. Stu.G. and Stu.Mrs.). In addition, each equipment taken into service was allotted an 'Sd.Kfz.' number of its own, within the band allotted to the tank or vehicle forming the basis of the equipment.

2. **Development of Operational equipments.**

German ideas and methods with regard to S.P. guns underwent considerable modification between the introduction of the first assault equipment (Sturmgeschütz - 7.5 cm. K.(L/24) on Stu.G.III) in 1940, and the end of the war. These changes may be directly traced to the German War situation at the time and the changes in the tactical roles of such equipments dictated thereby. Apart from the one specifically-designed equipment mentioned above, the chassis of the then obsolete Pz.Kpfw.I was utilised for the improvised mounting of the 15 cm. heavy infantry howitzer 15 cm. s.I.G.33 and the 4.7 cm. Czech A.tk. gun (4.7 cm. Pak.(t)). From this period almost to the end of the War, S.P. equipments were of two main types: (i) those specifically designed for the purpose or (ii) those improvised, to make possible the S.P. mounting of as many guns as possible in the shortest possible time. Both types were based on existing tank chassis, the first on current designs and the second on obsolescent designs of chassis. The 7.5 cm. K(L/24) on Stu.G.III falls into the first class, and remained in service (apart from modifications in the armament) until the end of the War. In the second class fall all the equipments introduced up to December 1942, many of which were based on the chassis of the French 'Lorraine' tractor, the Czech Pz.Kpfw.38(t) and various semi-tracked vehicles. These equipments are characterized by their slightly- or un-modified tank chassis, their light, bulletproof, open-topped superstructures and the armament, practically unmodified from the field mounting version. The specifically-designed equipments are characterized by their thick armour and roofed-in fighting compartments, low silhouettes and the modified or re-designed tank chassis on which they are based.

From January, 1943, equipments introduced into service were divided fairly evenly between the first and second types, the latter coming well to the fore in the last part of 1944 early '45 as the need for as many mobile, heavily armoured A.tk. guns as possible became more urgent.

In addition to classification by overall type of design, equipments may be classified according to the type of armament carried i.e., whether low velocity HE firing, high velocity anti-tank, or AA weapons. In the period Sept. 1939 - Dec. 1943, when the war situation was more favourable, the need for the first two types was about equal and that of the last type almost non-existent. Approximately equal proportions of the first two types and a very small number of the third were therefore employed, but in the subsequent phase up to the end of the war the emphasis was placed more and more on A.tk. and AA equipments with a consequent falling-off in the number of low velocity H.E. firing types.

It is impossible to attempt to cover the war-time history of the S.P. equipment of the German Army in any more detail in this short space, as there was a total of at least 66 such equipments in service during the war. Below, however, is a list of all known operational equipments giving German nomenclature and approximate date of introduction, classified both by calibre of gun and type of chassis, together with outline specifications of the more important equipments and photographs, where those available are suitable for reproduction.

- 38 -

(1) LIST OF S.P. EQUIPMENTS TAKEN INTO SERVICE (Classified by calibre of guns)

German Nomenclature	Sd.Kfz.No.	British Nomenclature	Approx.date of Introduction	Role in which employed	Remarks
M.G.151/15 oder 151/20 Drilling auf m.Schtz. Pz.Wg.	251/21	15mm. or 2cm. triple A.A. M.G.151 on 3-ton semi-tracked vehicle	Oct.1944	Light A.A.convoy protection with secondary light A.Tk.role	
2cm.Flak 30 oder Flak 38 auf Zgkw 1 t.	10/4	2 cm.AA gun 30 or 38 on 1-ton semi-tracked vehicle	1942	"	
2cm.Flak 38 auf Mannsch Kw.	Kfz.70	2cm. AA gun 38 on 4-whld.medium car	1942	"	
2cm.Flak 38 auf Pz.Kpfw.38(t) (le.Flak Pz.38(t))	140	2 cm.AA gun 38 on Czech light tank 38(light AA tank 38(T))	Oct.1943	"	
2 cm.Flakvierling 38 auf Zgkw 8 t.	7/1 and 7/2	2cm.Quadruple AA gun 38 on 8-ton semi-tracked veh.	1942	"	2 versions produced - one mounted in multi-sided turret and other on flat topped super-structure with raised hinged sides.
2 cm.Flakvierling 38 auf Pz.Kpfw.IV (Flak Pz.IV - Wirbelwind)		2cm.quadruple AA gun 38 on Pz.Kpfw.IV chassis (AA tank IV - Whirlwind)	Dec.1943	"	
m.Schtz.Pz.Wg.(2cm)	251/17	2cm.Tank gun 38 on 3-ton semi-tracked veh.	1944	Light mobile A.Tk.for reconnaissance	
2.8cm.s.Pz.B.41 auf le Schtz.Pz.Wg.	250/11	2.8cm.light anti-tk.gun 41 on 1-ton semi-tracked veh.	1942	"	
3cm.M.K.103 Zwilling auf Pz.Kpfw.IV (Flak Pz.IV - Kugelblitz)		Twin 3cm.M.K.103 on Pz.Kpfw.IV (AA tank IV - Kugelblitz)	Apr.1944	Light-medium AA protection of armoured convoys and static harbours	Totally enclosed armoured turret, with powered traverse and elev. Interim solution, pending development of "Kugelblitz" on Pz.Jag.38D chassis and medium AA on Panther.
3.7cm.Flak 18 oder 36 on Zgkw.5 t	6/2	3.7cm AA gun 18 or 36 on 5-ton semi-tracked veh.	1941	"	
3.7cm.Flak 38 auf Zgkw.8t	7/2	3.7cm AA gun 36 on 8-ton semi-tracked veh.	1941	"	
3.7cm.Flak 43 auf Flak Pz.IV (Möbelwagen)		3.7cm AA gun 43 on AA tank IV ("Furniture Van")	Mar 1944	"	Two types produced, one mounting gun in octagonal turret and other on flat, turretless platform with raisable sides.
3.7cm.Pak(sf)auf Inf.Schlepper UE(f) (Chenillette)		3.7cm A.Tk.gun on French Inf.Carrier UE' (Chenillette)	1940	Light,fast,mobile A.Tk. for reconnaissance.	
3.7cm.Pak(St) auf m.Schtz.Pz.Wg.	251/10	3.7cm.A.Tk.gun on 3-ton semi-tracked veh.	1942	"	
3.7cm.Pak.auf le.Schtz.Pz.Wg.	250/10	3.7cm A.Tk.gun on 1-ton semi-tracked veh.	1942	"	
3.7cm.Pak.auf Fahrgestell Bren Carrier'		3.7cm.A.Tk.gun on British Bren carrier chassis	1940	"	
4.7cm.Pak(t) auf Pz.Mg.I	101	4.7cm.Czech A.Tk.gun on Pz.Kpfw.I chassis	1939	Light, fairly mobile,S.P.A.Tk.	
4.7cm.Pak(t) auf Pz.Kpfw 35R(f)		4.7cm.Czech A.Tk.gun on French Renault R.35 Tank Chassis	1940	"	
4.7cm.Pak(f)auf Pz.Jäg.Lr.S.		4.7cm.French A.Tk.gun on French Lorraine carrier chassis	1941	"	
7.5cm.K(L/24)auf StuG.III	142	7.5cm.assault gun (L/24) on modified Pz.Kpfw.III chassis.	May 1940	Assault and breakthrough of prepared positions	
7.5cm.K.51 oder K.51/1(L/24) auf le.Schtz.Pz.Wg.	250/8	7.5cm.gun 51 or 51/1(L/24) on 1-ton semi-tracked veh.	1944	Fairly heavy anti-personnel weapon on light,fast mounting	
7.5cm.K.37(L/24)auf s.Pz.Sp.Wg. (8 rad)	233	7.5cm.gun 37(L/24)on heavy 8-wheeled A.C.	Oct 1942	"	
7.5cm.K.51 oder K.51/1(L/24) auf m.Schtz.Pz.Wg.	251/9	7.5cm.gun 51 or 51/1(L/24) on 3-ton semi-tracked veh.	1944	"	
7.5cm.K.51 oder K.51/1(L/24) auf s.Pz.Sp.Wg. (8 rad)	234/3	7.5cm.gun 51 or 51/1(L/24) on heavy 8-whld. armoured car	1944	"	

German Nomenclature	Sd.Kfz.No.	British Nomenclature	Approx.date of Introduction	Role in which employed	Remarks
7.5cm.Stu.K.40(L/43) auf Stu.G.III	142	7.5cm.assault gun 40(L/43) on modified Pz.Kpfw.III chassis	Jul.1942	Heavily armoured assault anti-tank weapon.	
7.5cm.Stu.K.40(L/48) auf Stu.G.III	142/1	7.5cm.assault gun 40(L/48) on modified Pz.Kpfw.III chassis (Stu.G.III)	Feb.1943	"	
7.5cm.Stu.K.40(L/48) auf Stu.G.IV	167	7.5cm.assault gun 40(L/48) on modified Pz.Kpfw.IV chassis (Stu.G.IV).	Oct.1943	"	
7.5cm.Pak 40/3(L/46) auf Pz.Jäg.38(t) (Harder 38(t))	138	7.5cm.A.Tk.gun 4C/3(L/46) on Pz.Kpfw.38(t) chassis (Marten 38(t)).	Jun.1942 (Later type, Mar.1943)	Lightly armoured mobile S.P. A.Tk.	2 version produced, 1 with engine at rear end gun forward (early type) and the other with engine mounted forward and gun at rear.
7.5cm.Pak 40/2(L/46) auf Pz.Jäg.II Ausf. A-C u.F (Marder II)	131	7.5cm.A.Tk.gun 40/2(L/46) on Pz.Kpfw.II(Models A-C and F).	Jun.1942	"	
7.5cm.Pak 4C(L/46) auf Pz.Jäg.II Ausf.Du E.	132	7.5cm.A.Tk.gun 40(L/46) on Pz.Kpfw.II(Models D and E).	Jun.1942	"	
7.5cm.Pak 40/1(L/46) auf Pz.Jäg.Lr.S.(f) (Marder I)	135	7.5cm.A.Tk.gun 40/1(L/46) on French Lorraine carrier chassis (Marten I).	Mid.1942	"	184 produced, converted by Alfred Becher of Krefeld.
7.5cm.Pak 40(L/46) auf Zgkw.Somua (f)		7.5cm.A.Tk.gun 40(L/46) on Somua (French) semi-tracked veh.	Mid.1942	"	16 produced, converted by Alfred Becher of Krefeld.
7.5cm.Pak 4C(L/46) auf Pz.Kpfw.39H(f)		7.5cm.A.Tk.gun 40(L/46) on French Hotchkiss H.39 tank chassis.	Mid.1942	"	24 produced, converted by Alfred Becher of Krefeld.
7.5cm.Pak 40(L/46) auf Pz.Jäg FCM(f)		7.5cm.A.Tk.gun 40(L/46) on French FCM tank chassis.	Mid.1942	"	10 produced, converted by Alfred Becher of Krefeld.
7.5cm.Pak 40(L/46) auf Pz.Jäg.R.S.O.		7.5cm.A.Tk.gun 40(L/46) on Raupenschlepper OST tracked lorry.	1944	"	
7.5cm.Pak 40(L/46) auf m.Schtz.Pz.Wg.	251/22	7.5cm.A.Tk.gun 40(L/46) on 3-ton semi-tracked veh.	Nov.1944	"	
7.5cm.Pak 40(L/46) auf s.Pz.Sp.Wg. (8-rad)	234/	7.5cm.A.Tk.gun 40(L/46) on 8-whld. armoured car.	Nov.1944	"	
7.5cm.Pak 39(L/48) auf Pz.Jäg.38(t) (Hetzer)		7.5cm.A.Tk.gun 39(L/48) on Tank Destroyer 38(t) (Baiter)	May 1944	Light, fast, well armoured tank destroyer with low silhouette.	7.5cm.Pak 39(L/48) has same piece as 7.5cm.KW.K.40(L/48) and 7.5cm.Stu.K. 40(L/48) and has also the same ballistics and fires the same ammunition. It is not, however, fitted with a muzzle brake.
7.5cm.Pak. 39(L/48) auf Pz.Jäg.IV	162	7.5.cm.A.Tk.gun 39(L/48) on Tank Destroyer IV.	Jan.1944	"	
7.5cm.Stu.K.42(L/70) auf Pz.Jäg.IV	162	7.5cm.Assault gun 42(L/70) on Tank Destroyer IV.	Aug.1944	"	7.5cm. StuK.42(L/70) has same piece, ballistics and fires same ammunition as the 7.5cm. KW.K.42 (L/70) fitted in Pz.Kpfw. Panther. No muzzle brake is fitted, however.
7.62cm.F.K.296(r) auf Pz.Jäg.II(Ausf. D u.E)	132	7.62cm. Russian field gun 296 on Pz.Kpfw.II chassis (Models D and E).	Jul.1942	Lightly-armoured, fairly mobile S.P. A.Tk.	
7.62cm.Pak 36(r) auf Pz.Jäg.II (Ausf. D u.E.)	132	7.62cm.Russian A.Tk.gun 36 on Pz.Kpfw.II chassis (Models D and E.).	Oct.1942	"	
7.62cm.Pak 36(r) auf Pz.Jäg.II (Ausf.A-C u.F).	131	7.62cm.Russian A.Tk.gun 36 on Pz.Kpfw.II chassis (Models A-C and F.).	Mid.1942	"	
7.62cm.Pak 36(r) auf Pz.Jäg.38(t)	139	7.62cm.Russian A.Tk.gun 36 on Pz.Kpfw.38(Czech) chassis.	Oct.1941	"	
7.62cm.Pak 36(r) auf Zgkw.5t	6	7.62cm.Russian A.Tk.gun 36 on 5-ton semi-tracked veh.	Oct.1941	"	
8cm.s.Gr.W.34 auf Pz.Kpfw.35R(f)		8cm.mortar on French R35 tank chassis.	Feb.1944	Mobile mortar with protection against S.A.A.	
8cm.R-Vielfachwerfer auf gep.Mannschaft Wg.Maultier		8cm.multiple rocket projector on 2-ton armoured semi-tracked vehicle Maultier.		"	

- 40 -

German Nomenclature	Sd.Kfz.No.	British Nomenclature	Approx.date of introduction	Role in which employed	Remarks
8.8cm.Pak 43/1(L/71) auf Pz.Jäg.III/IV ('Nashorn', fruher Hornisse').	164	8.8cm.A.Tk.gun 43/1 on Tank Destroyer III/IV ('Rhinoceros', formerly 'Hornet').	Nov.1942	Lightly-armoured mobile heavy A.Tk.	
8.8cm.Pak 43/2(L/71) auf Pz.Jäg.Tiger(P) (Elefant', fruher 'Ferdinand')	184	8.8cm.A.Tk.gun 43/2 on Tank Destroyer 'Tiger' (Porsche) ('Elephant', formerly 'Ferdinand').	Nov.1942	Heavily-armoured, assault, heavy A.Tk.	90 produced. Converted from Prosche-designed Kz. 4501 (or Tiger (P)) by Nibelungenwerke.
8.8cm.Pak 43/3(L/71) auf Pz.Jäg. Panther (Jagdpanther)	173	8.8cm.A.Tk.gun 43/3 on Tank Destroyer 'Panther' (Jagdpanther).	Jan.1944	Heavily-armoured, heavy tank destroyer with low silhouette.	
10.5cm. Stu.H.42 (L/28) auf Stu.G.III	142/2	10.5cm.Assault Howitzer 42 on modified Pz.Kpfw.III chassis (Stu.G.III).	Aug.1942	Assault on prepared positions. Anti-personnel and anti-concrete.	
10.5cm.le.F.H. 18/2 auf Gw.II (Wespe)	124	10.5cm.gun.how.18 on Pz.Kpfw.II chassis (Wasp).	Dec.1942	Lightly armoured mobile gun how.	
10.5cm.le.F.H.18 auf Gw.39H(f)		10.5cm.gun how.18 on Pz.Kpfw.H.39 tank chassis (French).	Mid.1942	"	48 produced. Converted by Alfred Becher of Krefeld.
10.5cm.le.F.H.18/3 auf Gw.B.2(f).		10.5cm. gun how. 18/3 on Pz.Kpfw.B.2 tank chassis (French).	1942	"	Converted by Rheinmetall-Borsig.
10.5cm.le F.H.18 auf Gw. Lr.S.(f)		10.5cm.gun how.18 on French 'Lorraine' carrier chassis.	Mid.1942	"	24 produced. Converted by Alfred Becher of Krefeld.
10.5cm.le F.H.16 auf Gw.F.C.M.(f)		10.5cm.gun how.16 on French F.C.M. chassis	Mid.1942	"	24 produced. Converted by Alfred Becher of Krefeld.
10.5cm.le F.H.18/1 auf Gw.IV.b	165/1	10.5cm.gun how.18/1 on modified Pz.Kpfw.IV chassis.	Nov.1942	"	Only 8 made - not up to requirements.
12.8cm.Pak.44(L/55) oder Pack 80(L/55) auf Pz.Jäg. Tiger Ausf.B (Jagdtiger)	186	12.8cm.A.Tk.gun 44 or 80 (L/55) on Tiger Model B tank destroyer (Jagdtiger).	Feb.1944	Heavily armoured, slow moving, heavy A.Tk. gun. Mobile pill box.	Produced only by Henschel and Nibelungenwerke. Nibelungenwerke version fitted with Porsche design of suspension. 150 order, 70 completed by end of war.
15cm.s.I.G.33 auf Pz.Kpfw.I Ausf.B	101	15cm.heavy Inf.how.33 on chassis of Pz.Kpfw.I Model B.	1939	Lightly armoured mobile heavy how.	
15cm.s.I.G.33 auf Pz.Kpfw.II	121	15cm.heavy Inf.how.33 on chassis of Pz.Kpfw.II	Early 1942	"	
15s.F.H.13 auf.Gw.Lr.S.(f)	135/1	15cm, medium how.13 on French 'Lorraine' carrier chassis.	Mid.1942	"	102 produced. Converted by Alfred Becher of Krefeld.
15cm.s.F.H.18 auf Gw.III/IV ('Hummel')	165	15cm.medium how.18 on composite Pz.Kpfw.III and IV chassis (Bumble Bee).	Oct.1942	"	
15cm.Stu.H.43(L/12) auf Stu.G.IV(Stu.Pz.43 - 'Brumbaer')	166	15cm.Assault How.43(L/12) on assault chassis IV (Assault veh.43 - 'Grizzly Bear').	Apr.1943	Heavily armoured heavy assault how.	
15cm.Pz.W.42(15cm. No.W.10-ring 42 auf Panzerwerfer)	4/1	10-barrelled 15cm.rocket projector on 2-ton armoured semi-tracked vehicle Maultier.	May.1944	Medium range area bombardment.	
15cm.s.I.G.33 auf Gw.38(t)	138/1	15cm.heavy Inf.How.33 on Czech Light Tank chassis 38.	Sep.1942	Lightly armoured mobile heavy how.	2 versions produced - earlier one with engine at rear and later one with engine forward and gun at rear.
38cm.R.W.61 auf Stu.Mrs.Tiger		38cm.rocket projector 61 Assault How. on Tiger Model E chassis.	Aug.1944	Heavily armoured, very heavy mobile assault How., Anti-personnel and Anti-concrete.	10 built. Converted by Alkett, Ex-Naval anti-submarine gun on modified Tiger E.
54cm.Mrs.KARL (Gerat 041)		54cm.E.S.f.Howitzer KARL (Equipment 041).	Jun - Jul. 1944	Heavy, long range, mobile siege gun.	6 built, numbered I to VI. 54cm. and 60cm. barrels interchangeable.
60cm.Mrs.KARL (Gerat 040)		60cm.S.P.Howitzer KARL (Equipment 040).	1942	"	

3. **Unsuccessful and unfinished projects**

As the number of projected designs is as great as, if not greater than the number taken into service, it is not proposed to describe in detail equipments other than those intended for future production had the war continued The other projects all fall into one or other of the classifications mentioned in Chapter 2, although characterized generally by their mounting guns of larger calibre than those carried in corresponding equipments taken into service.

The most outstanding development in S.P. gun design, planned for production in 1945, was the rigid mounting, (i.e. less recoil system) of the gun in the vehicle front plate. Several guns were to have been so mounted, including the 7.5 cm. Pak 39/1(L/48) in the Pz.Jag. 38(t) and 38(d), the 7.5 cm. Pak 42 (L/70) in the Pz.Jag 38(d), the 10.5 cm. Stu.H.42(L/28) in the Pz.Jag 38(t) and the 8.8 cm. Pak 43 (L/71) in the 'Jagdpanther'. The rigidly-mounted 7.5 cm. Pak 39/1 (L/48) on Pz.Jag 38(t) chassis was just about to commence production at the close of the war.

As will be seen from the above reference, the introduction of a new S.P. gun carriage, the Pz.Jag 38(d) was also contemplated. This was a purely German redesigned and enlarged version of the Pz.Jag 38(t), powered by a new Tatra diesel engine, of which very large production was intended and which bore little resemblance to any existing tank chassis.

A project for combining the fire power and mobility of an S.P. gun with the traverse of a tank gun and the low silhouette of a gun on its field carriage was the series of "Waffenträger' or gun carriers also planned for production in late 1945. These equipments consisted of anti-tank, field or medium guns mounted, on their field carriages, on lightly armoured chassis built up of standard (38(t), 38(D) or Pz.Kpfw.IV) components, in such a manner as to give, in most cases, 360° traverse. In addition, the gun was demountable to permit of firing from its field carriage on the ground. Most of these projects never progressed further than the drawing board, but a few reached the mock-up stage and one or two (such as the 'Grille' equipment, consisting of a 17 cm gun (17 cm. K.) on a lengthened Royal Tiger chassis) had advanced to the building of a prototype by the end of the war.

A further naval development, sponsored by the German Navy from 1939 onwards, was the series (typified by the R2, of which a photograph is included in '5' below) of S.P. coast defence guns R1 to R14. These guns ranged in calibre from 15 cm. to 38 cm. and were fired from the tracked carriage on a 360° traverse turntable.

4. **Outline Specifications of Operational Equipments.**

(i) <u>Anti-Tank</u>

(a) 4.7 cm. Czech A.Tk. gun on chassis of Pz.Kpfw.I Model B (4.7 cm. Pak (t) auf Pz.Jäg.I Ausf.B. (Sd.Kfz.101)).

<u>Wt. in action</u>	7.5 tons
<u>Crew</u>	3
<u>Armament</u>	4.7 cm. Pak(t)
Elevation	-8° to +12°
Traverse	30° (15°L and 15°R)
Calibre	47 mm. (1.85 ins.)
Overall length of piece	187.5 ins.
M.V. (A.P. shot)	2540 f.s.
Penetration of homogeneous armour at 30°:-	

Range (yds)	Thickness (mm)
500	55
1000	47

Ammunition
    Types   A.P., A.P.40 (C/R. with T.C. core) and H.E.
    Wt. of A.P. projectile   3.68 lbs.
    No. of rds carried   74

Armour
    Vertical and near vertical plates   15 mm.
    Horizontal and near horizontal plates   8 mm.

Power plant   Maybach NL38TR
                               Output 100 BHP at 3000 r.p.m.

Drive   )
Steering   )
Suspension)   As for Pz. Kpfw. I Model B (See 'Section I – Tanks')
Tracks   )

Dimensions
    Overall length   14 ft. 6 ins.
    " width   6 ft. 9 ins.
    " height   7 ft. 0 ins.
    Ground clearance   11½ ins.
    Track centres   5 ft. 6 ins.
    Track on ground   8 ft.

Performance
    Max. speed (roads)   24 m.p.h.
    " " (cross-country)
    Radius of action (roads)   95 miles
    " " " (cross-country)   70 miles
    Trench   4 ft. 7 ins.
    Step   1 ft. 2 ins.
    Fording Depth   1 ft. 11 ins.
    Gradient   30°

(b) <u>7.5 cm. A.Tk. Gun 40/3 (L/46) on Czech L.T.H. Light tank chassis (Marten 38(t) – 7.5 cm. Pak 40/3 (L/46) auf Pz. Jag 38(t) Marder 38 (t)).</u>

Weight in action   10 tons 16 cwt. (engine forward).
                                         10 tons 12 cwt. (engine rear).

Crew   4

Armament   7.5 cm. Pak 40/3
                                         Elevation −10° to +25°
                                         Traverse 60° (30° L and 30° R).
                                         Calibre 75 mm. (2.95 in.).
                                         Length in calibres (excl. M.B) 46.
                                         M.V. (APCBC) 2,600 f.s.

Ammunition
Types APCBC, A.P.40 (C.R. with T.C. core), H.E. and hollow charge.
No. of rounds carried 41 (engine forward).
                         38 (engine rear).
Wt. of APCBC projectile 15 lbs.
Penetration of Homogeneous armour at 30°:-

Range (yds)	Thickness (mm).
500	104
1000	89

Armour
11 mm – 16 mm. (engine front).
14.5 mm – 25 mm. (engine rear).

Power Plant
Type   TNHP petrol O.H.V., water cooled, 6 cyl.
Output 124 BHP at 2,200 r.p.m.

Transmission
Mechanical, with pre-selective epicyclic 'Wilson' type gearbox giving 5 speeds forward and 1 reverse.

Steering
Clutch/brake type.

Drive
Front sprocket.

Suspension
4 large rubber-tyred bogie wheels per side, sprung in pairs on semi-elliptic springs. 2 returned rollers per side.

Tracks
Single-link (dry) pin, cast, skeleton type with central wheel path and 2 guide horns. Single integrally-cast spud. 2 driving bushes.

Dimensions
Overall length (incl. gun – Engine forward 17 ft. 2 ins.
                                "   rear   18 ft. 11 ins.
Overall width   7 ft. 1 in.
  "   height   Engine forward 7 ft. 3 ins.
                        "   rear   8 ft. 3 ins.
Ground clearance   1 ft. 3 in.
Track centres   5 ft. 9½ in.
Track on ground   8 ft. 6¾ in.

Performance
Max. speed (roads)   25 m.p.h.
 "   "   (cross country)
Radius of action (roads) 115 miles
 "   "   " (cross country) 87 miles.
Trench   6 ft 10 ins.
Step   2 ft. 9 ins.
Fording depth   3 ft 0 ins.
Gradient   30°

(c) 8.8 cm. A.Tk. gun 43/1(L/71) on tank destroyer III/IV ('Rhinoceros', formerly 'Hornet') – 8.8 cm. Pak 43/1(L/71) auf Pz.Jäg. III/IV ('Nashorn', früher 'Hornisse') (Sd.Kfz. 169)).

<u>Wt. in action</u>	24 tons
<u>Crew</u>	5
<u>Armament</u>	8.8 cm. Pak 43/1 (L/71)
Sight	Sfl.Z.F.1a.
Elevation	-5° +20°
Traverse	30° (15°L & 15°R)
Calibre	88 mm (3.45 in)
Length in calibres (excl. M.B.)	71
M.V. (APCBC)	3280 f.s.
Penetration of homogeneous armour at 30° (APCBC):-	

Range (yds)	Thickness (mm)
500	184
1000	169

<u>Ammunition</u>
    No. of rds. carried   48
    Types   APCBC shell H.E., A.P.40 (C.R. with T.C. core) and Hollow Charge.
    Wt. of APCBC projectile   22 lbs.

<u>Armour</u>
  Hull
    Upper nose plate   30 mm at 12°
    Lower " "   20 mm at 60°
    Glacis plate   15 mm at 70°
    Sides   20 mm vertical
  Superstructure
    Front   10 mm at 30°
    Sides   10 mm at 16°

<u>Power plant</u>)
<u>Transmission</u>) As for Pz.Kpfw. III
<u>Drive</u>)   ) See "Section I - Tanks"
<u>Suspension</u>) As for Pz.Kpfw. IV
<u>Tracks</u>)

<u>Dimensions</u>
    Overall length (incl. gun)   27 ft. 8¾ in.
    " width   9 ft. 8⅛ in.
    " height   9 ft. 7¾ in.
    Ground clearance   1 ft. 3¾ in.
    Track centres   7 ft. 11 in.
    Track on ground   11 ft 6 in.

<u>Performance</u>
    Max. speed (roads)   25 m.p.h.
    " " (cross country)   15 m.p.h.
    Radius of action (roads)   160 miles.
    " " " (cross country)   80 miles.
    Trench
    Step
    Fording depth   2 ft 7½ in.
    Gradient   30°

(d) 7.5 cm. A.Tk.Gun 39(L/48) on redesigned Czech "L.T.H" light tank chassis - 'Baiter' (7.5 cm. Pak 39 (L/48) auf Pz.Jag.38(t) - 'Hetzer', oder 'Jagdpanzer 38')

<u>Wt. in action</u>	15 tons 15 cwt.
<u>Crew</u>	4
Armament (i) Main	7.5 cm. Pak 39 (L/48)
	Sight Sfl.Z.F.1a
	Elevation -6° to +12°
	Traverse 16° (5°L & 11°R)
	Calibre 75 mm. (2.95 in.)
	Overall length of piece 48 calibres.
	M.V. (APCBC) 2461 f.s.
	Penetration of homogeneous armour at 30°:-

Range (yds)	Thickness (mm)
500	90
1000	80

(ii) <u>Subsidiary</u> Roof-mounted 7.92 mm. M.G. 34.
Traverse 360°
Sight   Periscopic (Magnification x 3
                          Field 8°).

<u>Ammunition</u>

(i) 7.5 cm. Types APCBC shell, A.P.40. (C.R. with T.C. core), H.E., Smoke & hollow charge
No. of rounds carried   40
Wt. of APCBC projectile   15 lbs.

(ii) 7.92 mm. No. of rounds carried   600

<u>Armour</u>
Glacis plate	60 mm. at 70°
Lower nose plate	60 mm. at 40°
Hull side	20 mm. at 15°
Superstructure side	20 mm. at 40°
Upper tail plate	8 mm. at 70°
Lower tail plate	20 mm. at 15°
Roof	8 mm. horizontal
Belly	10 mm. "

<u>Power plant</u>
Type O.H.V. 6 cyl. petrol, water cooled.
Maker E.P.A. (Czech).
Output 150 B.H.P. at 2600 r.p.m.

<u>Transmission</u>
Mechanical. Manually operated Wilson type preselector gearbox giving 5 speeds forward and 1 reverse.

<u>Steering</u>
Mechanical clutch/brake type.

<u>Drive</u>
Front sprocket.

Suspension
4 large diameter, rubber-tyred single bogie wheels per side, sprung in bogie pairs on semi-elliptic springs. One rubber tyred return roller per side, between bogies.

Tracks
Single-link single-pin cast skeleton type with single central wheel path and twin guide horns. Twin driving bosses.

Dimensions
Overall length (incl. gun)	15 ft. 7 in.
" width (over skirting plates)	8 ft. 7½ in.
" height (over M.G. Mtg.)	7 ft. 1½ in.
" " (excl. " ")	6 ft. 3¼ in.
Ground clearance	1 ft. 6½ in.
Track centres	7 ft. 0¾ in.
Track on ground	8 ft. 10 in.

Performance
Max. speed (roads)	26 m.p.h.
Average speed (cross country)	9 m.p.h.
Radius of action (roads)	124-145 miles
" " " (cross country)	62-80 miles
Trench	4 ft. 3 in.
Step	2 ft. 1 in.
Fording depth	3 ft. 7¼ in.
Gradient	25°

(c) 8.8 cm. A.Tk. gun 43/3 (L/71) on 'Panther' tank destroyer - 8.8 cm. Pak. 43/3 (L/71) auf. Pz.Jag. Panther (Sd.Kfz.173 - Jagdpanther).

Weight in action	44 tons 16 cwt.
Crew	5

Armament
(i) Main — 8.8 cm. Pak 43/3 (L/71)
   Elevation — -8° to +14°
   Traverse — 26° (13°L & 13°R)
   Sights — Sfl.Z.F.1a on Z.E. 37 sight bracket.
   Calibre — 88 mm. (3.45 in).
   Length of piece in cals (excl. M.B.) — 71
   M.V. (APCBC) — 3280 f.s.
   Penetration of homogeneous armour at 30° (APCBC):-

Range (yds)	Thickness (mm)
500	184
1000	169

(ii) Subsidiary. — 7.92 mm. M.G.34 ball-mounted in off-side of front glacis plate.

Ammunition
(i) 8.8 cm. — Types APCBC, A.P.40 (C.R. with T.C. core), H.E. and Hollow Charge.
   No. of rds. carried — 28 APCBC
   29 HE
   Total 57
   Weight of APCBC projectile — 22.4 lbs.

(ii) 7.92 mm. — No. of rounds carried.

(ii) 7.92 mm.   No. of rounds carried.

Armour
   Glacis plate   80 mm at 55°
   Lower nose plate   60 mm at 55°
   Hull sides   40 mm vertical
   Superstructure sides   45 mm at 30°
   Tail plate   40 mm at 30°
   Superstructure rear   40 mm at 30°
   Roof   17 mm at 85°
   Belly   15 (rear)   } horizontal.
                             20 + 13 (front) }

Power plant   )
Transmission   )
Drive   )   As for Pz.Kpfw.Panther (See 'Section I - Tanks').
Suspension   )
Tracks   )

Dimensions
   Overall length (incl. gun)   32 ft. 4 ins.
   "   width   10 ft. 9 ins.
   "   height   8 ft. 3 ins.
   Ground clearance   1 ft. 10 ins.
   Track centres   8 ft. 7$\frac{1}{8}$ ins.
   Track on ground   12 ft. 10 ins.

Performance
   Max. speed (roads)   18 m.p.h.
   "   "   (cross country)   10 m.p.h.
   Radius of actions (roads)
   "   "   "   (cross country)
   Trench
   Step   3 ft. 0 ins.
   Fording   4 ft. 7 ins.
   Gradient   30°

(f) 12.8 cm. A.Tk. gun 44 or 80 (L/55) on Pz.Kpfw. Tiger Model B Tank Destroyer - 12.8 cm. Pak 44 oder Pak 80 (L/55) auf Pz.Jäg. Tiger Ausf. B (Sd.Kfz.186) - Jagdtiger.

Wt. in action   70 tons 12 cwt. (with Henschel suspension)
                      68 tons 17 cwt. (with Porsche suspension).

Crew   6

Armament
  (i) Main: 12.8 cm. Pak 44 (L/55) or Pak 80 (L/55)
      (Note: These two guns have identical pieces and ballistics, and fire the same ammunition. 12.8 cm Pak 44 was the original gun and Pak 80 the later type, introduced about March 1945. Approx. 25-50 of these vehicles were fitted with the 8.8 cm. Pak 43/3 (as mounted in Jagdpanther - see (e) above) pending the introduction of the Pak 80)

Sight   W.Z.F. 2/1
Elevation $-7.5°$ to $+15°$
Traverse $20°$ ($10°$L and $10°$R).
Calibre   128 mm. (5.04 in).
Length of piece in calibres   55

M.V.(APCBC)   3020 f.s.
Penetration of homogeneous armour at $30°$ (APCBC):-

Range (yds)	Thickness (mm).	
547	215	) German figures,
1094	202	) from range table.

(ii) Subsidiary: 7.92 mm. M.G. 34 ball-mounted in offside of front glacis plate.

Ammunition

(i) 12.8 cm.
    Types: APC, APCBC, H.E. (APC was abandoned soon after introduction)
    No. of rds. carried   38
    Wt. of APCBC projectile   62.5 lbs.

(ii) 7.92 mm.
    No. of rds. carried.

Armour
Hull

Glacis plate   150 mm at $50°$
Lower nose plate   100 mm at $50°$
Sides   80 mm vertical
Tail   80 mm at $30°$
Belly   80 mm at $30°$

Superstructure

Front   250 mm at $15°$
Sides   80 mm at $25°$
Rear   80 mm at $10°$
Roof   30 mm Horizontal

Power Plant)
Transmission)   as for Pz.Kpfw. Tiger Model B (See 'Section I - Tanks').
Steering)
Drive)

Suspension.

    Vehicles built by Henschel were fitted with Henschel suspension as fitted to Pz.Kpfw. Tiger Model B (for details see 'Section I - Tanks'). Those built by Nibelungenwerk of St. Valentin were fitted with a Porsche design of suspension, incorporating longitudinal torsion bars, similar in principle to that on the V.K.4501 (P) (see 'Section I - Tanks'). Porsche suspension has 8 small diameter, steel-tyred single bogie wheels per side, mounted in bogie pairs and sprung on single longitudinal torsion bars. No return rollers.

Tracks

Two types of track, one similar to that on Pz.Kpfw. Tiger Model B (see 'Section I – Tanks') and other, generally similar, but with 3-piece main links and 4-piece connecting links. Narrow (transportation) and wide (operational) tracks also provided.

Dimensions

	Porsche Suspension	Henschel Suspension
Overall length (incl. gun)	34 ft. 0⅜ in.	34 ft. 11½ in.
Overall width – over narrow tracks (for loading)	10 ft. 8¾ in.	10 ft. 8¾ in.
Overall width – over skirting plates (for operations)	11 ft. 9⅜ in.	11 ft. 10¾ in.
Overall height – Porsche suspension	9 ft. 7 in.	9 ft. 3 in.
Ground clearance – Porsche suspension	1 ft. 10 in.	1 ft. 6 in.
Track centres	9 ft. 2 in.	
Track on ground – Porsche suspension	14 ft. 2⅞ in.	13 ft. 11 in.

Performance

Max. speed (roads)	23.6 m.p.h.
" " (cross country)	9–12 m.p.h.
Radius of action (roads)	105.6 miles
" " " (cross country)	75 miles
Trench	8 ft. 2 in.
Step	2 ft. 9½ in.
Fording depth	5 ft. 11 in.
Gradient	35°

(ii) Field and Medium, and Assault.

(a) 7.5 cm. gun (L/24) on Assault Gun Carriage III (Modified Pz.Kpfw. III). – 7.5 cm. K(L/24) auf Stu.G. III (Sd.Kfz. 142).

Wt. in action	19.9 tons
Crew	4
Armament	7.5 cm. (L/24)
Sight	Sfl.Z.F.1
Elevation	–10° to +20°
Traverse	12½° L and 12½° R
Calibre	75 mm. (2.95 ins.)
Length of piece in cals.	24
M.V. (H.E.)	1378 f.s.
Max. range (H.E.)	6758 yds.

Ammunition
Types: H.E., Hollow charge, Smoke and APCBC
Wt. of H.E. Projectile 12.6 lbs.
No. of rds. carried in stowage 44

Armour
Hull
    Front vertical plate   50 mm at 10°
    " glacis   "   26 mm at 84°

- 50 -

Upper nose plate	50 mm at 52°
Lower " "	50 mm at 21° and 20 mm at 74° (lower portion)
Side plate	30 mm vertical
Tail "	30 mm at 30° and 10° (lower)
Roof "	17 mm at 85° (front) and 75° (rear)
Belly "	16 mm horizontal

Superstructure

Front	50 mm at 15°
Sides	30 mm vertical (fighting compartment protected by extra 8 mm plate at 20° and 31°)
Rear	30 mm undercut 30°
Roof	11 mm at horizontal and 82° (centre and at 80° and 78° (sides)

Power Plant)
Transmission)
Steering)   As for Pz.Kpfw.III (See 'Section I – Tanks').
Drive)
Suspension)

Dimensions

Overall length	18 ft. 0 ins.
" width	9 ft. 8 ins.
" height	6 ft. 4½ ins.
Ground clearance	1 ft. 2 ins.
Track centres	8 ft. 2½ ins.
Track on ground	9 ft. 4½ ins.

Performance

Max. speed (roads)	29 m.p.h.
" " (cross country)	15 m.p.h.
Radius of action (roads)	102 miles.
" " " (cross country)	59 miles
Trench	
Step	
Fording depth	2 ft. 7½ ins. (early models) 2 ft. 11 ins. (later models)
Gradient	30°

(b) 10.5 cm Gun How. 18/2 on modified Pz.Kpfw II chassis 'Wasp' (10.5 cm le. F.H. 18/2 auf Gw II – 'Wespe', Sd.Kfz.124)

Weight in action	10.8 tons
Crew	5

Armament
  One 10.5 cm le.F.H. 18/2, with double baffle muzzle brake
  Sight: Sfl.Z.F. 1 on Z.E.34 sight bracket.
  Elevation -5° to +42°
  Traverse 17° L and 17° R
  Calibre 104.9 mm (4.14 ins)
  Length in calibres (excl. M.B.) 26
  M.V.(H.E. charge 'F') 1772 f.s. (Charge 'F' is an extra long range charge only used when the gun is fitted with a muzzle brake).
  Max. range (H.E., charge 'F') 14,530 yds.

Ammunition
    Types H.E., Hollow Charge & Smoke
    Wt. of H.E. projectile. 32 lbs. 11 oz.
    No. of rds. carried   30

Armour
  Hull
    Driver's compartment   20 mm at $15°$, $22°$ & $30°$
    Glacis Plate   10 mm at $75°$
    Lower nose plate   30 mm at $15°$
    Sides   15 mm vertical
    Belly   5 mm horizontal
    Roof   10 mm   "
    Tail upper   8 mm vertical
    " lower   15 mm at $10°$
  Superstructure
    Internal Mantlet   10 mm at $24°$
        Front   12 mm at $21°$
        Sides   10 mm at $17°$
        Rear   8 mm at $16°$

Power Plant
    As for Pz. Kpfw II Model F, but mounted amidships on offside
    of hull.

Transmission)
) As for Pz. Kpfw II Model F (See 'Section I - Tanks')
Drive   )

Suspension
    As for Pz. Kpfw. II Model F except only three return rollers per
    side instead of four.

Tracks
    As for Pz. Kpfw. II Model F.

Dimensions
    Overall length   15 ft. $8\frac{1}{2}$ in.
    " width   7 ft. 4 in.
    " height   7 ft. $7\frac{1}{2}$ in.
    Ground clearance   1 ft. 2 in.
    Track centres   6 ft. 2 in.
    " on ground   7 ft. $10\frac{1}{2}$ in.

Performance
    Max. speed (roads)   24 m.p.h.
    " " (cross country)
    Radius of action (roads) 127 miles
    " " " (cross country) 72 miles
    Trench
    Step
    Fording depth   3 ft.
    Gradient $30°$

(c) 10.5 cm Assault Howitzer 42 (L/28) on Assault Gun Chassis III
     (10.5 cm Stu. H. 42 (L/28) auf Stu. G. III - Sd. Kfz. 142/2)

Wt. in action   23.5 tons

Crew   4

Armament
   One 10.5 cm Stu.H.42 (L/28)
   Sight   Sfl.Z.F.1a on Z.E. 37 sight bracket.
   Elevation $-6°$ to $220°$
   Traverse $20°$ ($10°$ L and $10°$ R)
   Calibre   104.9 mm (4.13 in.)
   Length of piece in cals.
     (excl. M.B.)   28
   M.V. (H.E. charge 6)   1771 f.s.
   Max. range
     (H.E. charge 6)   13480 yds.

(Note: In later models, an auxiliary, roof-mounted 7.92 mm M.G.34,
       similar to that on the Pz.Jag.38(t) (See '(i) A.Tk. - (d)'
       above) was provided).

Ammunition
   Types. H.E., Hollow Charge and Smoke.
   Wt. of H.E. projectile. 32 lbs. 11 1z.
   No. of rds. carried. 36

Armour
   Hull
      Glacis plate   26 mm
      Nose plate   50 mm
      Lower nose plate   50 mm
      Side plate   30 mm
      Roof   26 mm
      Belly (front and rear)   30 mm
      Belly (centre)   16 mm
      Tail plate   50 mm
   Superstructure
      Front   50 + 30 mm
      Mantlet   50 mm
      Sides   30 mm
      Rear   30 mm
      Roof   20 mm

Power Plant   )
Transmission   )
Steering   ) As for Pz.Kpfw.III (See 'Section I - Tanks').
Drive   )
Suspension   )
Tracks   )

Dimensions
   Overall length (incl. gun) 20 ft. $1\frac{3}{4}$ ins.
     "   width   9 ft. $8\frac{1}{2}$ ins.
     "   height   6 ft. $5\frac{1}{8}$ ins.
   Ground clearance)
   Track centres   ) As for Pz.Kpfw.III (See 'Section I - Tanks).
   Track on ground   )

Performance
  Max. speed (roads)   25 m.p.h.
   "   "   (cross country)
  Radius of action (roads)   105 miles
    "   "   "   (cross country)   56 miles
  Trench   8 ft. 6 in.
  Step   2 ft. 0 in.
  Fording depth   2 ft. 9 in.
  Gradient   27°

(d) 15 cm. How. 13 on French 'Lorraine' carrier chassis (15 cm. s.F.H.13 auf Gw.Lr. S.(f) – Sd.Kfz.135/1)

Wt. in action   8 tons approx.

Crew   5

Armament   One 15 cm. s.F.H.13
  Elevation   –1° 25' to +40°
  Traverse   5°L & 5°R.(Approx)
  Calibre   149.7mm (5.9 ins)
  Length of piece in cals. 17
  M.V.(H.E.)   1250 f.s.
  Max. range (H.E.)   9300 yds.

Ammunition
  Types: H.E., Anti-concrete and Smoke.
  Wt. of H.E. projectile.   92.4 lbs.
  No. of rounds carried.

Armour
  Hull
    Driver's front plate   9 mm at 35°
    Glacis plate   6 mm at 80°
    Nose plate   8 mm rounded
    Sides   9 mm vertical
    Tail (upper)   9 mm at 36°
     "   (lower)   9 mm at 11°
    Belly   5 mm horizontal
    Roof   6 mm horizontal
  Superstructure
    Front   10 mm at 18°
    Sides (Upper)   9 mm at 12°
      "   (lower)   9 mm at 10°
    Rear (upper)   7 mm at 12°
      "   (lower)   9 mm at 11°

Power plant
  6 cyl. in line water cooled petrol engine, Delahaye 103 – TT.
  Output approx. 80 B.H.P.

Transmission
  Mechanical with crash type manually-operated gearbox giving 5 speeds forward and 1 reverse.

Steering
  'Cletrac' type controlled differential.

Drive
  Single-ring front sprocket.

Suspension
6 single rubber-tyred bogie wheels per side arranged in bogie pairs. Each pair sprung on semi-elliptic springs. 4 single rubber-tyred return rollers per side.

Tracks
Single link, dry, single-pin type. Links are steel stampings of recessed type, with 2/3 linkage, single central wheel path and 2 guide horns.

Dimensions
Overall length ('incl. spade)	17 ft. 5 in.
" width	6 ft. 2 in.
" height	6 ft. 10 in.
Ground clearance	7 in.
Track centres	4 ft. 4$\frac{5}{8}$ in.
Track on ground	9 ft.

Performance
Max. speeds (roads)	21 m.p.h.
Remainder not known	

(e) 15 cm. Assault howitzer 43 (L/12) on Assault Vehicle IV (armoured Assault Vehicle 43 'Grizzly Bear') - 15 cm Stu. H.43 (L/12) auf. Stu. G. IV (Stu. Pz. 43 - 'Brummbär' Sd. Kfz. 166).

Wt. in action	27 tons 3 cwt.
Crew	5
Armament	One 15 cm Stu.H .43 (L/12) (ballistically similar to s.I.G.33)
Sight	Sfl.Z.F.1a on Z.E.37 sight bracket.
Elevation	−8° 30' to + 30°
Traverse	8° L and 8° R (approx)
Calibre	150 mm (5.9 in).
Length of piece in cals.	12
M.V.(H.E.)	790 f.s.
Max. range (H.E.)	4,700 yds.

(Note: an auxiliary 7.92 mm M.G. 34 was ball-mounted to the left of the main armament in the superstructure front plate on some later models).

Ammunition
The 15 cm Stu. H.43 fires the same ammunition (separate) as the s.I.G.33.
Types: H.E., Hollow charge and Smoke.

Wt. of H.E. projectile	83.6 lbs.
No. of rds. carried	38

Armour
Hull
Driver's front plate	80 mm at 12°
Glacis plate	20 mm at 72°
Nose plate	50 + 50 mm at 15°
Lower nose plate	30 + 30 mm at 59°
Sides	20 + 20 mm vertical
Tail (upper) } 20 mm	10°
" (lower) }	8°

```
          Roof (front)      25 mm  ⎱ horizontal
           "   (rear)       10 mm  ⎰
          Belly                     10 mm horizontal
       Superstructure
          Front             100 mm at 40°
          Sides (forward)   60 mm at 25°
          Sides (centre)    50 mm at 18°
          Sides (rear)      20 mm at 12°
          Rear              30 mm at 26° and vertical
          Roof              20 mm at 84°
```

Power Plant ⎫

Transmission ⎬

Steering ⎬ As for Pz.Kpfw.IV (See 'Section I - Tanks').

Drive ⎬

Suspension ⎬

Tracks ⎭

Dimensions
   Overall length   19 ft. 4 in.
    "   width (over skirting plates)   10 ft. 2 in.
    "   height   8 ft. 2 in.
   Ground clearance $10\frac{1}{2}$ in.
   Track centres   8 ft. 1 in.
   Track on ground   11 ft. 6 in.

Performance
   No details available.

(f)   15 cm Armoured S.P. rocket projector 42 - 15 cm Panzerwerfer 42
      (15 cm Ne. W 10 - ling 42 auf Panzerwerfer)

Weight in action		7 tons 4 cwt.
Crew		3
Armament	(a) Main	10 barrelled 15 cm Nebelwerfer 42 (rocket projector 42)
		Elevation $-5°$ to $+45$
		Traverse $360°$
		Calibre 15 cm (5.9 ins.)
		Max. range 8,000 yds approx.
	(b) Subsidiary	One 7.92 mm. M.G.34 or 42.
Ammunition		
15 cm.		50 rds. (10 in projector, 40 in vehicle) on s.W.S. chassis. Unknown quantity carried on Maultier chassis.
7.92 mm.		1500 rds.
Armour		
s.W.S. chassis		6 mm. basis.
Maultier chassis		8 mm. basis.

Power Plant)
Transmission)
Steering) See 'Vehicles' section, under Maultier 4½ ton and
Drive)   s.W.S.
Suspension)
Tracks)

Dimensions
   As for Maultier 4½ ton and s.W.S. (See 'Vehicles' section) except:-
    Overall height   s.W.S. version   6ft. 8 in.
                   Maultier version

(g) 38 cm Rocket Projector 61 as Assault Howitzer on Modified Tiger Model E chassis - 38 cm R.W.61 auf Sturmmörser Tiger

---

Wt. in action.

Crew   5

Armament
  (a) Main   One 38 cm R.W.61
       Sight   Telescope Pak 3 x 8° on Marine - Pak ZE C/42 sight
                      bracket.
       Elevation   0° to +85°
       Traverse   10° R x 10° L
       Calibre   38 cm (15 in)
       Length of piece in cals   5.4
       M.V. of H.E. projectile 50 ft/sec. Max. velocity 300 ft/sec.
       Maximum range of H.E. projectile 6014 yds.

  (b) Auxiliary   One 7.92 mm M.G.34 ball mounted on offside of
                       superstructure front plate.

Ammunition

  (a) 38 cm. Types H.E. and Hollow Charge
       Wt. of H.E. Projectile   761 lbs.
       No. of rounds carried   13 (incl. one on loading tray).

  (b) 7.92 mm No. of rounds carried

Armour
  Hull - as for Pz.Kpfw Tiger Model E (See 'Section I - Tanks')

  Superstructure
    Front   150 mm at 45°
    Sides   84 mm at 20°
    Rear   84 mm at 10°
    Roof   40 mm Horizontal

Power Plant
Transmission
Steering   As for Pz.Kpfw. Tiger Model E (See 'Section I - Tanks')
Drive
Suspension
Tracks

Dimensions
    Overall length   20 ft. 8½ ins.
    "   width   12 ft. 3 ins.
    "   height (Incl. crane)   11 ft. 4 ins.

Ground Clearance
Track on Ground   As for Pz.Kpfw. Tiger Model E (See 'Section I - tanks')
Track Centres

Performance
    No details available.

(h)   60 cm. Self Propelled Howitzer 'Karl' - 60 cm. Mrs. Karl (Gerät 040)

Wt. in action	123 tons approx.

Crew

Armament   One 60 cm. Mrs. Karl
    Elevation $-10°$ to $+75°$
    Traverse $2°$ approx. L and R
    Calibre   59.8 cm. (23.6 ins.)
    Length of piece in cals.   8.44
    M.V. (H.E.)   928 f.s.
    Max. range (H.E.)   7,300 yds.
    Wt. of H.E. projectile   4,840 lbs.

Ammunition
    None carried on vehicle. Carried in Mun. Pz. Wg. IV (Pz.Kpfw IV Ammunition Carrier), provided with crane.

Armour
    Vehicle is unarmoured, but constructed of ½ in. thick steel plates. No protection is provided for the gun crew.

Power Plant.
    Daimler Benz 12 cyl. V water cooled diesel engine type MB507.

Transmission
    Voith torque converter, with direction-change gearbox.

Drive
    Front sprocket.

Suspension

Single torsion bar springing. Two types, one with eleven all steel twin bogie wheels and six twin rubber tyred return rollers per side, and other with 8 twin rubber tyred bogie wheels and eight rubber tyred return rollers per side. Hull may be lowered to the ground for firing by rotating the fixed ends of the torsion bars.

Tracks

Cast steel centre-guided type with single, dry pin, hollow guide horns and shallow spud.

Dimensions

Overall length	36 ft.	10 ins.
" width (for travel)	10 ft.	6 ins.
" " (in action)	13 ft.	9 ins.
" height (for travel)	14 ft.	8 ins.
" " (in action)	13 ft.	5 ins.

Performance

No details available.

5. INDEX TO ILLUSTRATIONS

Fig.1. M.G.151/15 or 151/20 Drilling (Triple Mounting) on 3-ton Armoured Semi-Tracked Vehicle Sd.Kfz.251/21.

Fig.2. 2cm. Flack 30 or 38 on chassis of Pz.Kpfw.38(t) - Sd.Kfz.140.

Fig.3. 3.2cm. Flakvierling 38 on 8-ton Semi-Tracked Vehicle Sd.Kfz.7/1.

Fig.4. 2.8cm.s.Pz.B.41 on light 4-wheeled Armoured Car Sd.Kfz.221.

Fig.5. 2cm. Flakvierling 38 (Top Vehicle) and 3.7cm. Flak 43 (bottom right) on Pz.Kpfw.IV chassis (Flak Pz.IV) - Wirbelwind (Whirlwind) and Mobelwagen(Furniture Van), respectively.

Fig.6. 3cm. MK103 Zwilling (Twin Mounting), on Flak Pz.IV - Kugelblitz (Ball Lightning).

Fig.7. 3.7cm. Pak(t) on British 'Bren' Carrier.

Fig.8. 3.7cm. Pak on Armoured Infantry Carrier 'UE'(f) (Chenillette).

Fig.9. 3.7cm. Pak on Light Armoured Semi-Tracked Vehicle Sd.Kfz.250/10.

Fig.10. 4.7cm. Pak(f) on French 'Lorraine' Carrier Chassis (Pz.Jäg.Lr.S.(f)).

Fig.11. 4.7cm. Pak(t) on Pz.Jäg.I(Sd.Kfz.101).

Fig.12. 4.7cm. Pak(t) on Chassis of French Renault R.35 Tank.

Fig.13. 7.5cm. K.(L/24) on Stu.G.III (Sturmgeschütz).

Fig.14. 7.5cm. K.37(L/24) on 8-wheeled Armoured Car Sd.Kfz.233.

Fig.15. 7.5cm. K.51 or K.51/1(L/24) on 8-wheeled Armoured Car Sd.Kfz.234/3.

Fig.16. 7.5cm. Pak 40(L/46) on Chassis of 'Raupenschlepper Ost'.

Fig.17. 7.5cm. Pak 40(L/46) on French Somua Armoured Semi-Tracked Vehicle.

Fig.18. 7.5cm. Pak 40(L/46) of French Lorraine Carrier.

Fig.19. 7.5cm. Pak 40/3(L/46) on Czech.Pz.Kpfw.38(t) Tank Chassis with engine forward - Marder 38(t).S.Kfz.138.

Fig.20. 7.5cm. Pak 40(L/46) on French 'F.C.M.' Tank Chassis.

Fig.21. 7.5cm. Pak 40(L/46) on Czech Pz.Kpfw.38(t) Tank Chassis with engine at rear.

Fig.22. 7.5cm. Pak 40(L/46) on French Hotchkiss H.35 Tank Chassis.

Fig.23. 7.5cm. Pak 40(L/46) on 3-ton Armoured Semi-Tracked Vehicle, Sd.Kfz.251/22.

Fig.24. 7.5cm. Pak 40(L/46) on 8-wheeled Armoured Car, Sd.Kfz.234 Series.

Fig.25. 7.5cm. Pak 40(L/46) on Chassis of Pz.Kpfw.II (Models A to C and F): Marder II (Sd.Kfz.131).

Fig.26. 7.5cm. Stu.K.40(L/43) and (L/48) on Stu.G.III.

Fig.27. 7.5cm. Pak 39(L/48) on Pz.Jäg. 38(t) - Hetzer.

Fig.28. 7.5cm. Pak 39(L/48) on Pz.Jäg.IV(Sd.Kfz.162).

Fig.29. 7.5cm.Stu.K.42(L/70) on Pz.Jäg.IV(Sd.Kfz.162).

Fig.30. 7.62cm. Pak 36(r) on Pz.Kpfw.II(Models D and E) chassis - Sd.Kfz.132.

Fig.31. 7.62cm. Pak 36(r) on Czech.Pz.Kpfw. 38(t) tank chassis.

Fig.32. 8.8cm. Pak 43/1(L/71) on Pz.Jäg.III/IV, known originally as 'Hornet' and later as 'Rhinoceros'. (Sd.Kfz.164).

Fig.33. 8.8cm. Pak 43/2(L/71) on Pz.Jäg.Tiger (P), Sd.Kfz.184. Formerly known as 'Ferdinand' and later as 'Eleffant'.

Fig.34. 8.8cm. Pak 43/3(L/71) on Pz.Jäg.Panther - Sd.Kfz. 173(Jagdpanther).

Fig.35. 10.5cm. le. F.H.18/2 on Gw.II(Wespe).Sd.Kfz.124.

Fig.36. 10.5cm. le. F.H.18/1 on Gw.IVb - Sd.Kfz.165/1.

Fig.37. 10.5cm. le.F.H. 18/2 on Chassis of French Char B2 Tank.

Fig.38. 10.5cm. Stu.H.42(L/28) on Stu.G.III - Sd.Kfz.142/2.

Fig.39. 10.5cm. le.F.H.18 on French Lorraine Carrier Chassis.

Fig.40. 10.5cm. le. F.H.18 on French F.C.M. Tank Chassis.

Fig.41. 10.5cm. le. F.H.18 on French Hotchkiss H.35 Tank Chassis.

Fig.42. 12.8cm. Pak 44 or Pak 80(L/55) on Pz. Jäg.Tiger Model B Sd.Kfz. 186 (Jagdteger).

Fig.43. 15cm. Stu.H.43(L/12) on Stu.Pz.IV(Brummbär - Grizzly Bear).

Fig.44. 15cm. s.I.G.33 on Chassis of Pz.Kpfw.38(t) with engine forward - Sd.Kfz.138/1.

Fig.45. 15cm.s.I.G.33 on Gw.38(t) with engine rear.

Fig.46. 15cm.s.F.H.13 on French Lorraine Carrier.

Fig.47. 15cm.s.I.G.33 on Pz.Kpfw.II - Sd.Kfz.121.

Fig.48. 15cm.s.F.H.18 on Gw.III/IV(Hummel - Bumble Bee), Sd.Kfz.165.

Fig.49. 38cm. Rocket Projector RW 61 Pz.Kpfw. Tiger Model E Chassis - Stu.Mrs.Tiger.

Fig.50. 60cm. Mrs. Karl - Gerät 040.

Fig.51. Vomag prototype of 7.5cm. Stu.K.42(L/70) on Pz.Jäg.IV.

Fig.52. Panzerjäger 38(t) with 7.5cm. Kw.K.42(L/70).

Fig.53. Rheinmetall-Borsig/Ardelt Waffenträger for 8.8cm. Pjk 43 or Kw.K.43-Prototype.

Fig.54. Krupp/Steyr Prototype of 8.8cm. Pak 43/3(L/71) Waffenträger high-angle.

Fig.55. Einheitswaffenträger, (G.P.) (Gun Carrier) with 8.8cm. Pak 43 (L/71).

Fig.56. Panzerjäger IV with 8.8cm. Pak 43/3 (L/71).

Fig.57. Krupp Prototype for S.P. 8.8cm. Flak 18 or 36 on high-angle mounting with all-round traverse.

Fig.58. Krupp early experimental Waffenträger, mounting 10.5cm. le F.H.18 on Gw.IVb Chassis. (Heuschrecke Series).

Fig.59. Heuschrecke IV6 (Grasshopper IVb) - 10.5cm. le F.H.18/6 on GW IV.

Fig.60. Model of Heuschrecke 15.

Fig.61. Mock-up of Krupp 'Grille' 10 mounting 10.5cm. le. F.H.43/35.

Fig.62. Prototype of first experimental 'Heuschrecke' Waffenträger by Krupp.

Fig.63. Prototype of 10.5cm. K.18 on Pz. Sfl. IVa.

Fig.64. Light Gun Carrier (Leichter Waffenträger) with 10.5cm. (L/28) le F.H.18/40.

Fig.65. Einheitswaffenträger (G.P. Gun Carrier) with 10.5cm. C.F.H.18/40 (L/28).

Fig.66. Jagdtiger mounting 12.8cm. (L/66) gun.

Fig.67. Panzerjäger Panther with 12.8cm. Pak 80(L/55).

Fig.68. Einheitswaffenträger (G.P. Gun Carrier) with 12.8cm. K.81(L/55).

Fig.69. Mock-up of 'Grille' 15 by Krupp, mounting 15cm. s.F.H.43 or 12.8cm. K.43.

Fig.70. Mittlerer Waffenträger (Medium Gun Carrier) with 12.8cm. K.81(L/55).

Fig.71. Mittlerer Waffenträger (Medium Gun Carrier) with 15cm. s.F.H.18 (L/29.5).

Fig.72. Einheitswaffenträger (G.P. Gun Carrier) with 15cm. s.F.H.18 (L/29.5).

Fig.73. Mock-up of 'Grille' 17/21 - Waffenträger for 17cm. K. or 21 cm. Mrs.

Fig.74. Krupp prototype of Naval mobile 28cm. Coast Defence Gun - R.2.

6. Bibliography

Examination reports by:-

D.T.D., Ministry of Supply.
M.C. of S.S.T.T. (Preliminary Reports)
M.I.10, H.Q., M.E.F. (Intelligence Summaries)
G.S.I. (tech). 21 Army Group (Technical Intelligence Summaries)
G-2 Tech.Int.Sec., H.A. & C.M. (Technical Intelligence Summaries)
G-2 (Tech.), S.H.A.E.F. (Technical Intelligence Summaries)
M.I.10, War Office (War Office Technical Intelligence Summaries)

German equipment handbooks ('D' - Vorschriften), held by F.V. Wing, M.C. of S.

German manufacturers' drawings and files, held by F.V. Wing M.C. of S. on behalf of B.I.O.S., Group V.

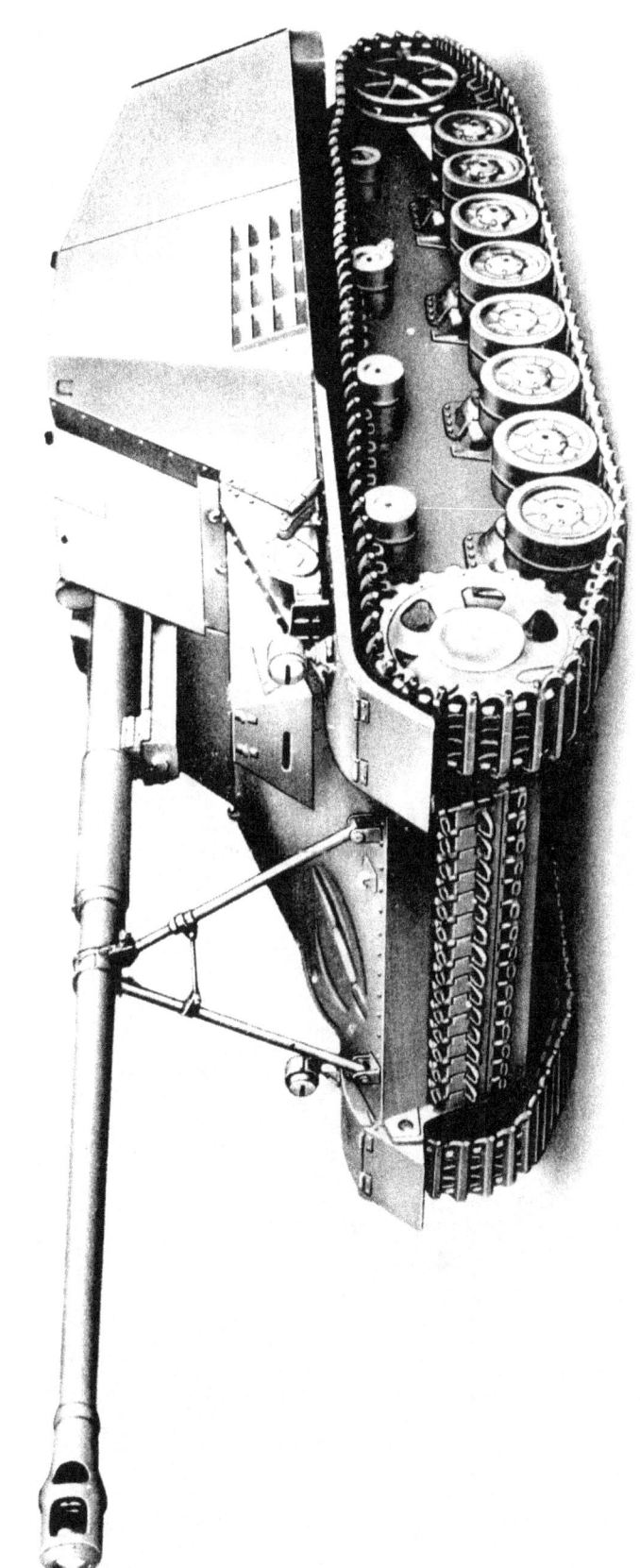

Fig.32. 8.8 cm. Pak 43/1 (L/71) on Pz.Jäg.III/IV, known originally as 'Hornet', and later as 'Rhinoceros'. (Sd.Kfz.164)

Fig. 31. 7.62cm. Pak 36(r) on Czech.Pz.Kpfw. 38(t) tank chassis.

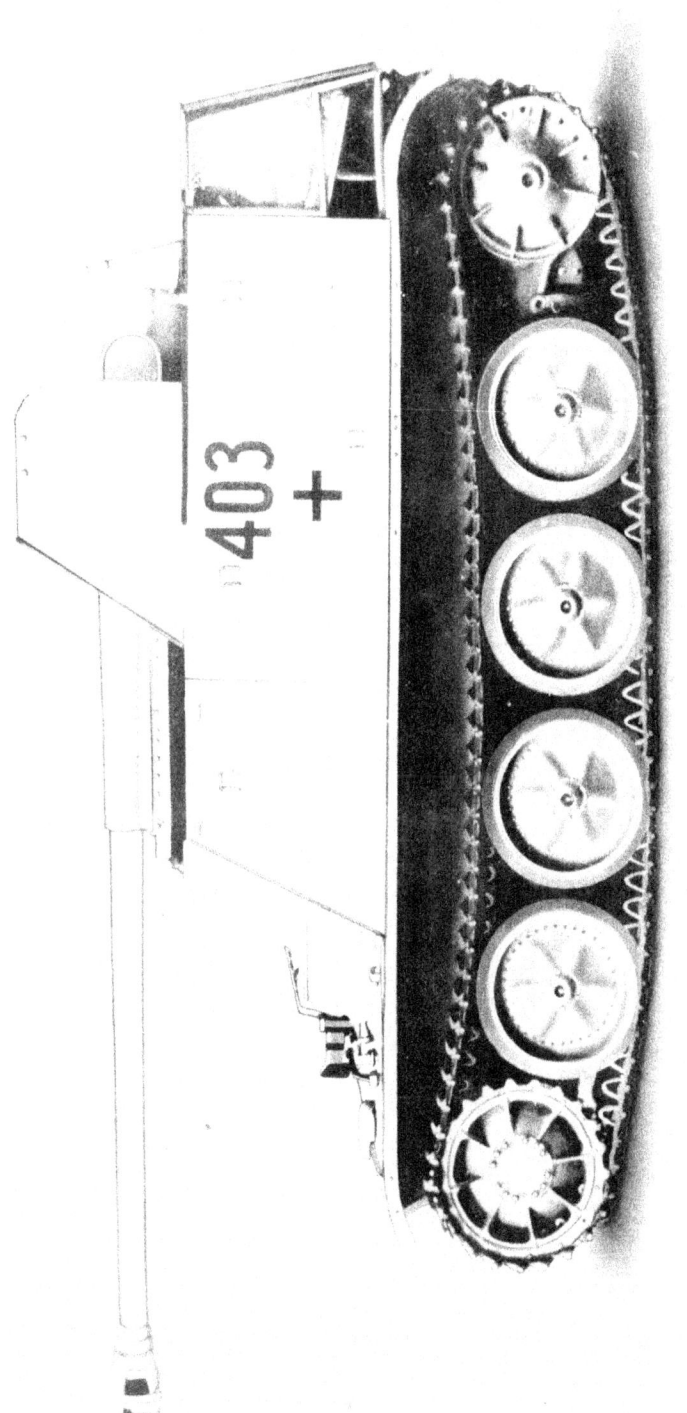

Fig. 30 7.62 cm. Pak.36(r) on Pz.Kpfw.II (Models D and E) Chassis - Sd.Kfz.132.

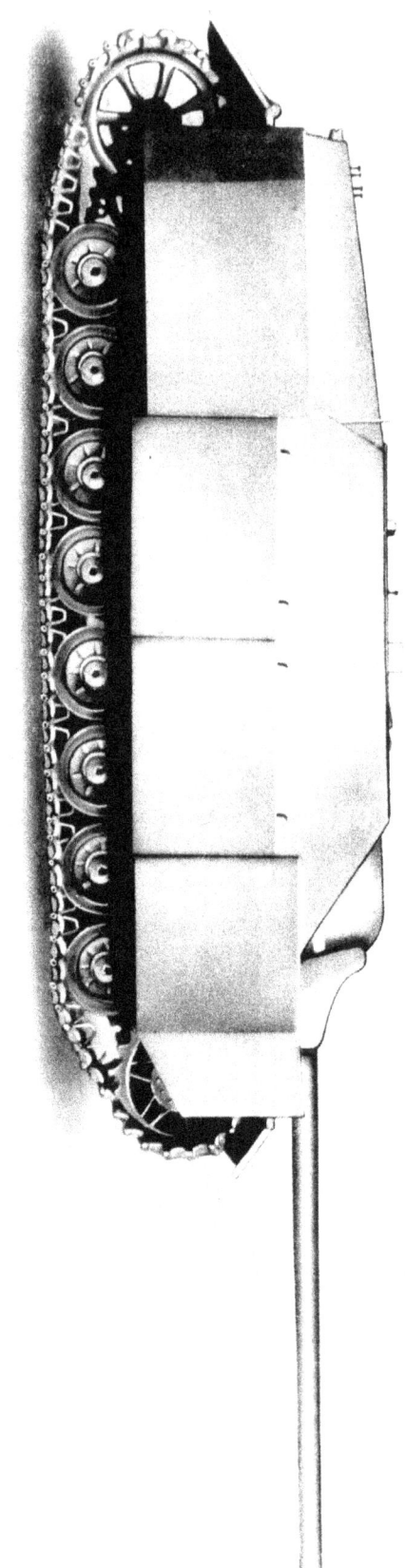

Fig. 29, 7.5 cm. Stu.K.42 (L/70) on Pz.Jäg.IV (Sd.Kfz.162).

Fig. 28. 7.5 cm. Pak 39 (L/48) on Pz.Jäg.IV (Sd.Kfz.762).

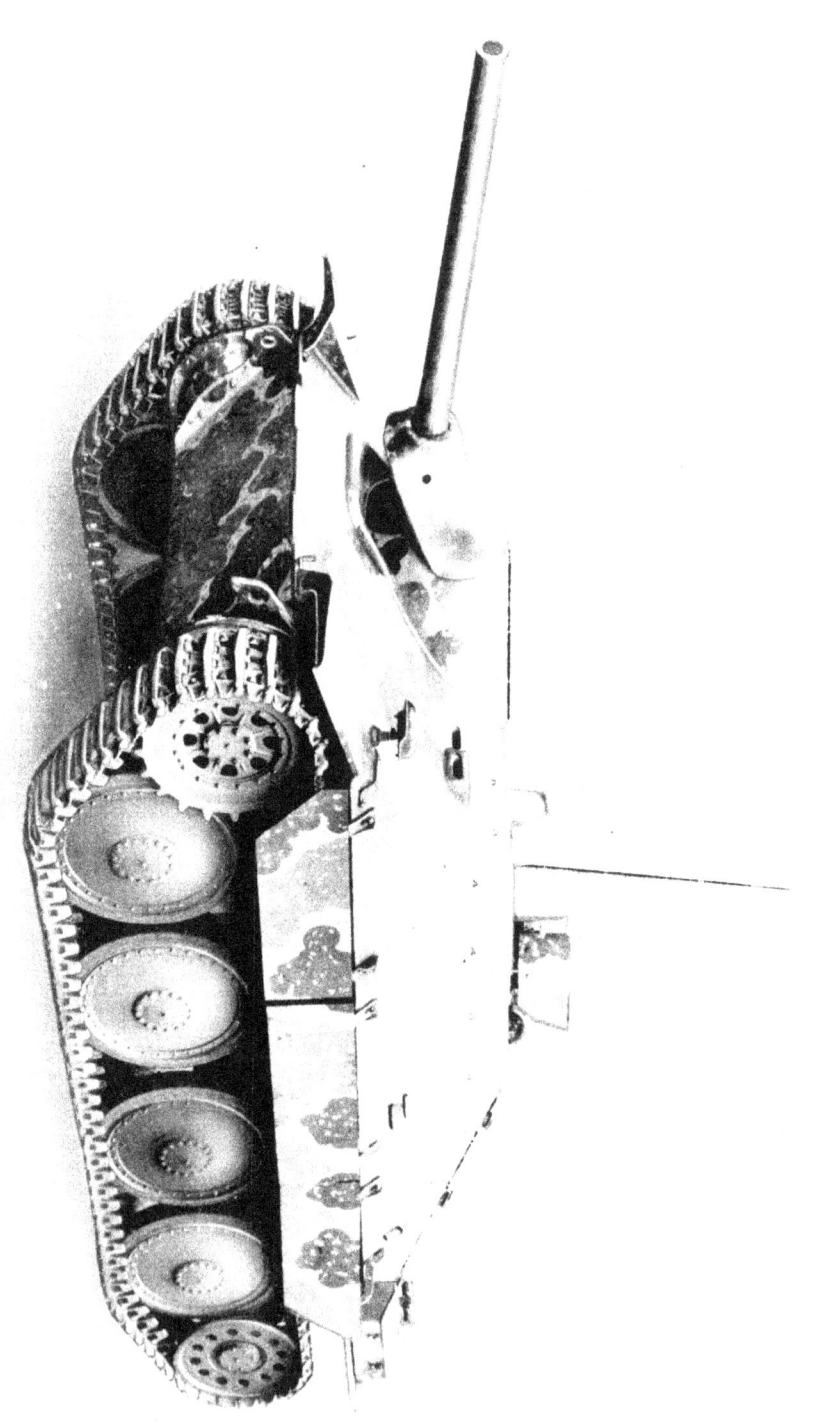

Fig. 27. 7.5 cm. Pak 39 (L/48) on Pz.Jäg. 38(t) - Hetzer.

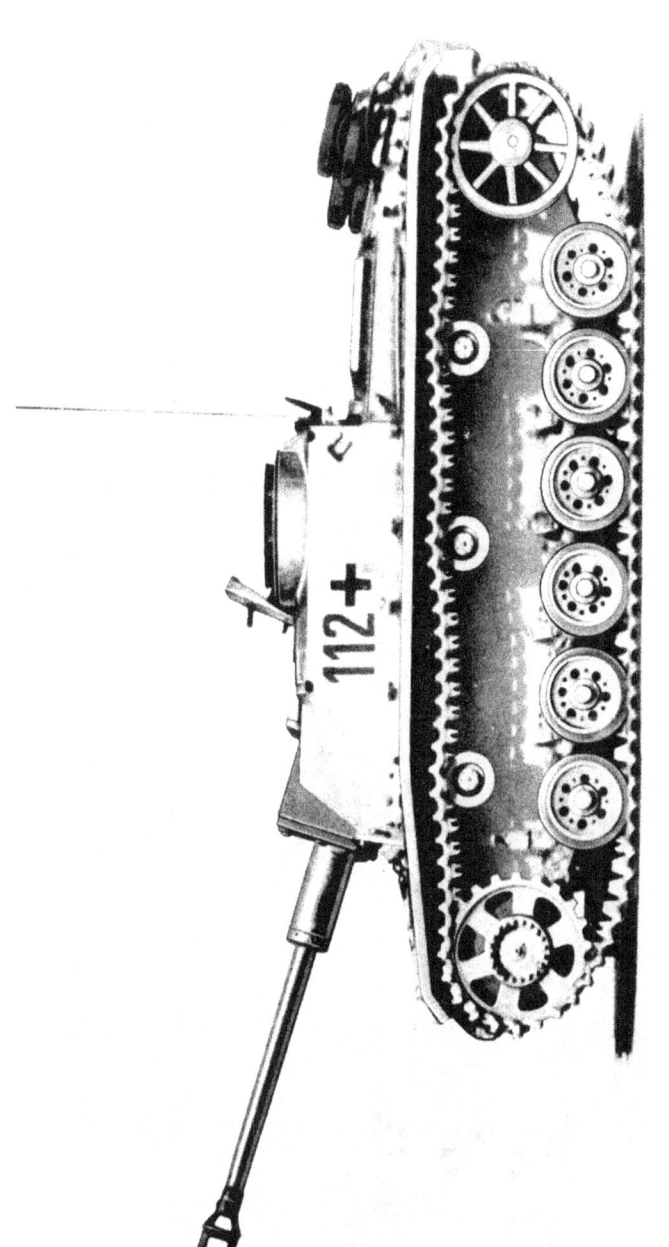

Fig. 26. 7.5. cm. Stu.K.40 (L/43) and (L/48) on Stu.G.III.

Fig. 25. 7.5 cm. Pak 40 (L/46) on Chassis of Pz.Kpfw.II (Models A to C and F): Marder II (Sd.Kfz.131).

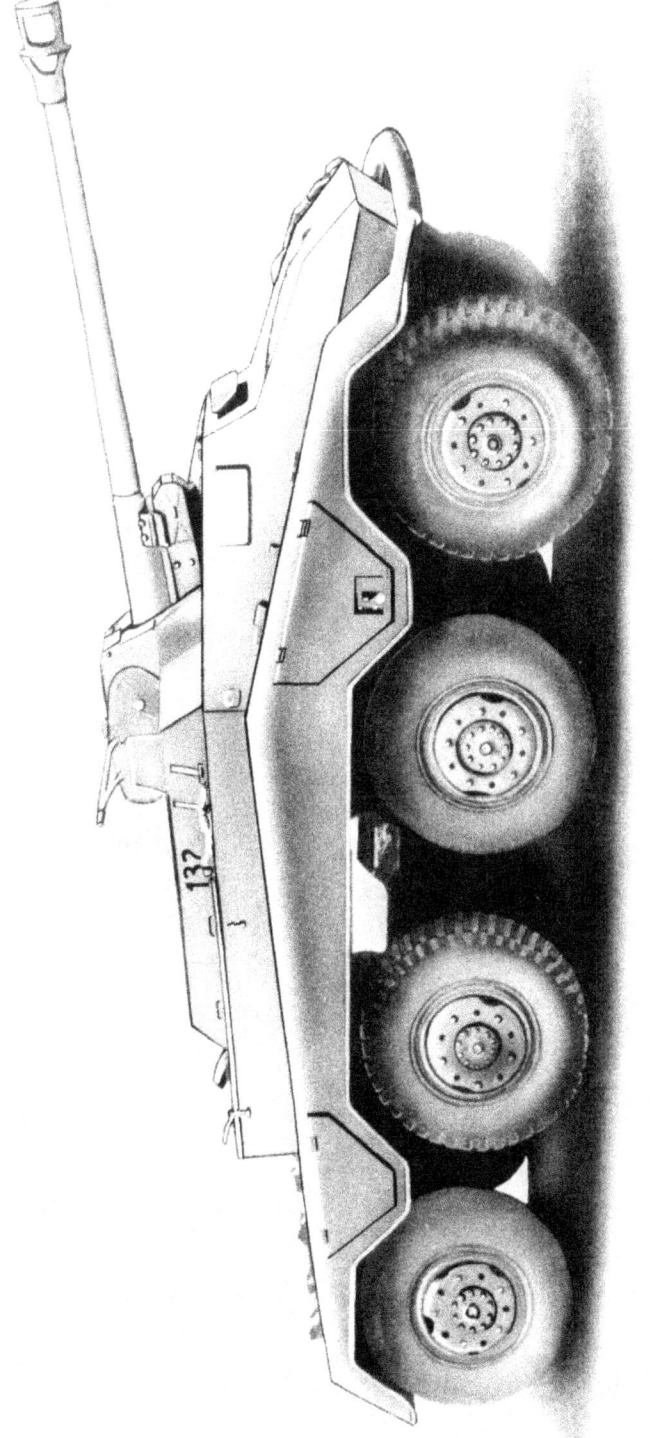

Fig. 24. 7.5 cm. Pak 40 (L/46) om 8-wheeled Armoured Car, Sd.Kfz.234 Series.

Fig. 23. 7.5 cm. Pak 40 (L/46) on 3-ton Armoured Semi-Tracked Vehicle, Sd.Kfz.251/22.

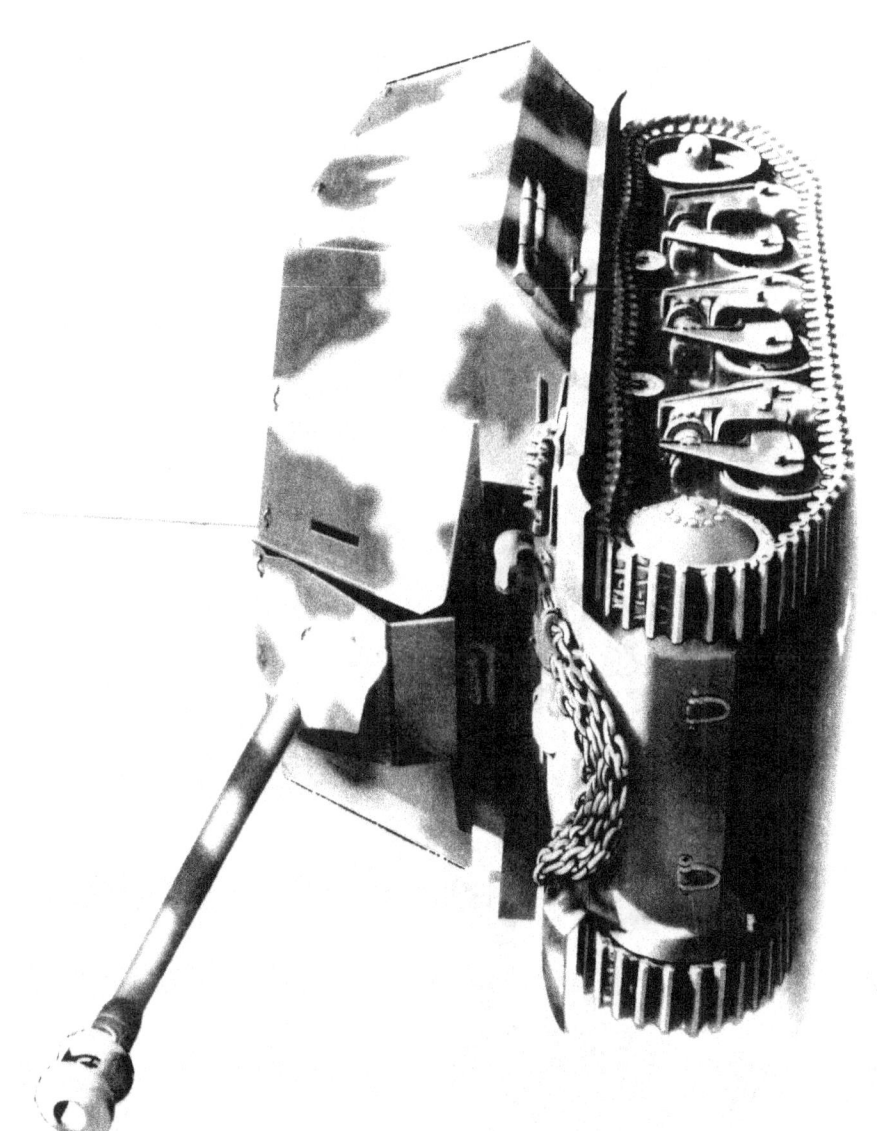

Fig. 22 7.5 cm. Pak 40(L/46) on French Hotchkiss H.35 Tank Chassis.

Fig.21 7.5 cm. Pak. 40 (L/46) on Czech Pz.Kpfw. 38(t) Tank Chassis with engine at rear.

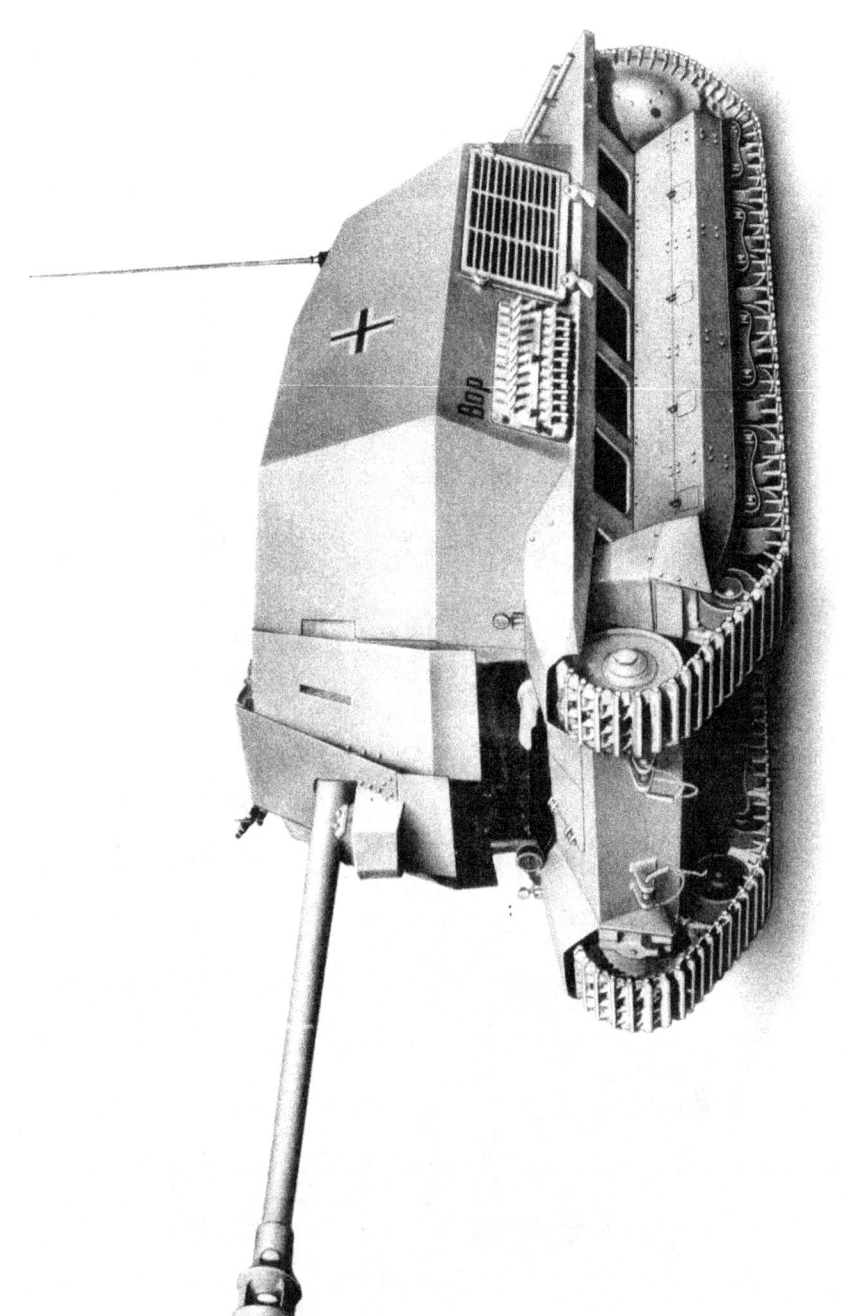

Fig.20. 7.5 cm. Pak 40 (L/46) on French 'F.C.M.' Tank Chassis.

Fig 29. 7.5 cm. P 40/3 (L/46) Czech Pz.Kpfw.38(t) Tank Chassis with engine forward-Marder 38(t), Sd.Pfz.138.

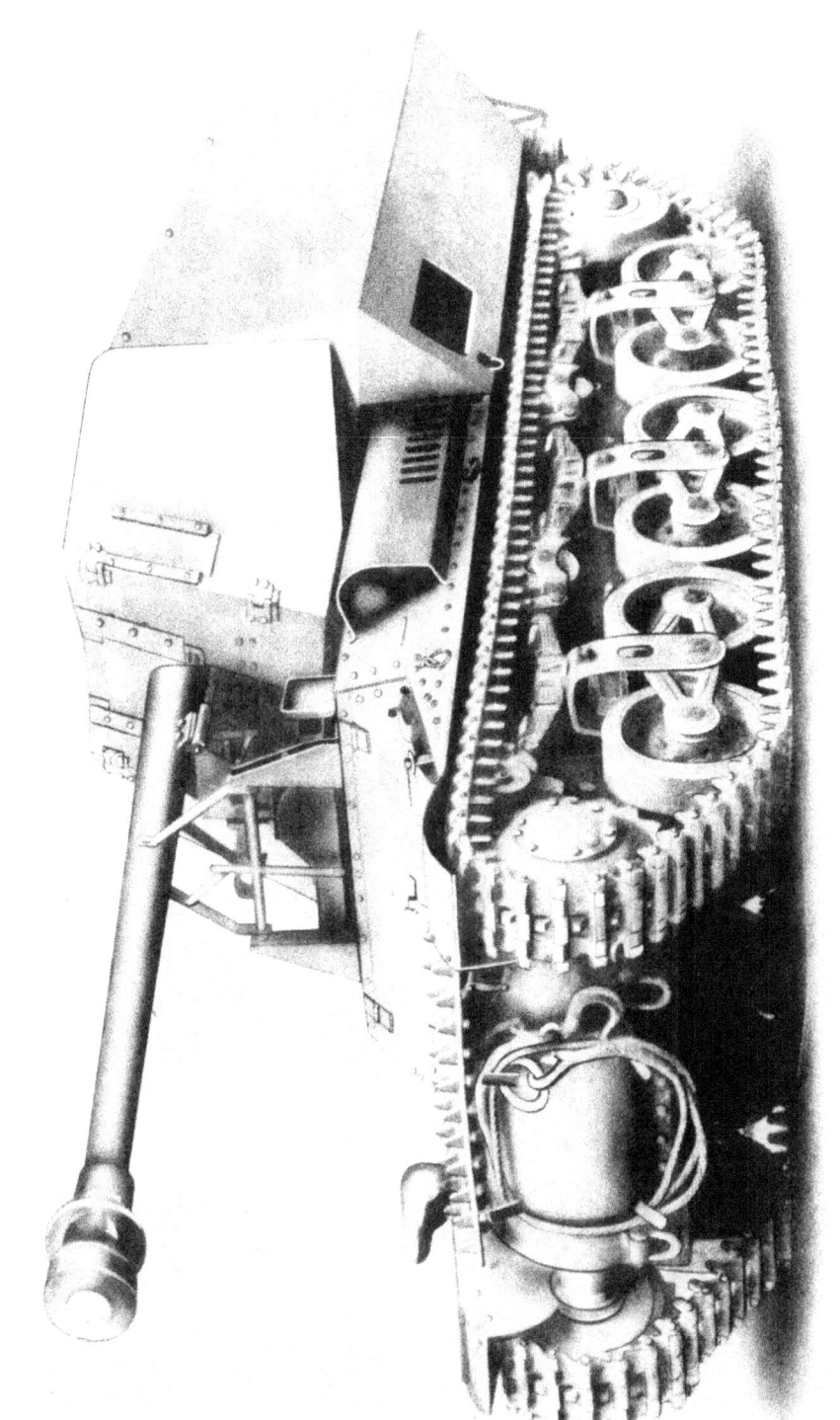

Fig. 18. 7.5 cm. Pak 40 (L/46) on French Lorraine Carrier.

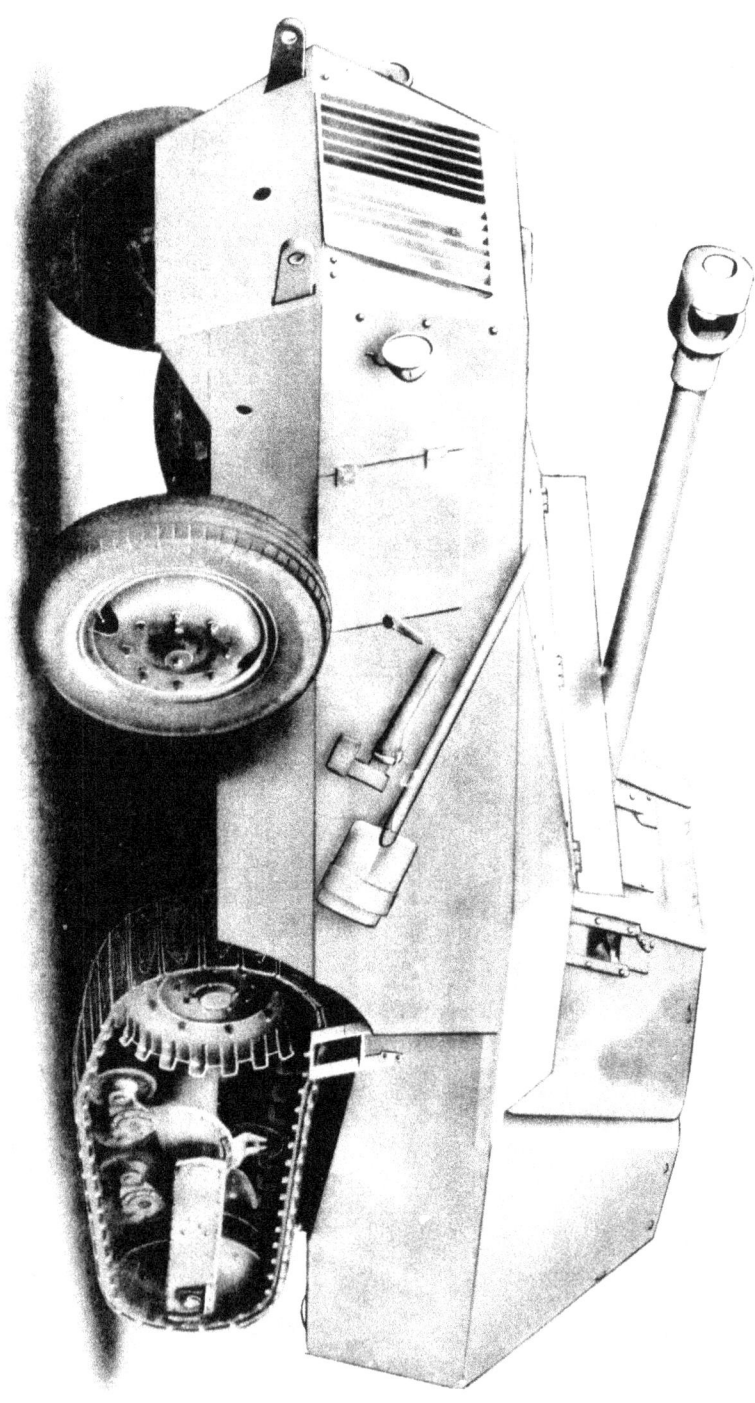

Fig.17. 7.5 cm. Pak 40 (L/46) on French Somua Armoured Semi-Tracked Tracked Vehicle.

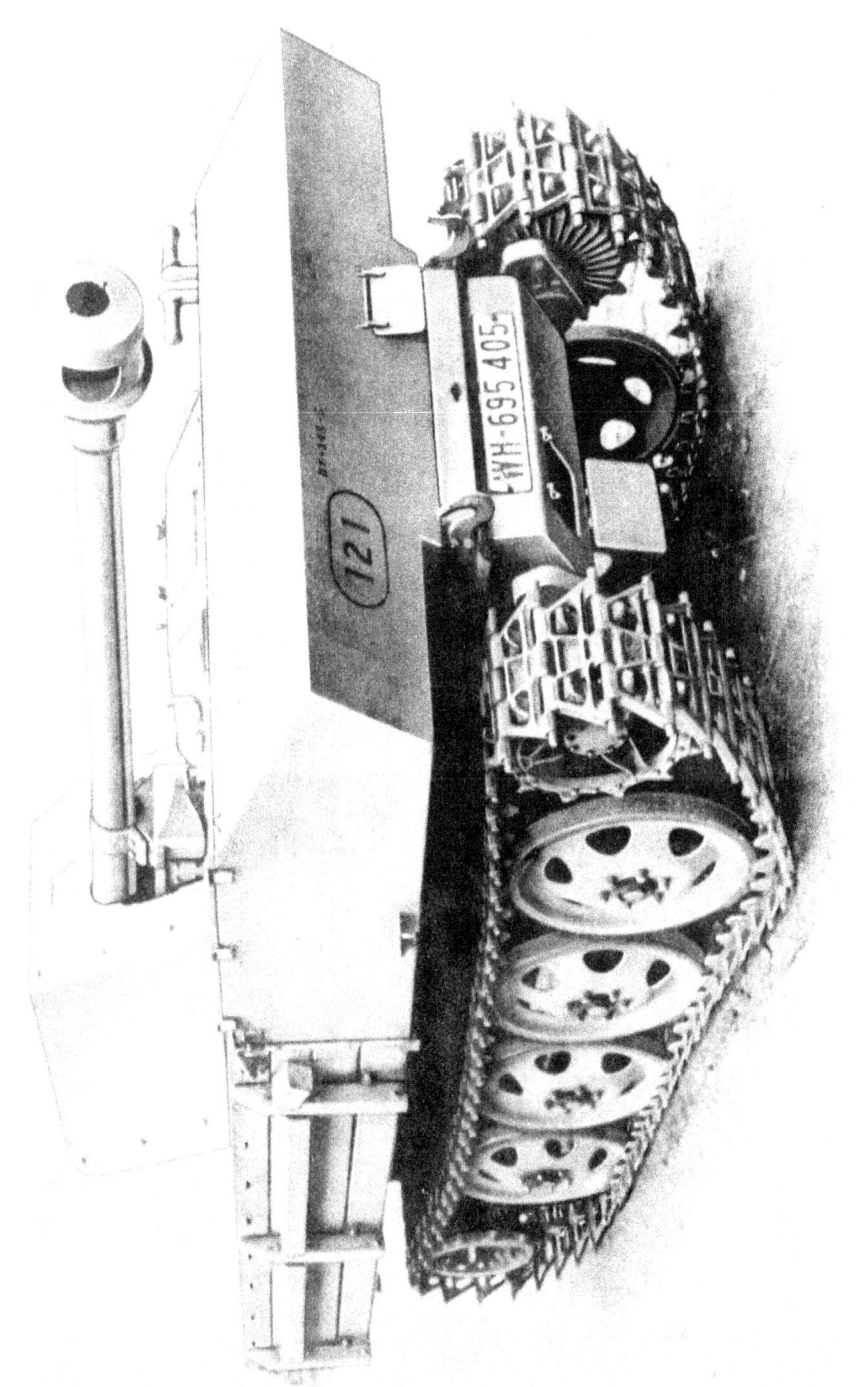

Fig. 16. 7.5 cm. Pak 40 (**L/46**) on Chassis of 'Raupenschlepper Ost'.

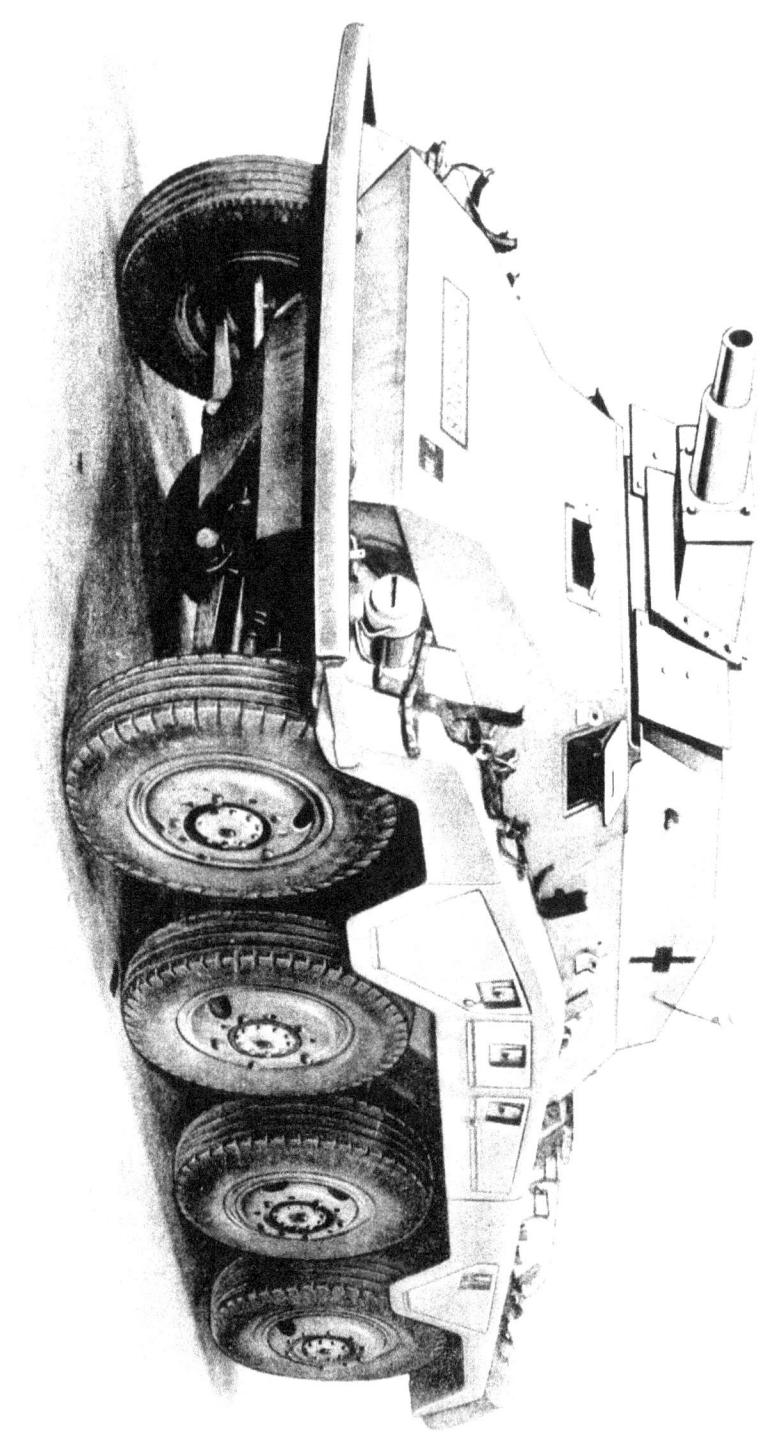

Fig. 15. 7.5 cm. K.51 or K.51/1 (L/24) on 8-wheeled Armoured Car Sd.Kfz. 234/3.

Fig.14. 7.5 cm. K.37 (L/24) on 8-wheeled Armoured Car Sd.Kfz.233.

Fig. 13, 7.5 cm.K.(L/24) on Stu.G.III (Sturmgeschütz)

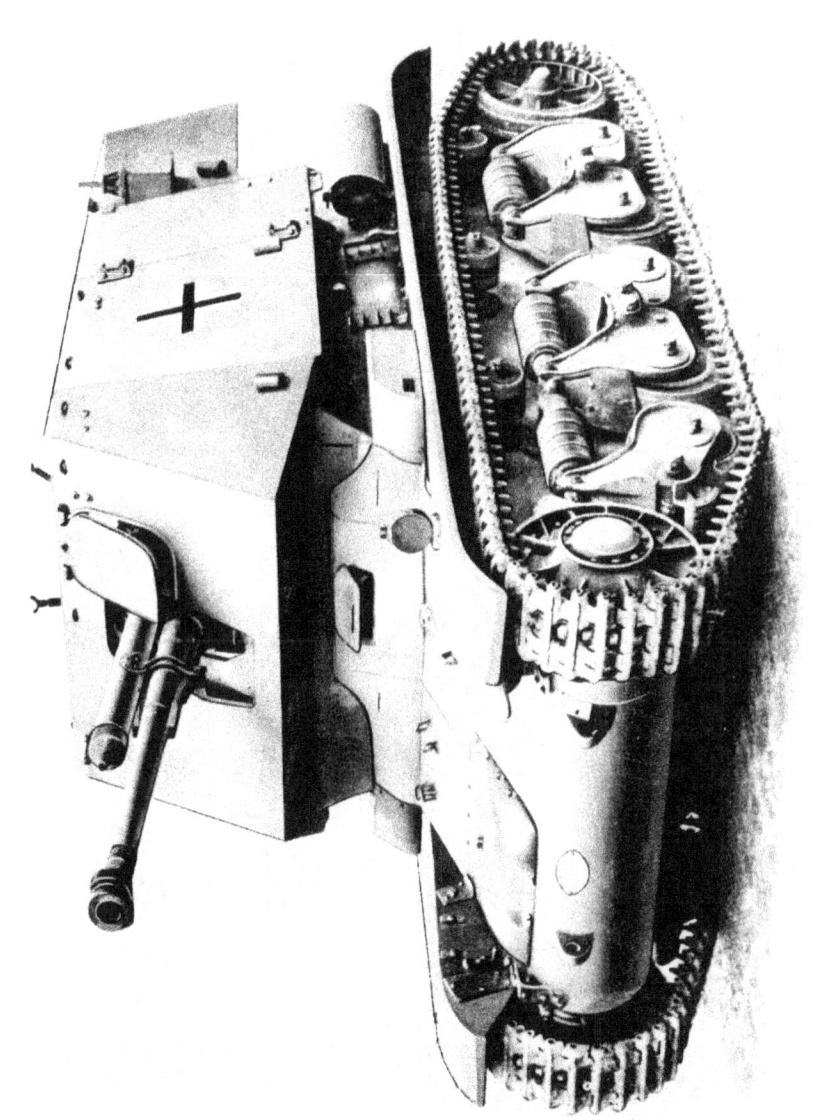

Fig.12. 4.7 cm. Pak(t) on Chassis of French Renault R.35 Tank.

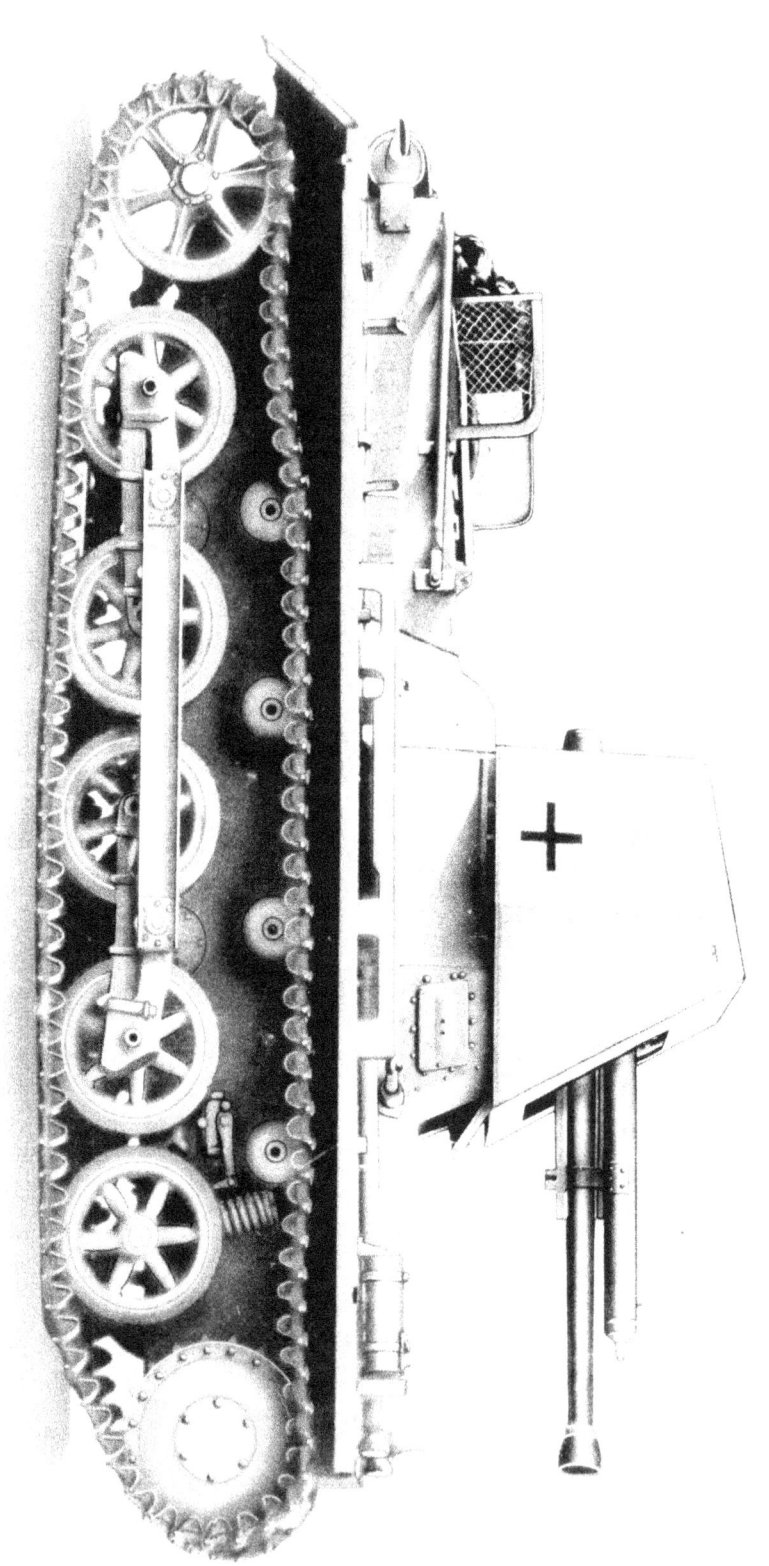

Fig.11. 4.7 cm. Pak(t) on Pz.Jäg.I (Sd.Kfz.101).

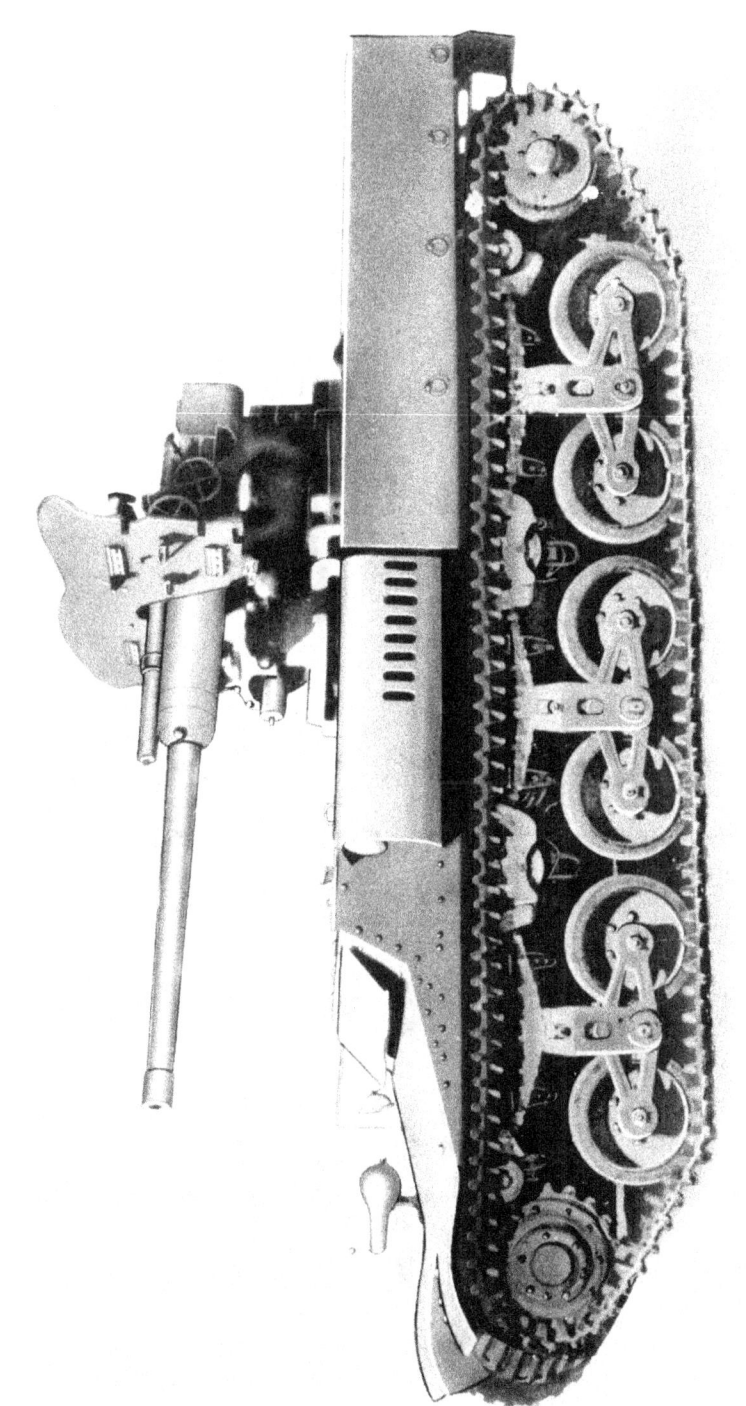

Fig. 10. 4.7 cm. Pak(f) on French 'Lorraine' Carrier Chassis (Pz.Jag.Lr.S.(f)).

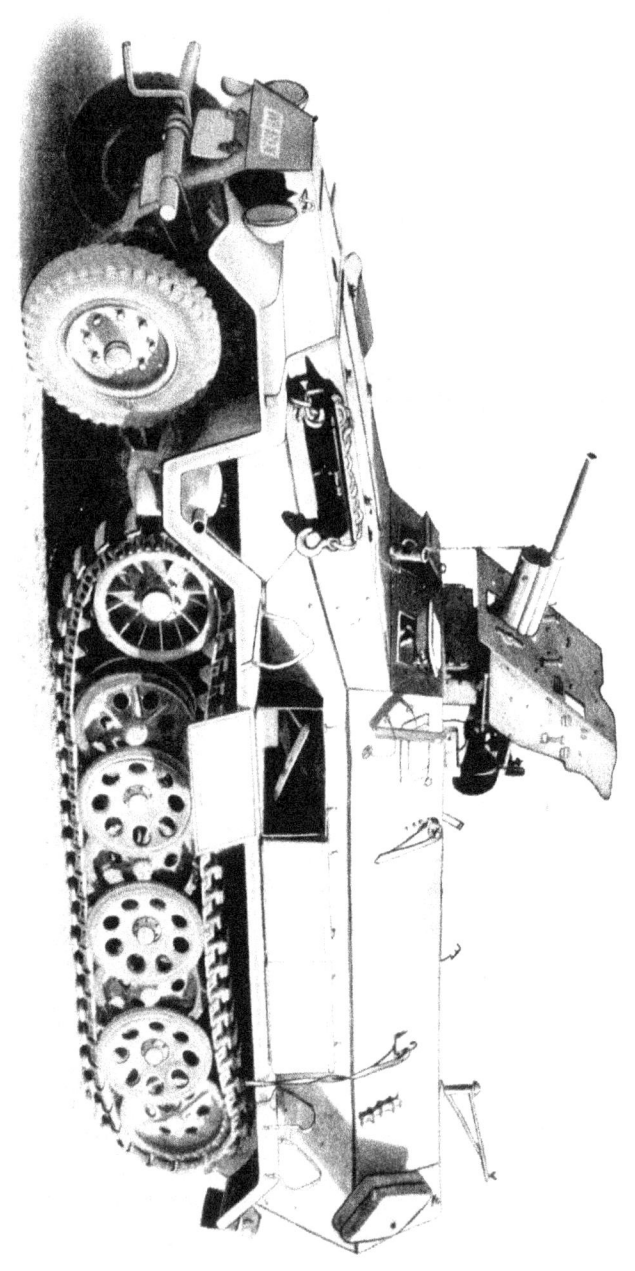

Fig.9. 3.7cm. Pak on Light Armoured Semi-Tracked Vehicle Sd.Kfz.250/10.

Fig.8. 3.7 cm. Pak on Armoured Infantry Carrier 'UE'(f) (Chenillette).

Fig.7. 3.7cm on British 'Bren' Carrier.

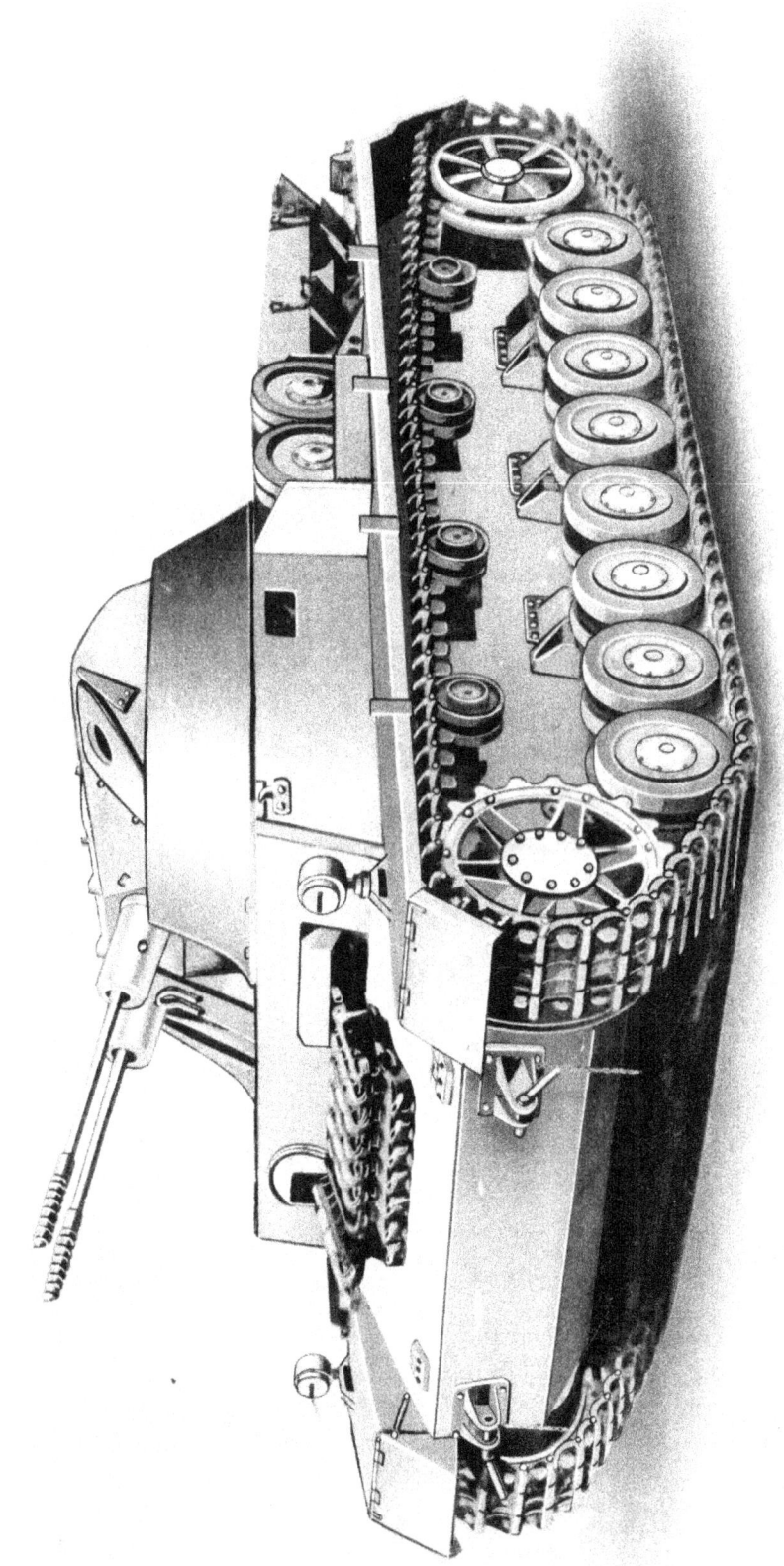

Fig. 6. 3 cm. MK103 Zwilling (Twin Mounting) on Flak Pz. IV – **Kugelblitz** (Ball Lightning).

Fig.5 2 cm. Flakvierling 38 (Top Vehicle) & 3.7 cm.Flak 43 (bottom right) on Pz.Kpfw.IV chassis (Flak Pz.IV) - Wirbelwind (Whirlwind) and Mobelwagen (Furniture Van) respectively.

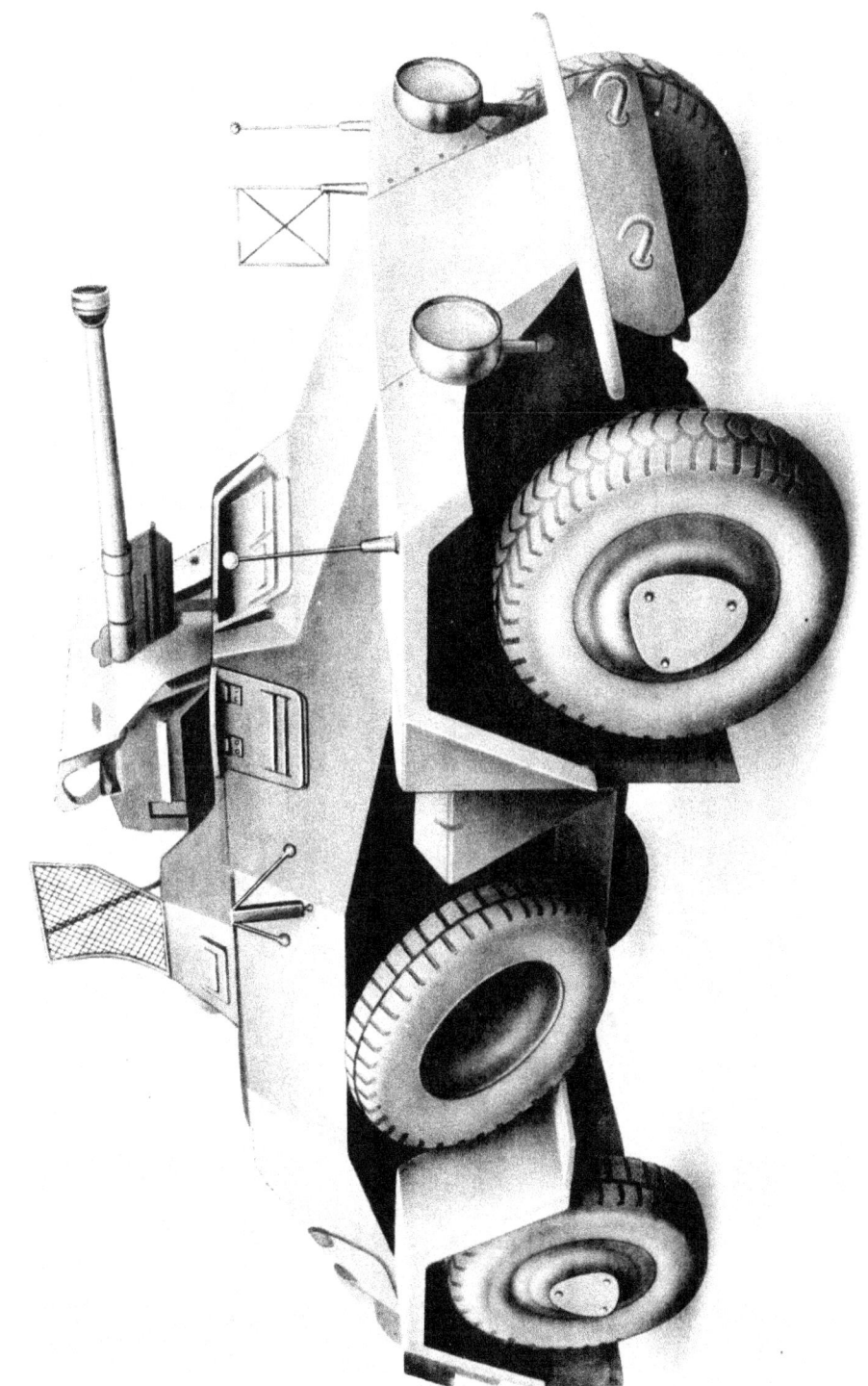

Fig.4.2.8 cm.z.Pz.B.41 on light 4-wheeled Armoured Car Sd.Kfz.221.

Fig. 3. 2 cm. Flakvierling 38 on 8-ton Semi-Tracked Vehicle Sd.Kfz.7/1.

Fig. 2 2 cm. Flak 30 or 38 on chassis of Pz.Kpfw.38(t) Sd.Kfz.140

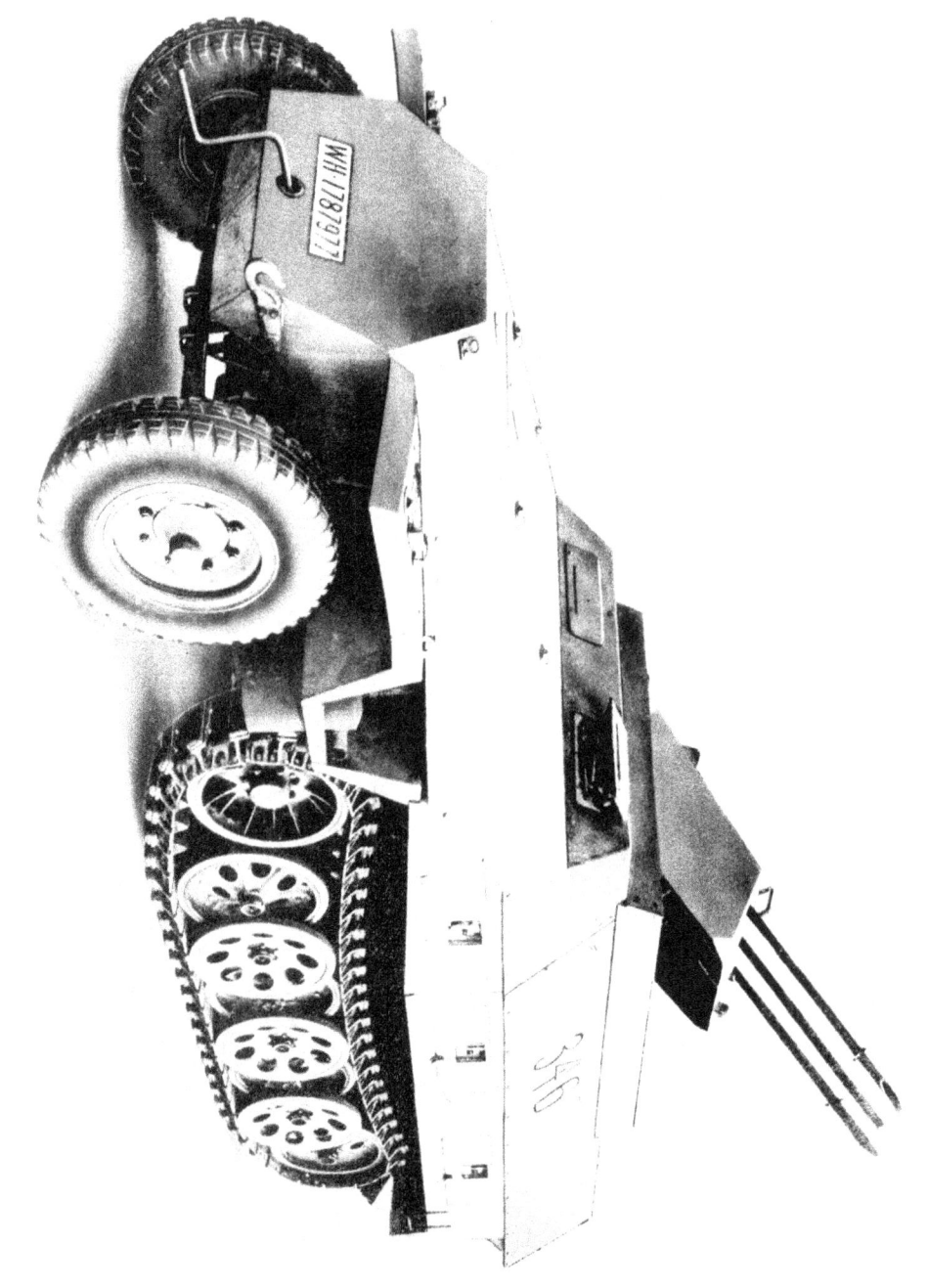

Fig.1. M.G.151/15 or 151/20 Drilling (Triple Mounting) on 3-ton Armoured Semi-Tracked Vehicle Sd.Kfz.251/21.

Fig. 33. 8.8 cm. Pak 43/2 (L/71) on Pz.JägTiger (P), Sd.Kfz.184 Formerly known as 'Ferdinand' and later as 'Elefant'.

Fig. 34. 8.8 cm. Pak 43/3 (L/71) on Pz. Jäg. Panther – Sd.Kfz. 173 (Jagdpanther).

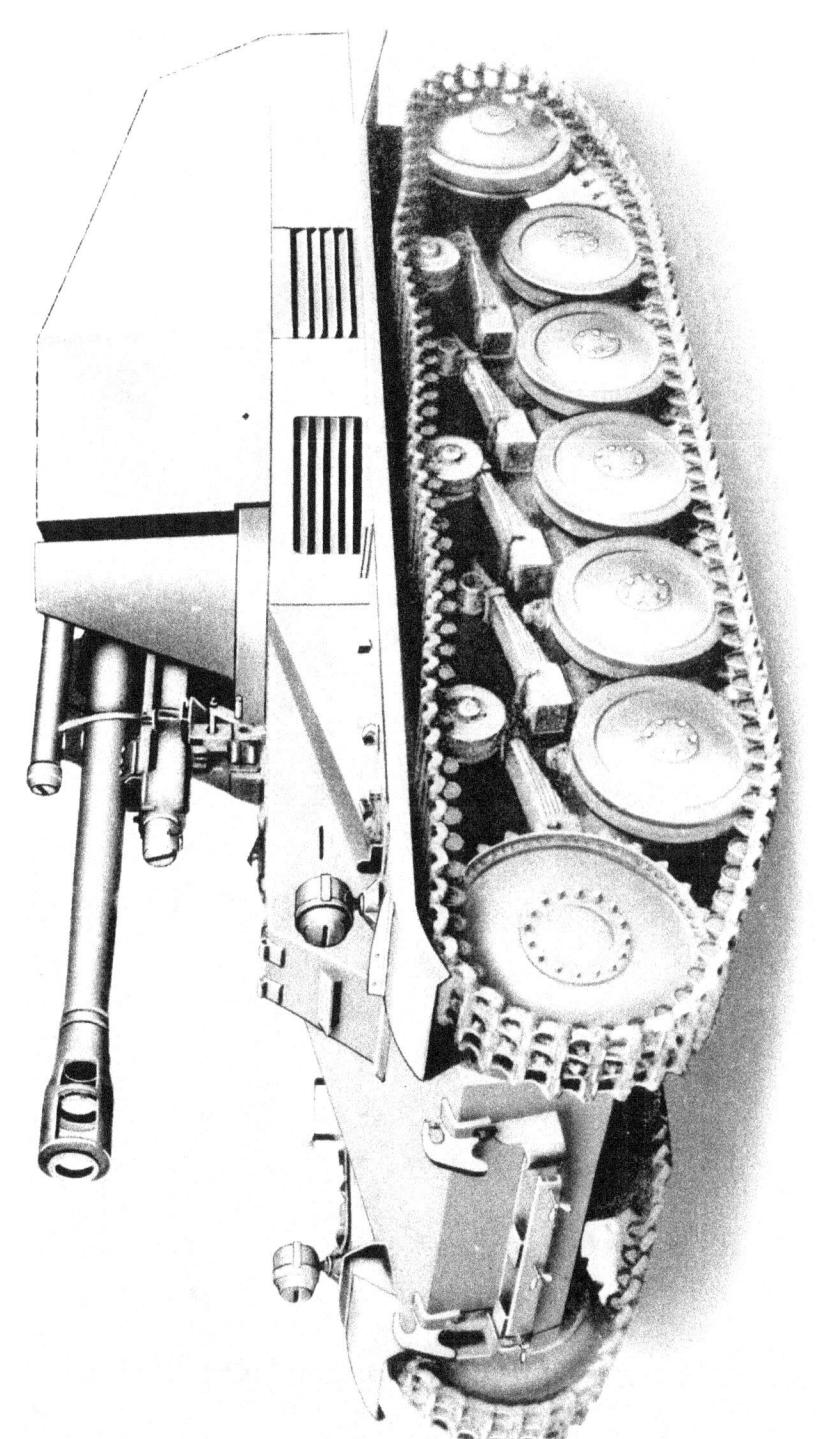

Fig. 35. 10.5 cm. le. F.H.18/2 on Gw.II(Wespe), Sd.Kfz.124.

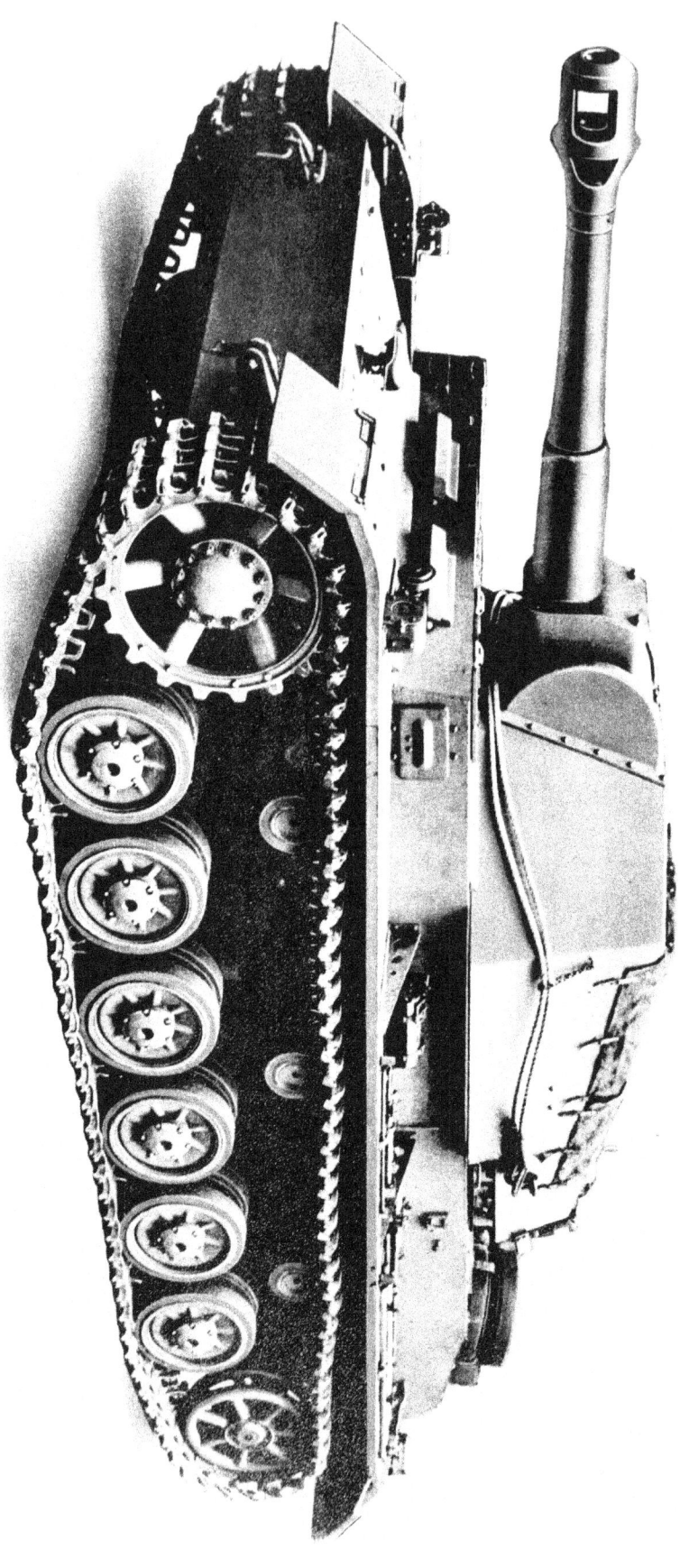

Fig. 36. 10.5 cm. le.F.H.18/1 on Gw.IVb - Sd.Kfz.165/1.

Fig. 37 10.5 cm. le F.H. 18/2 on Chassis of French Char B2 Tank.

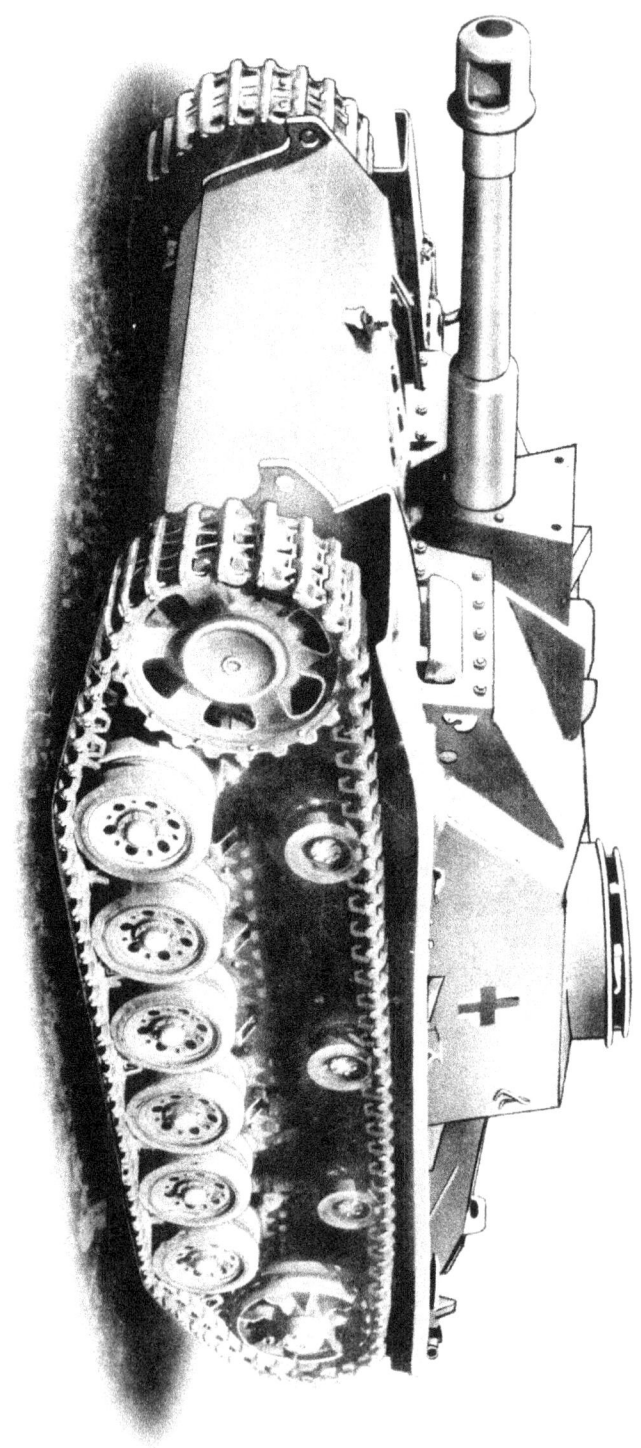

Fig. 38. 10.5 cm. Stu.H.42(L/28) on Stu.G.III - Sd.Kfz.142/2.

Fig. 39. 10.5 cm. le F.H.18 on French Lorraine Carrier Chassis.

Fig. 40 10.5 cm. le.F.H.18 on French F.C.M. Tank Chassis.

Fig. 41. 10.5 cm. le F.H.18 on French Hotchkiss H.35 Tank Chassis.

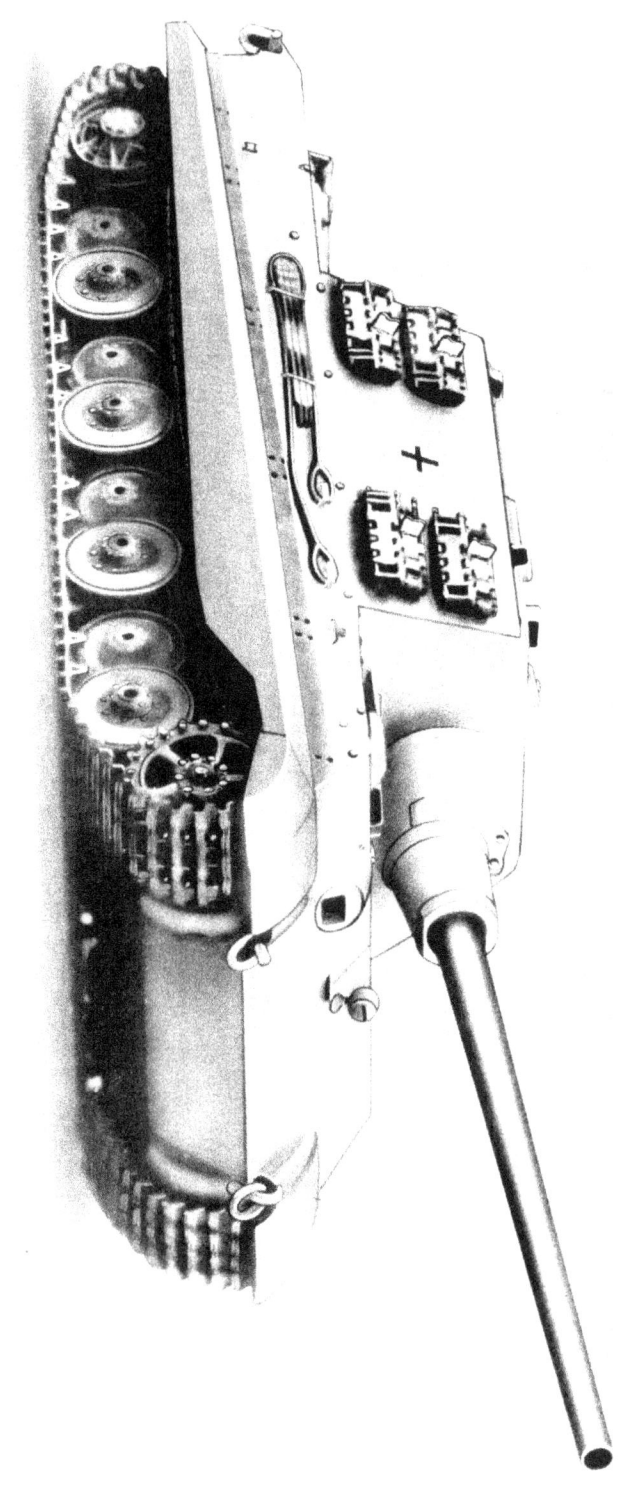

Fig. 42. 12.8 cm. Pak 44 or Pak 80(L/55) on Pz.Jäg.Tiger Model B - Sd.Kfz.186 (Jagdtiger).

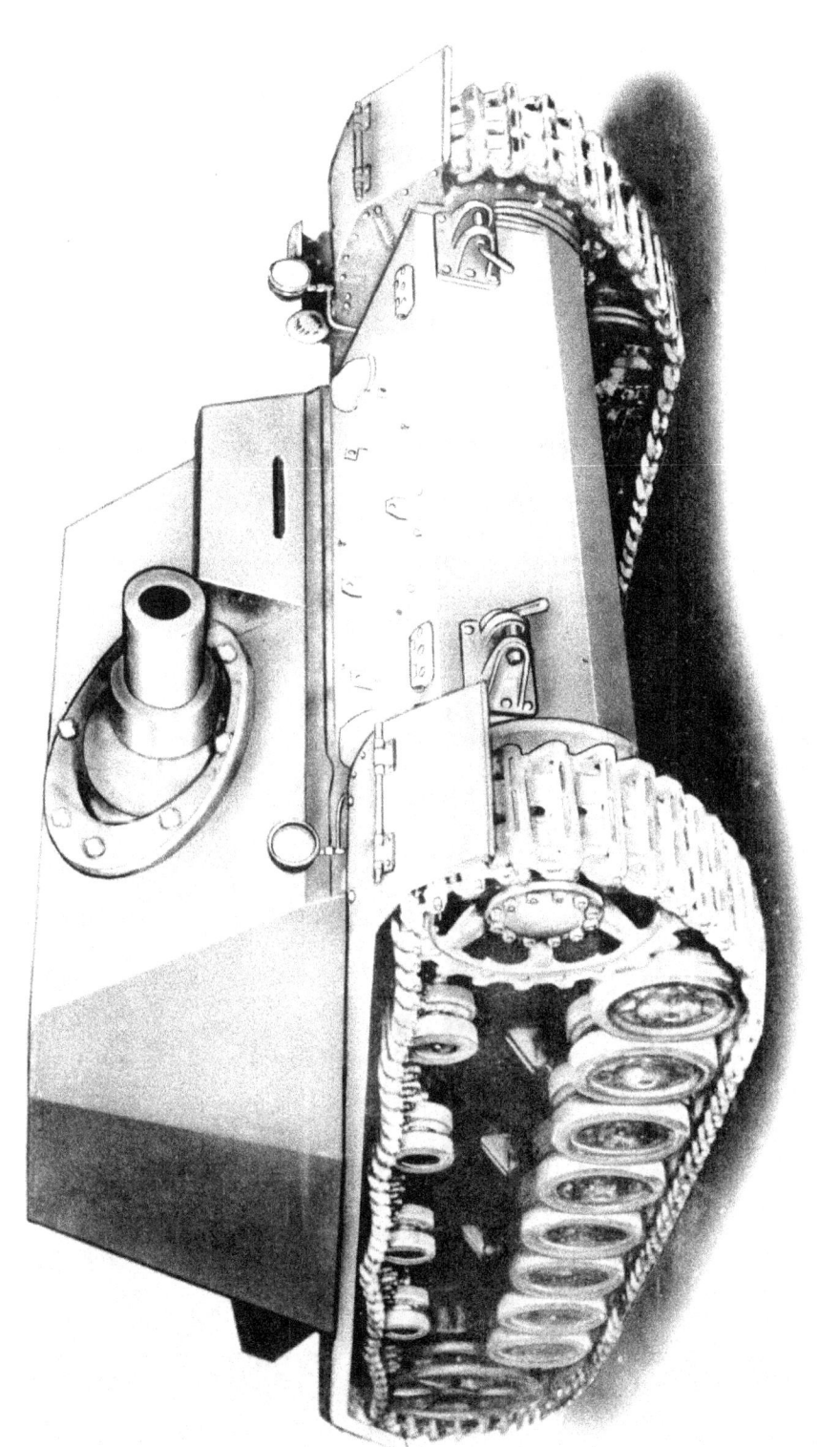

Fig. 43. 15 cm. Stu.H.43 (L/12) on Stu.Pz.IV (Brummbär – Grizzly Bear).

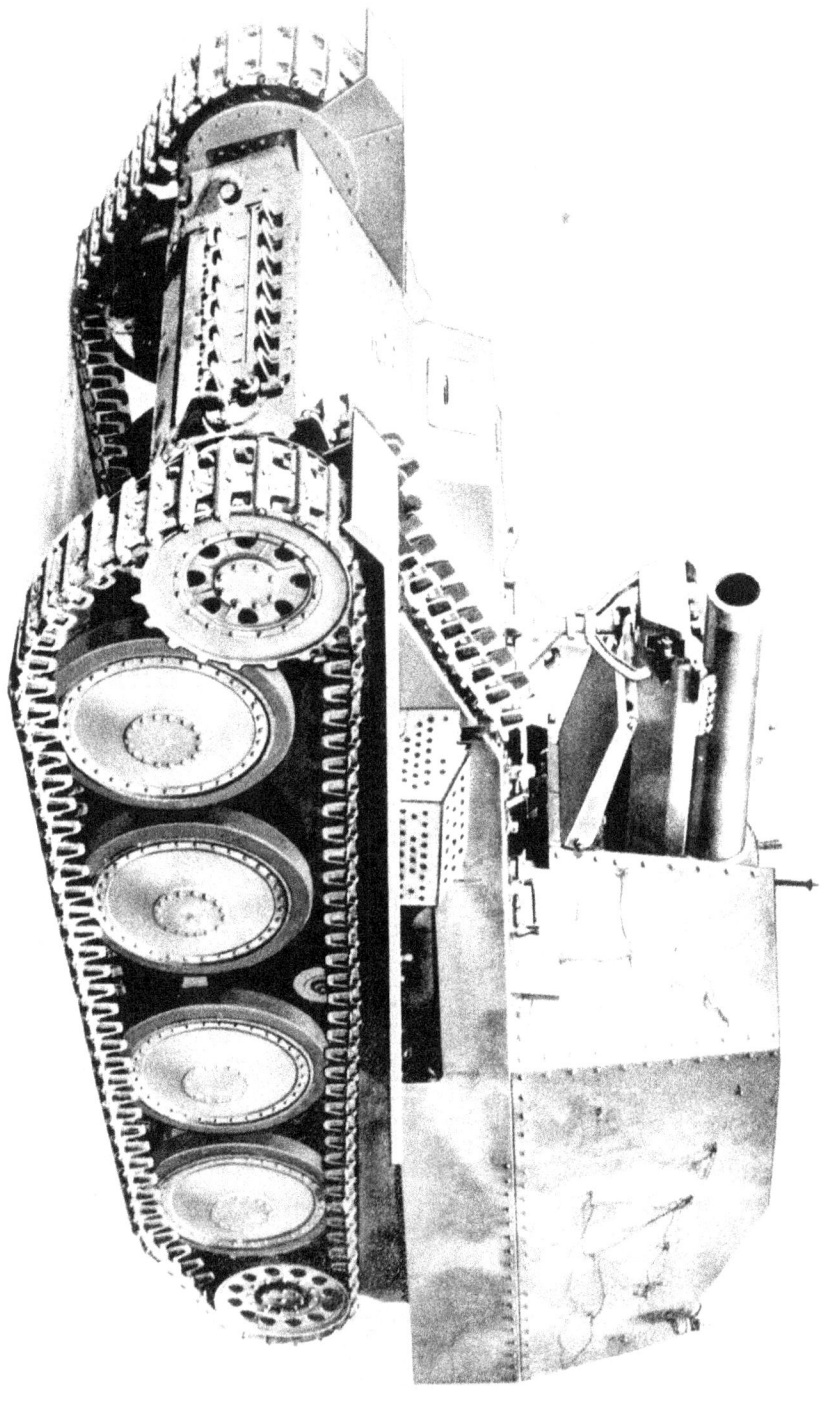

Fig. 44. 15 cm. s.I.G.33 on Chassis of Pz.Kpfw.38(t) with engine forward - Sd.Kfz.138/1

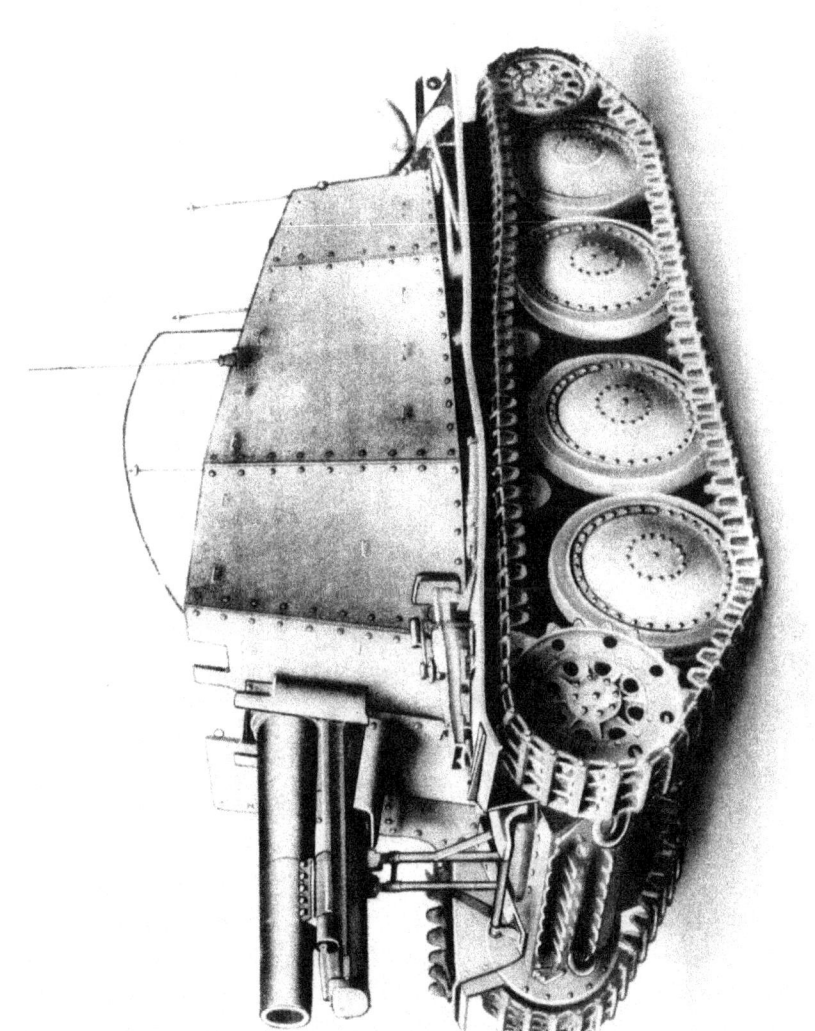

Fig. 45. 15 cm. s.I.G.33 on Gw.38(t) with engine rear.

Fig. 46 15 cm. s.F.H.13 on French Lorraine Carrier.

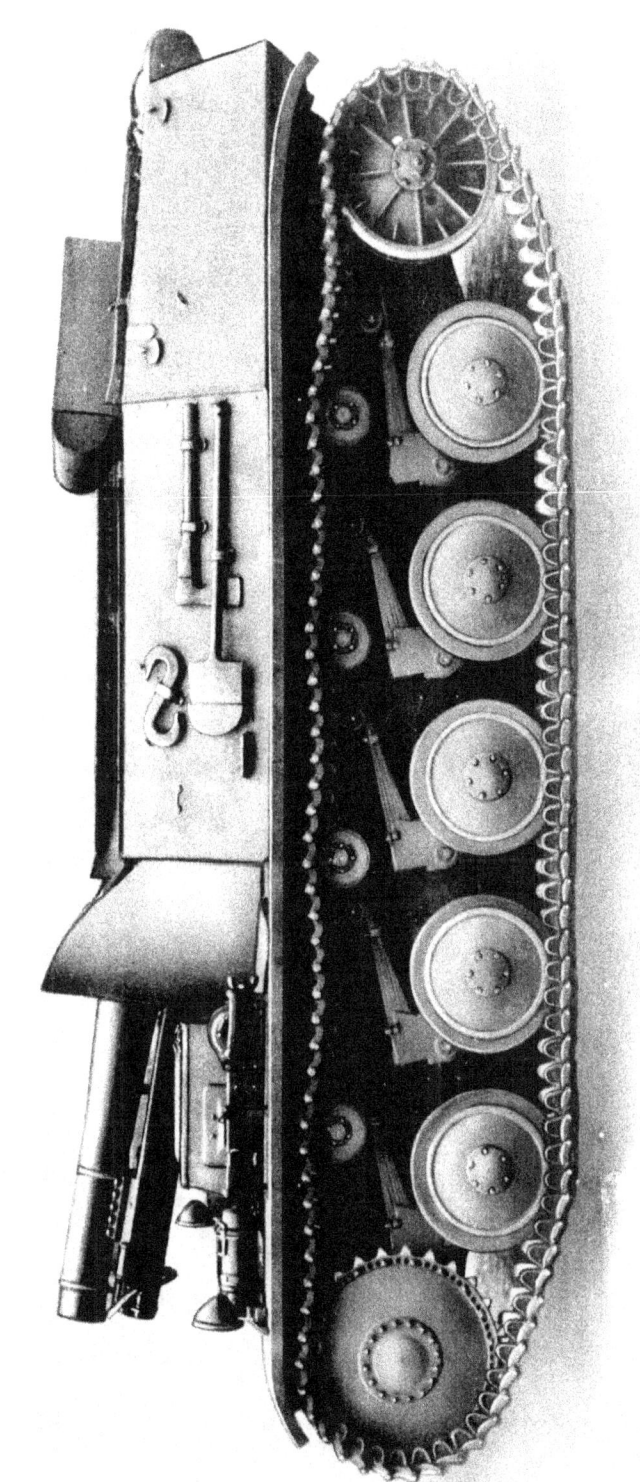

Fig. 47. 15 cm. s.I.G.33 on Pz.Kpfw.II- - Sd.Kfz.121.

Fig. 48. 15 cm. s.F.H.18 on Gw.III/IV (Hummel – Bumble Bee), Sd.Kfz.165.

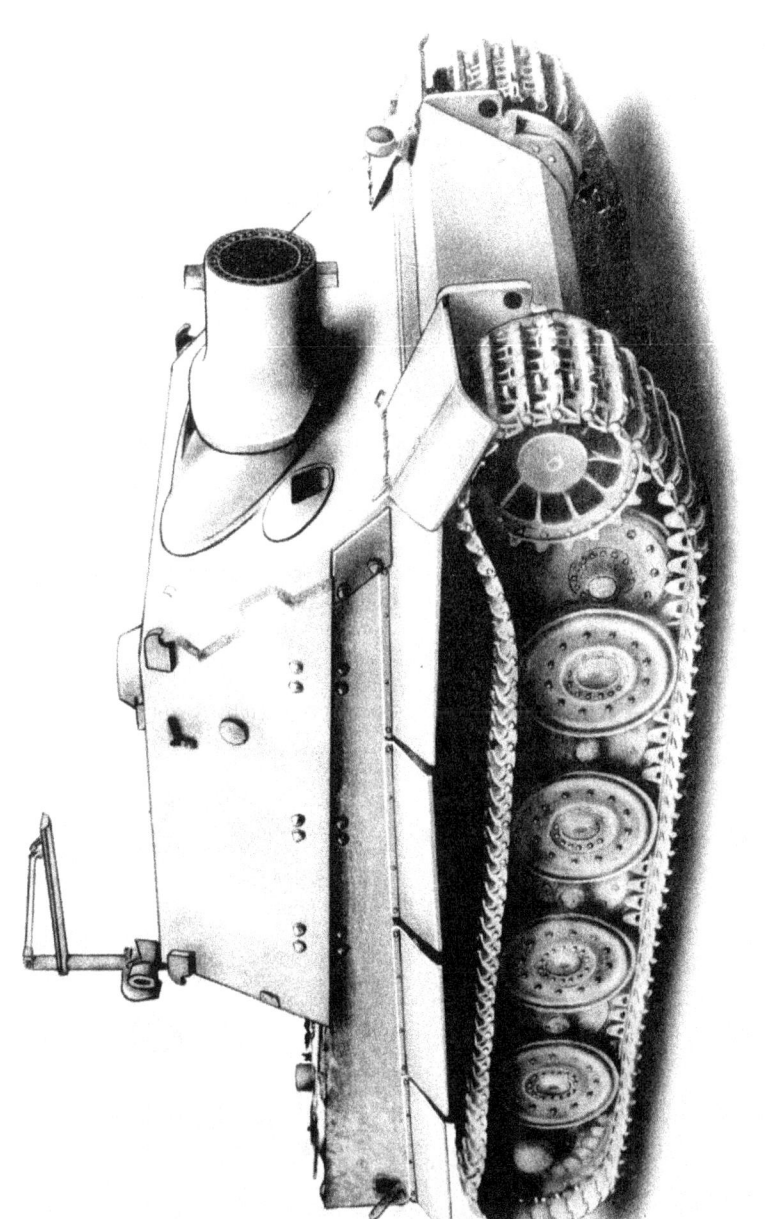

Fig.49. 38 cm. Rocket Projector RW 61 on Pz.Kpfw. Tiger Model E Chassis - Stu.Mrs.Tiger.

Fig.50. 60 cm. Mrs. Karl - Gerät 040.

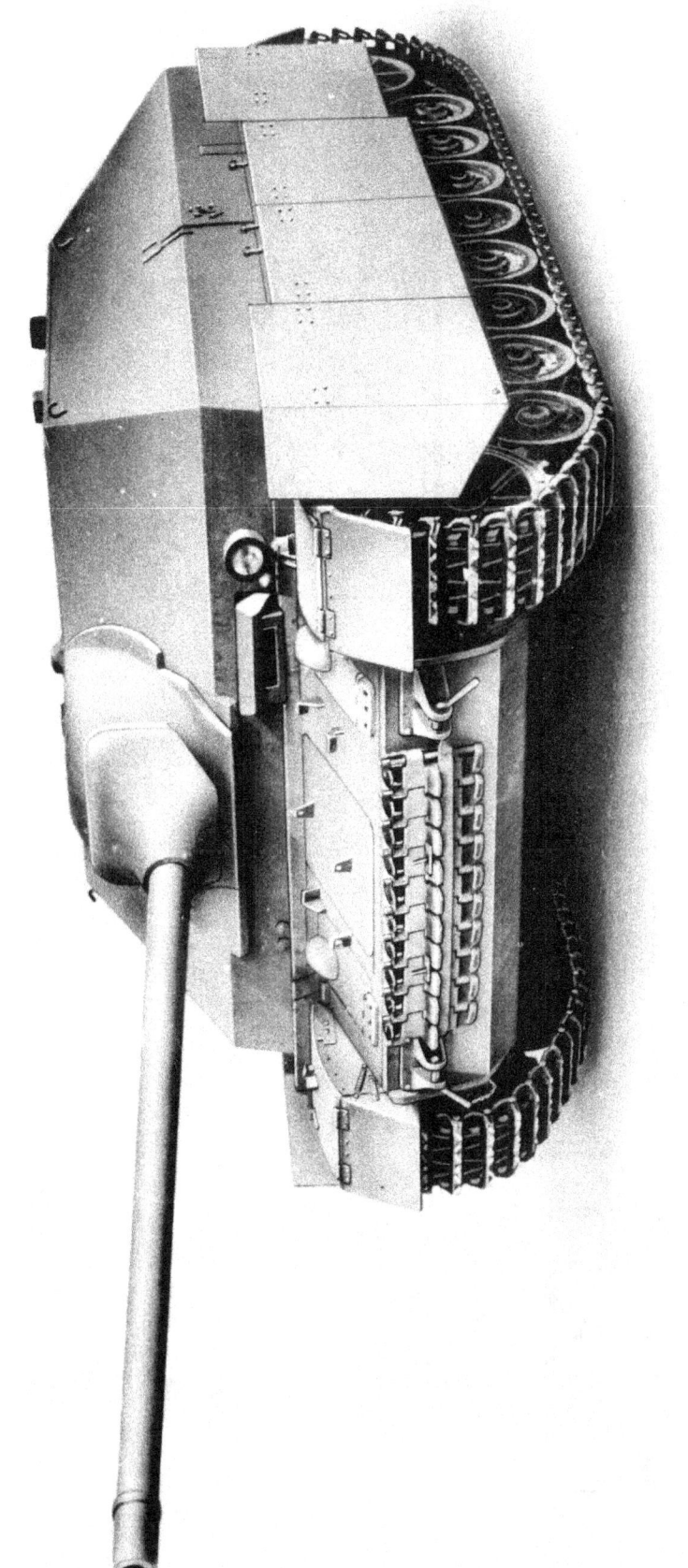

Fig. 51. Vomag prototype of 7.5 cm. Stu.K.42(L/70) on Pz.Jag.IV.

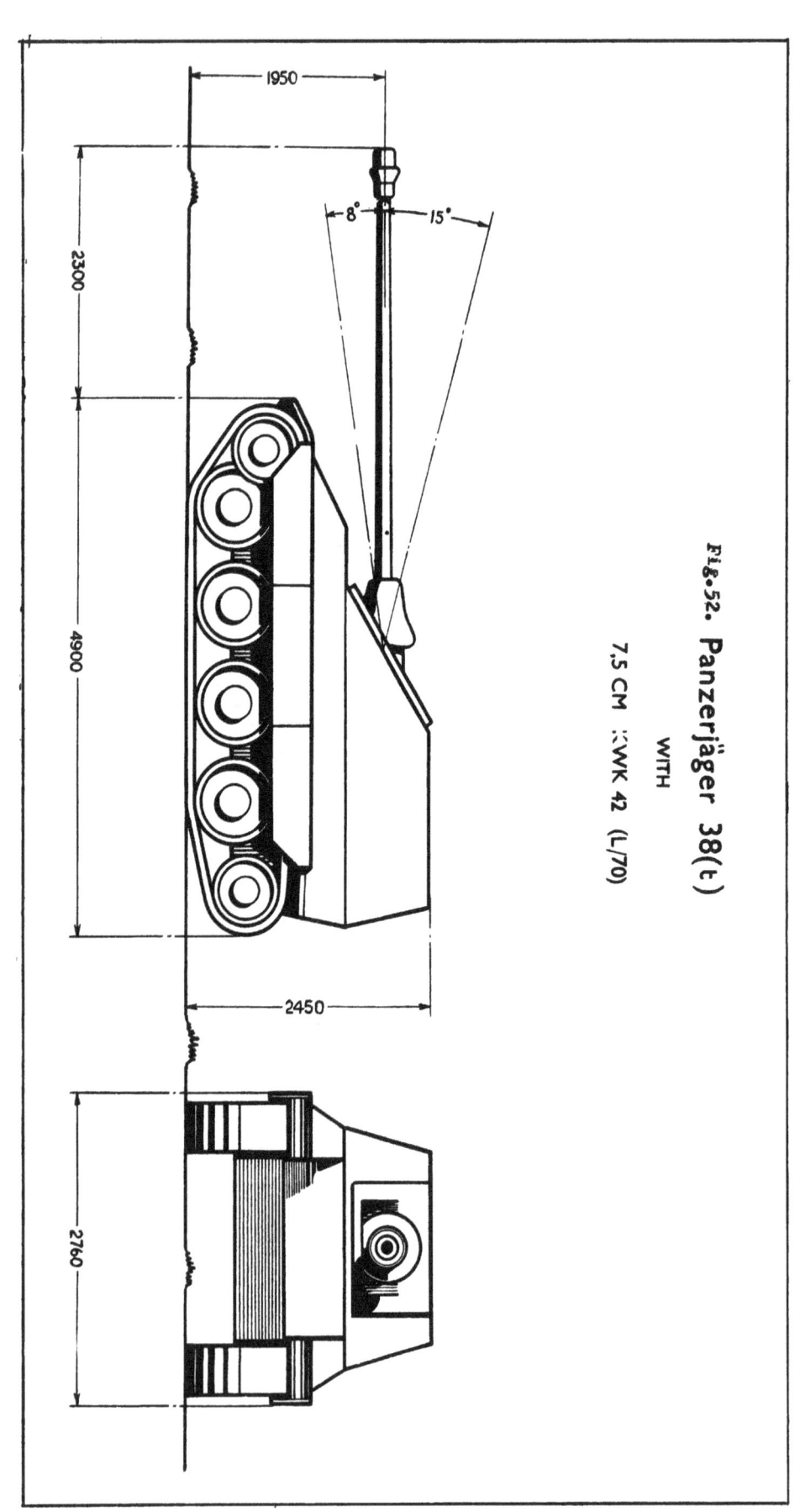

Fig. 52. Panzerjäger 38(t) with 7.5 CM KWK 42 (L/70)

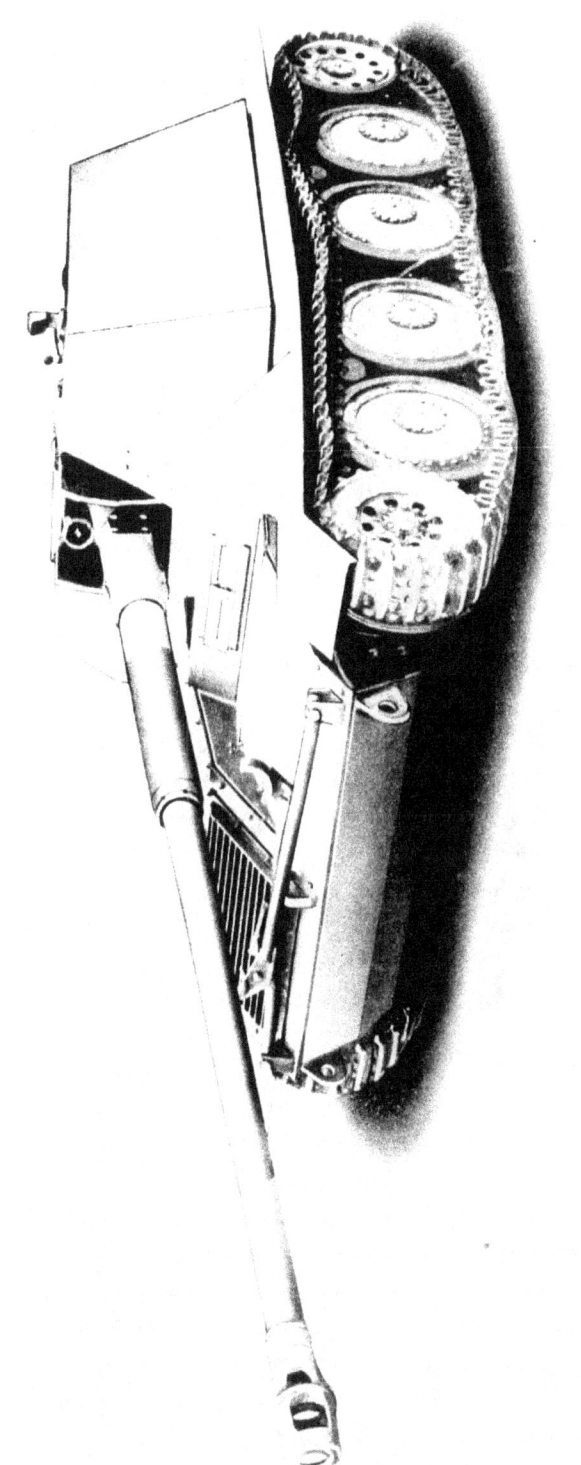

Fig.53. Rheinmetall-Borsig/Ardelt Waffenträger for 8.8 cm. Pjk.43 or Kw.K.43-Prototype.

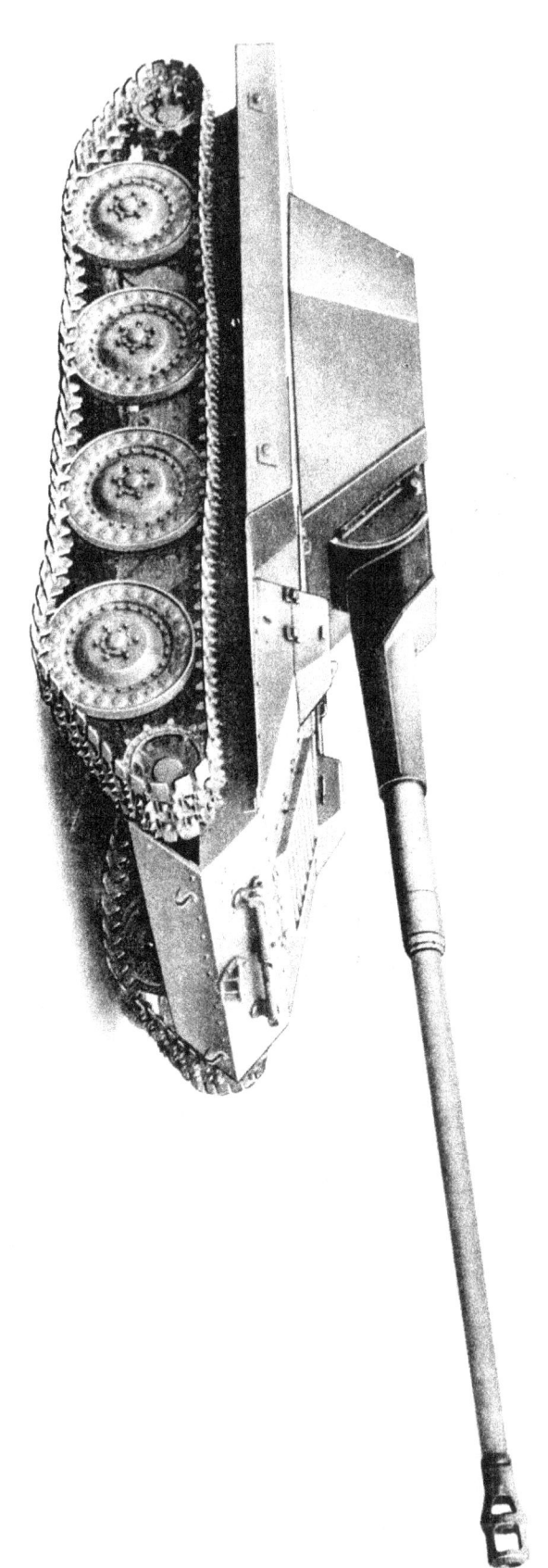

Fig. 54. Krupp/Steyr Prototype of 8.8 cm. Pak 43/3(L/71) Waffenträger.

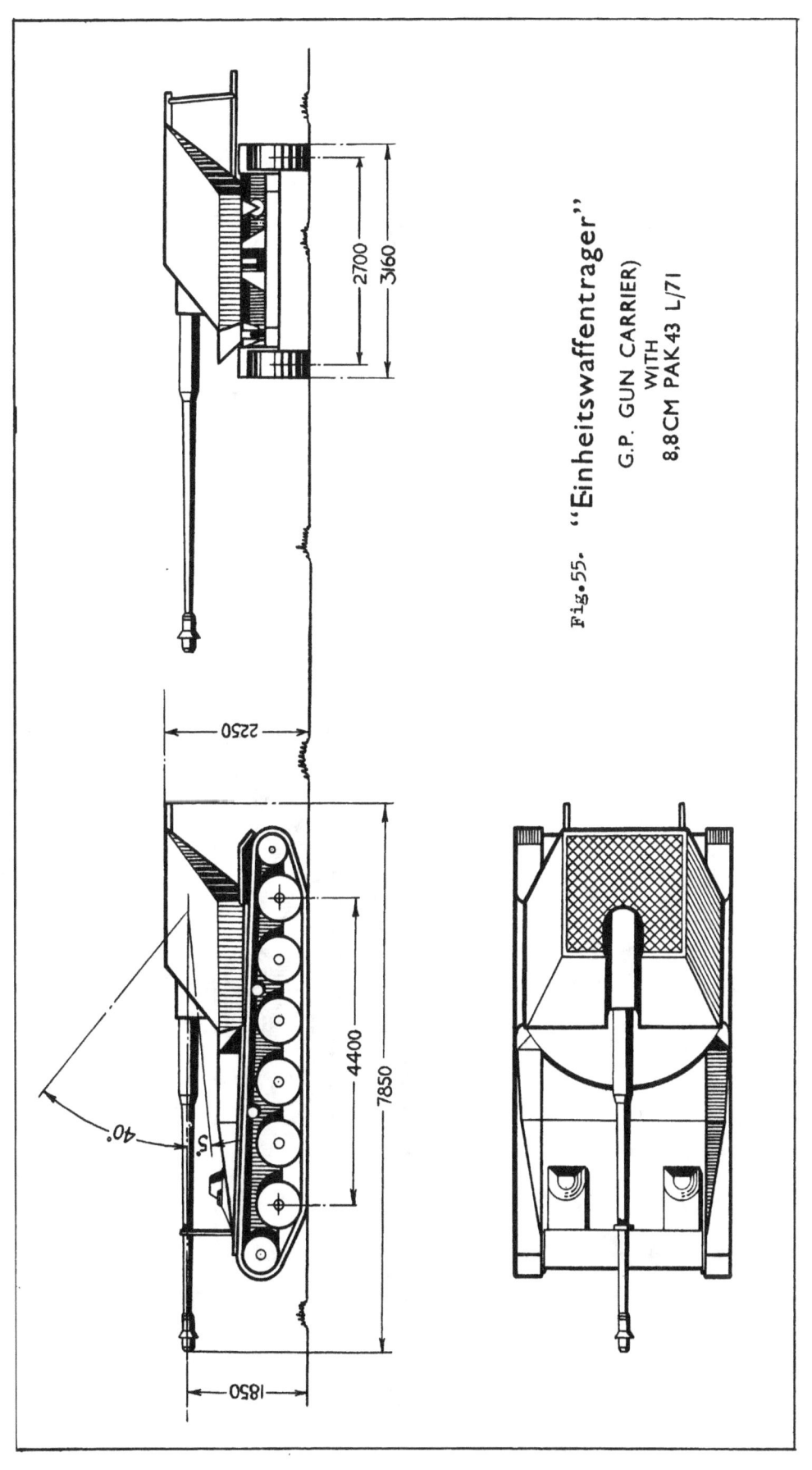

Fig. 55. "Einheitswaffentrager"
G.P. GUN CARRIER)
WITH
8,8 CM PAK 43 L/71

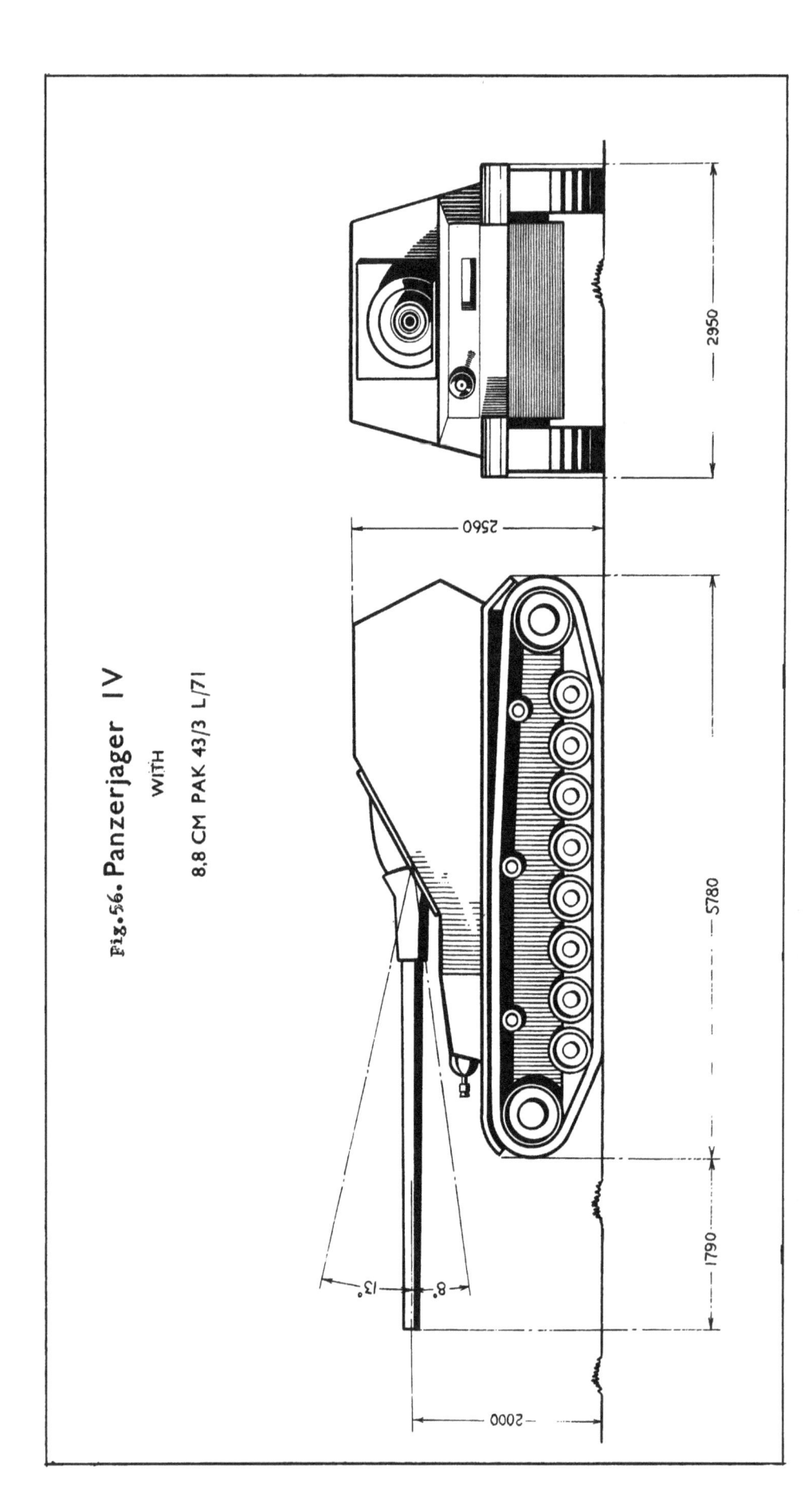

Fig. 56. Panzerjager IV with 8,8 cm PAK 43/3 L/71

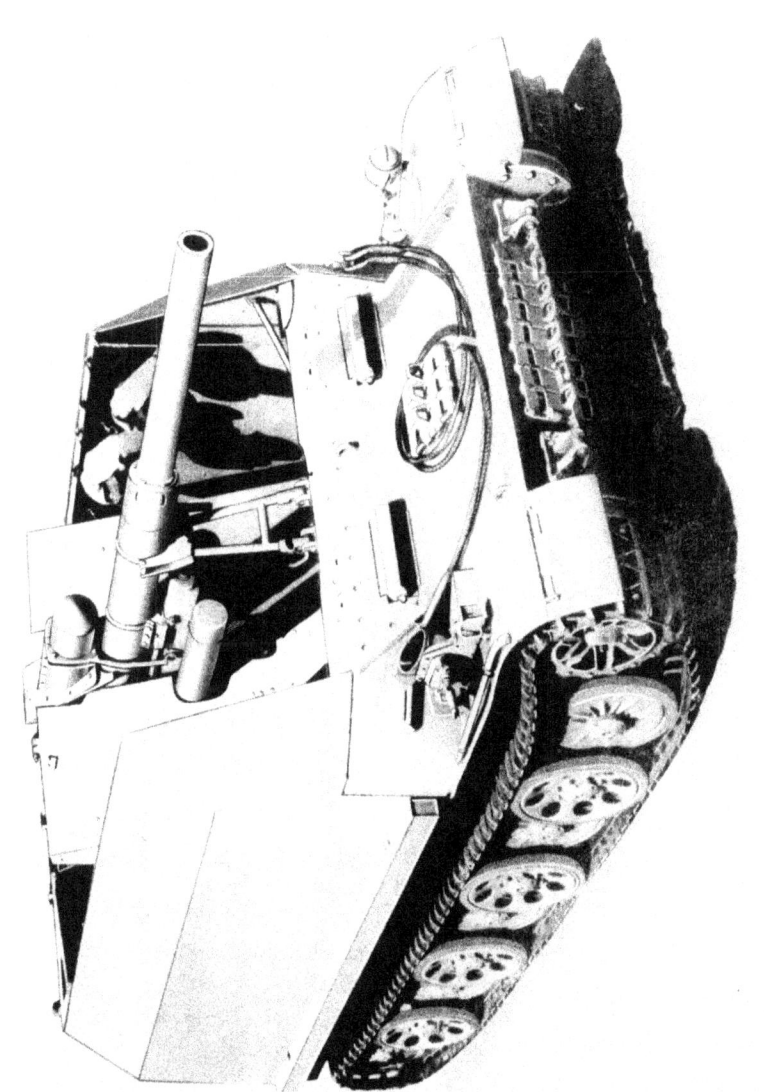

Fig. 57 Krupp Prototype for 'S.P.' 8.8 cm. Flak 18 or 36 on high-angle mounting with all-round traverse.

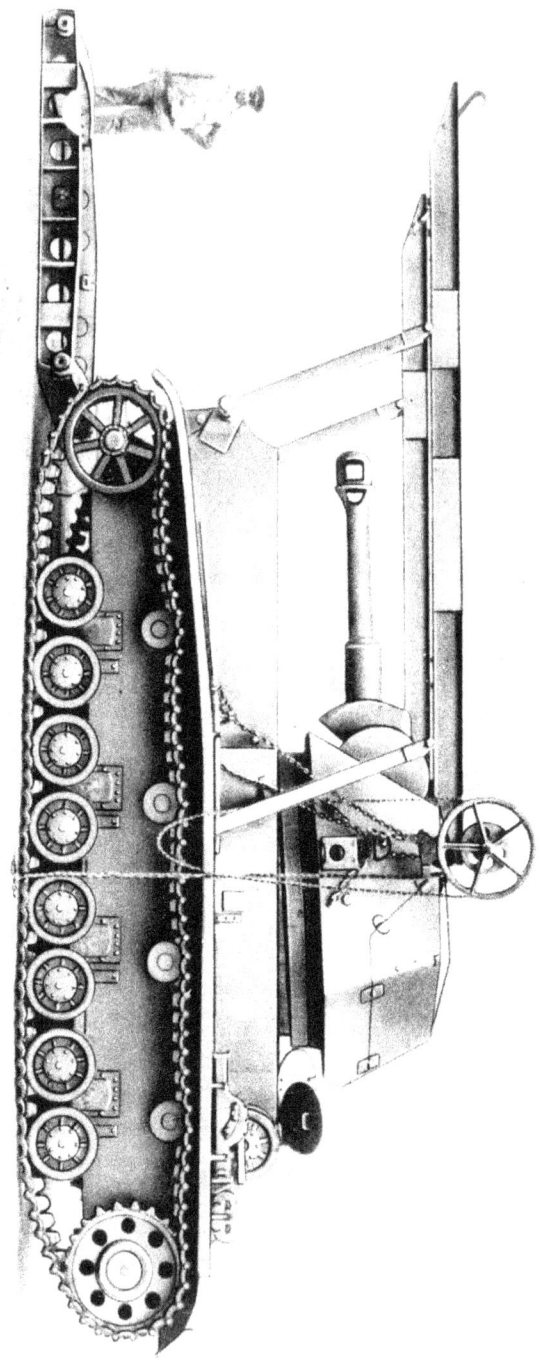

Fig. 58. Krupp early experimental Waffenträger, mounting 10.5 cm. le F.H. 18 on Gw. IVb Chassis. (Heuschrecke Series).

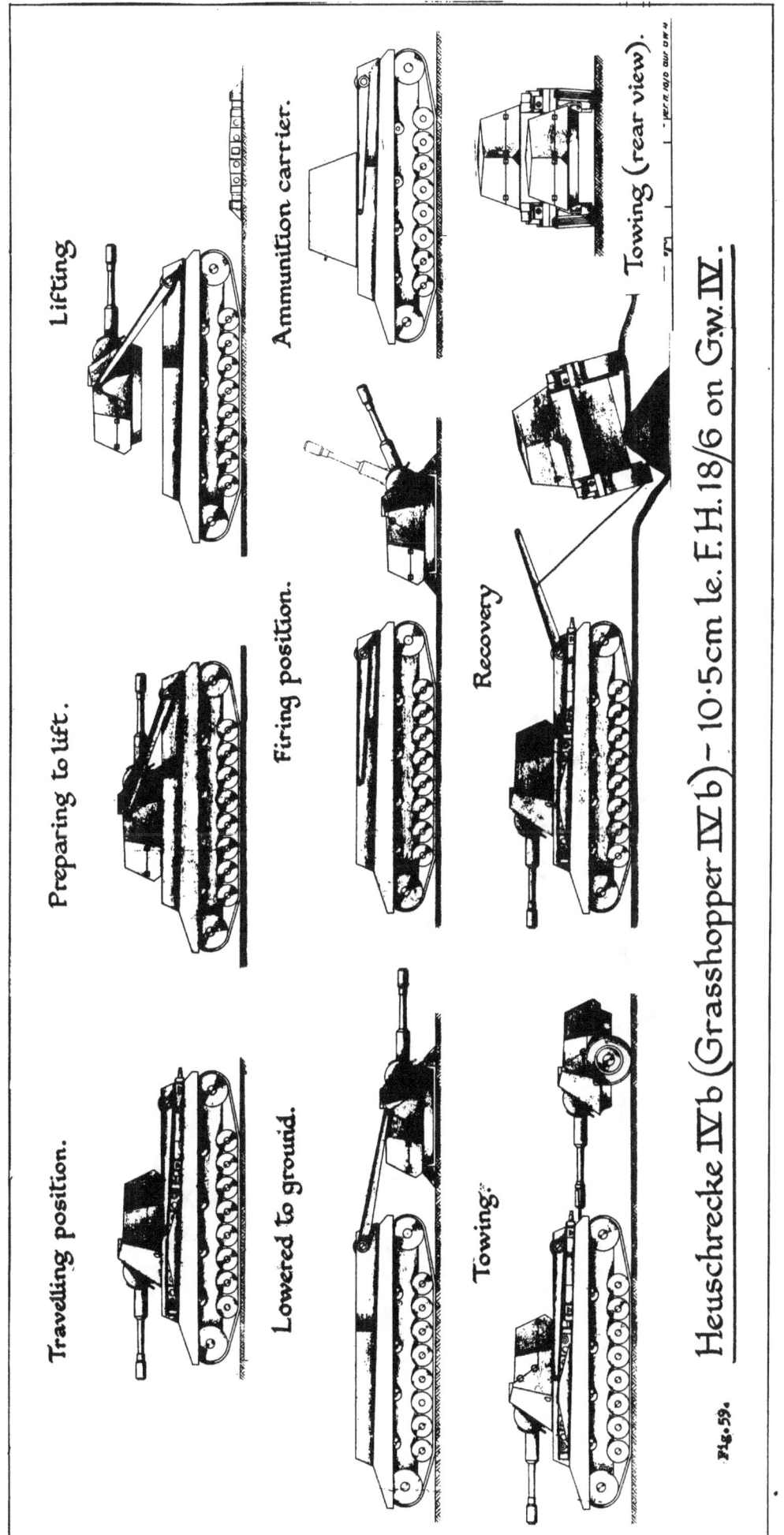

Fig. 59. Heuschrecke IVb (Grasshopper IVb) – 10.5cm le.F.H.18/6 on Gw.IV.

Fig. 60 Model of Heuschrecke 15.

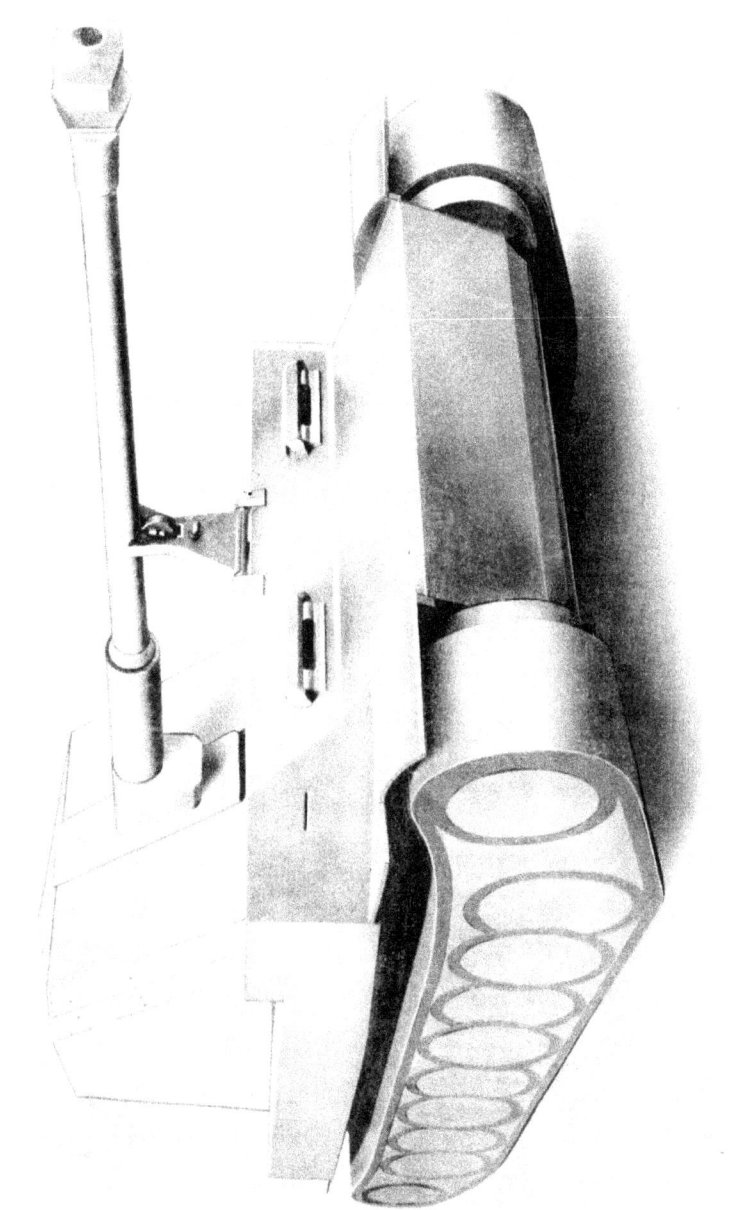

Fig. 61. Mock-up of Krupp 'Grille' 10 mounting 10.5 cm. le F.H.43/35

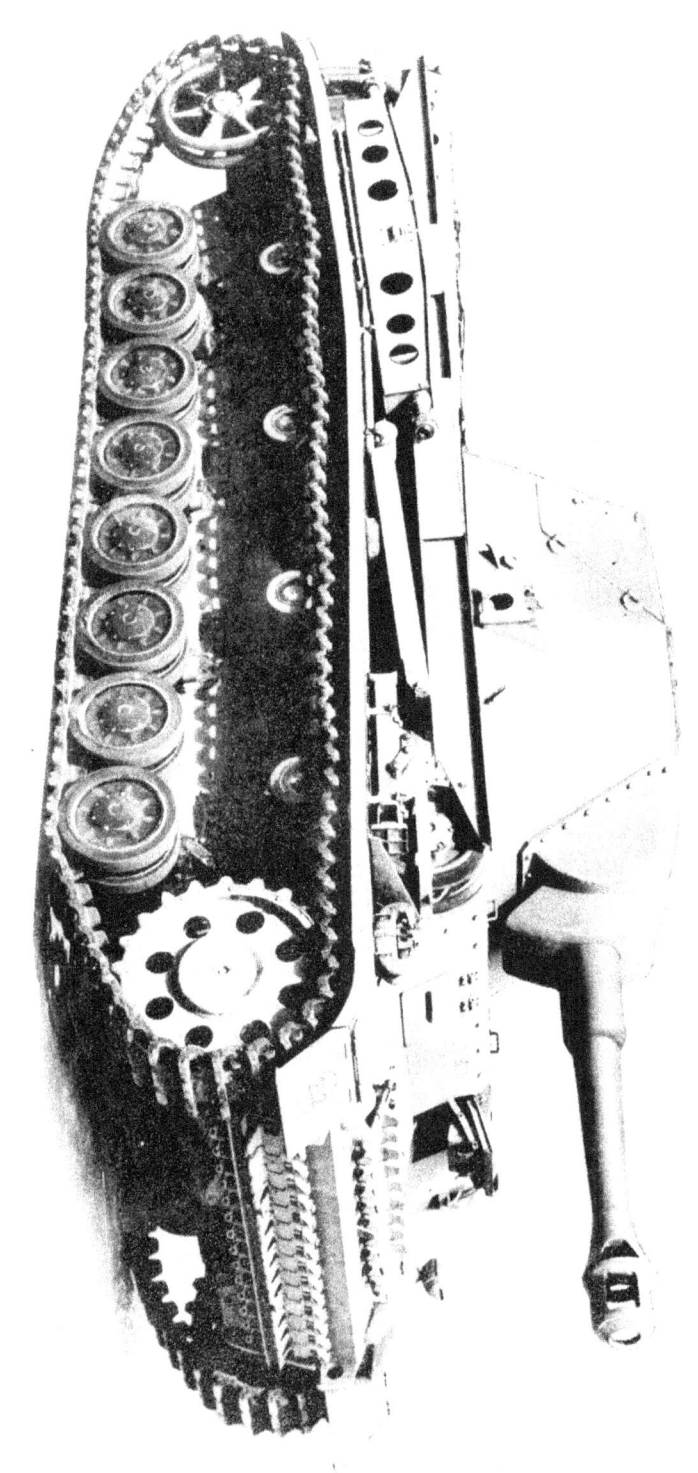

Fig. 62. Prototype of first experimental 'Heuschrecke' Waffenträger by Krupp.

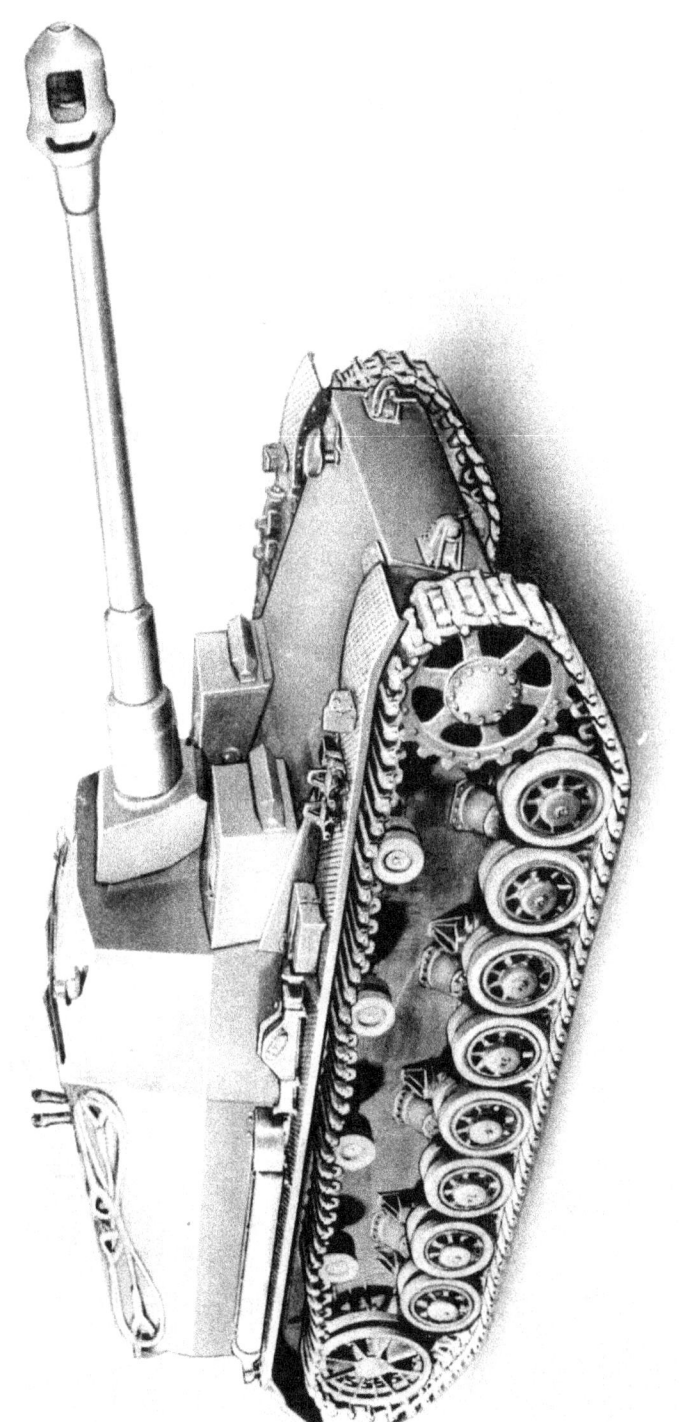

Fig.63. Prototype of 10.5 cm. K.18 on Pz. Sfl. IVa.

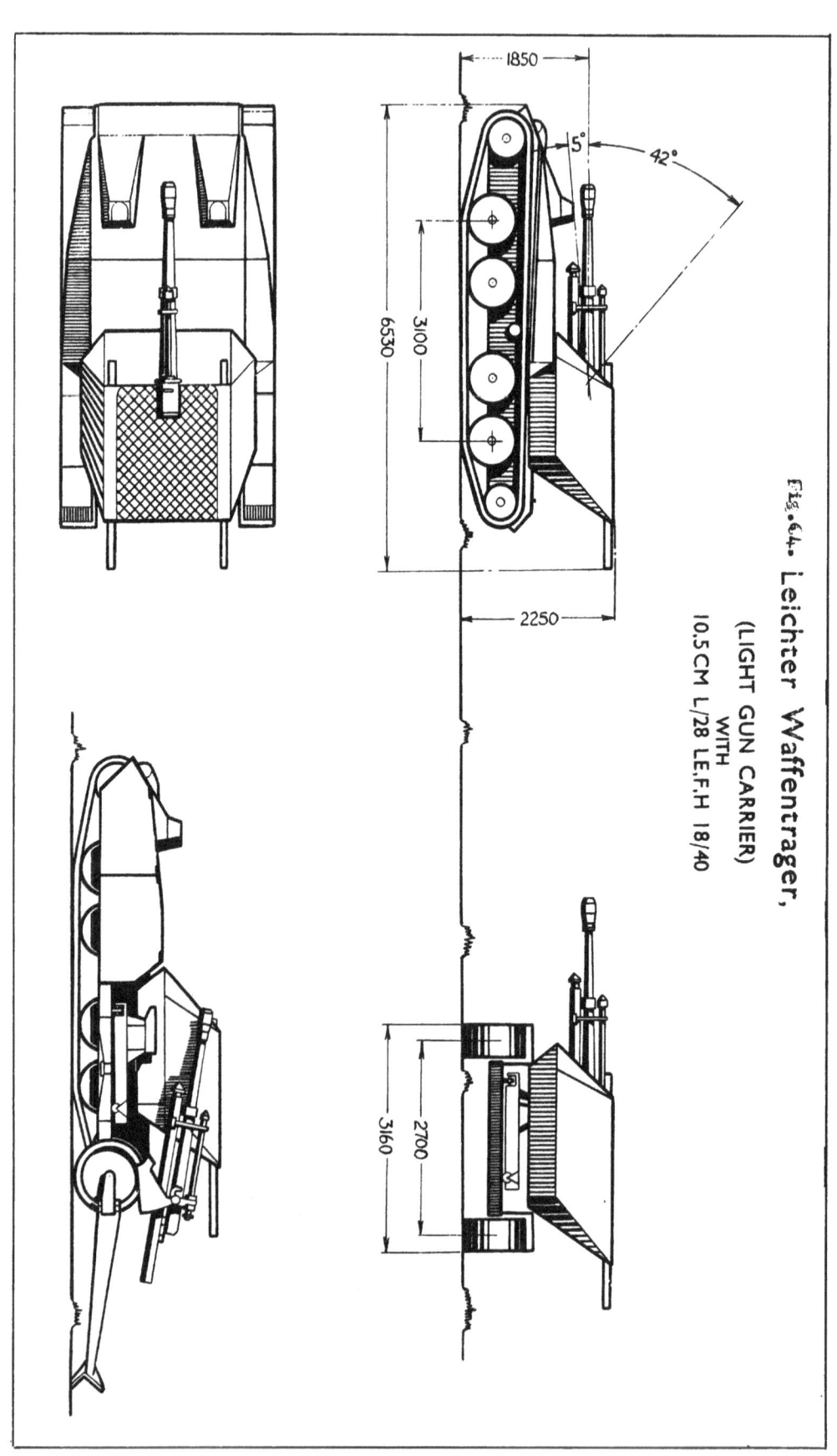

Fig. 64. Leichter Waffenträger, (LIGHT GUN CARRIER) WITH 10.5 CM L/28 LE.F.H 18/40

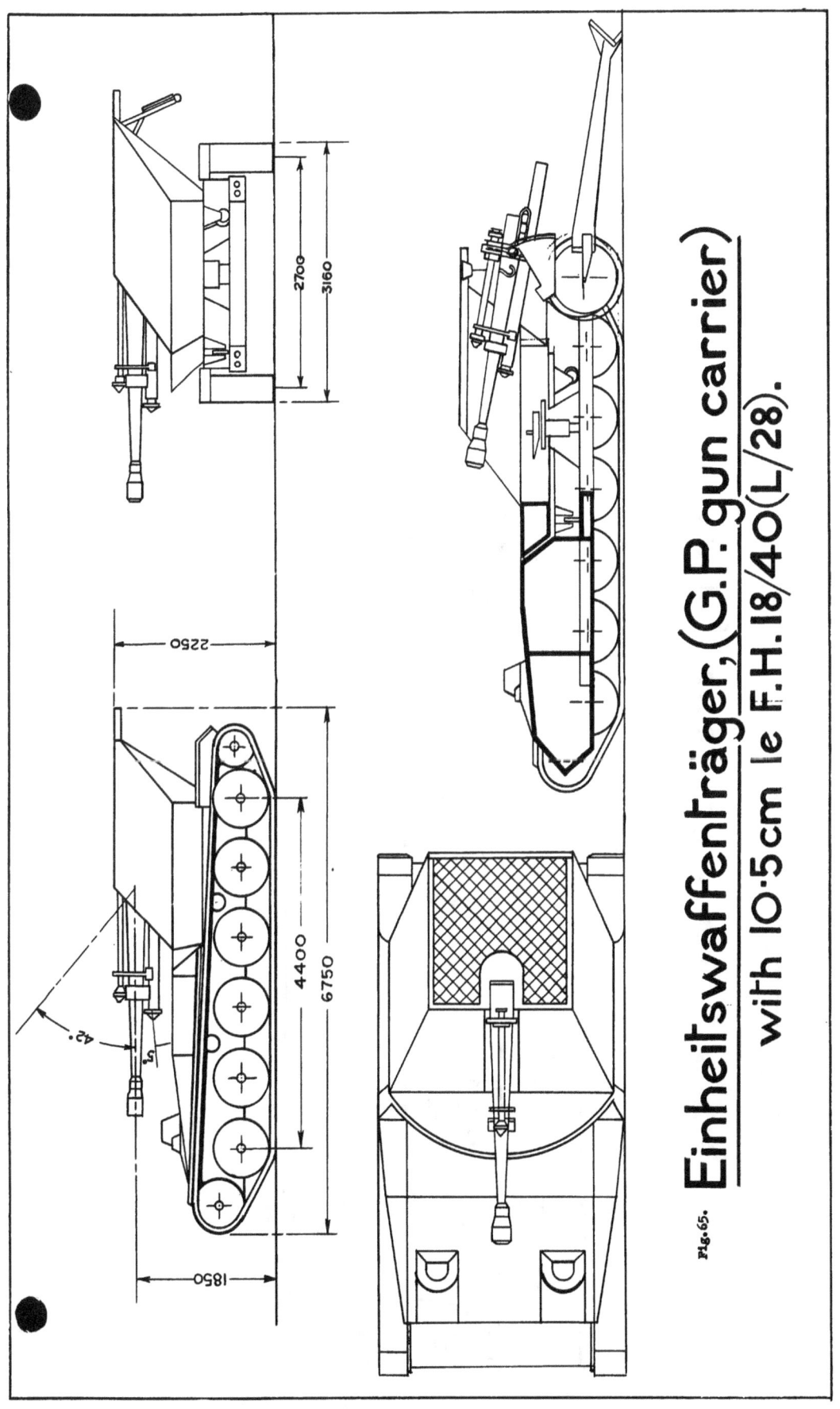

Fig. 65. Einheitswaffenträger, (G.P. gun carrier) with 10·5cm le F.H.18/40(L/28).

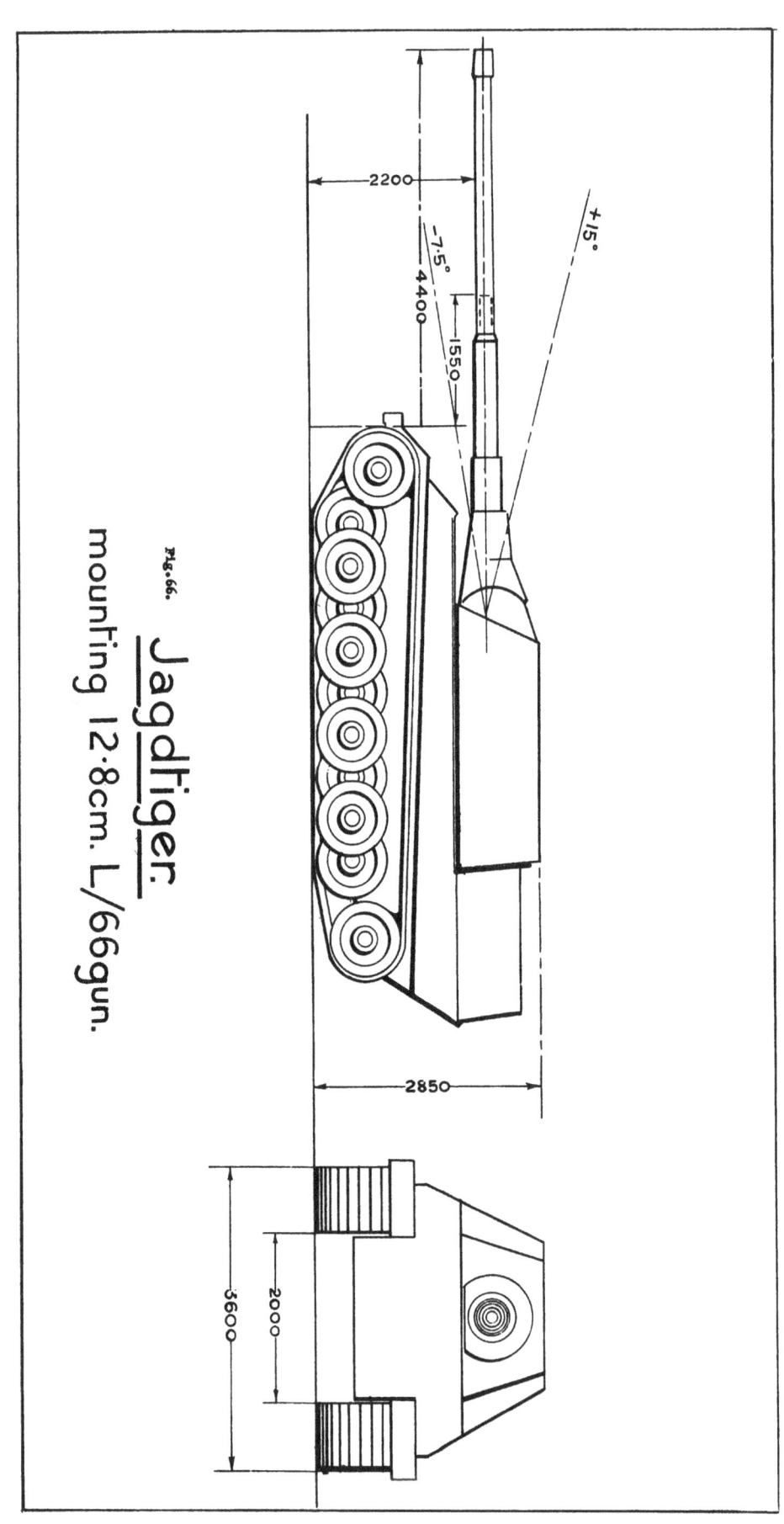

Fig. 66. **Jagdtiger.** mounting 12·8cm. L/66 gun.

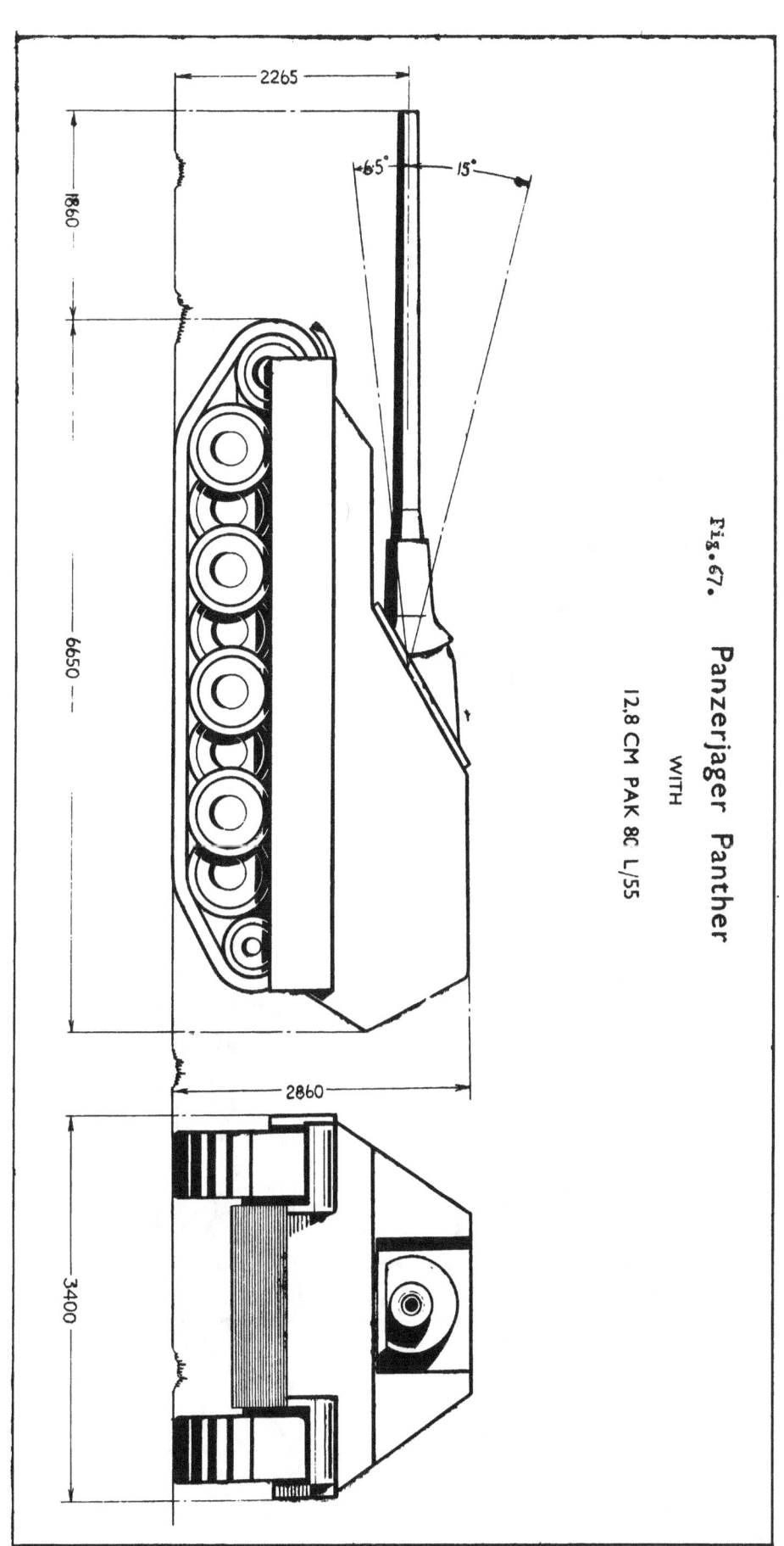

Fig. 67. Panzerjäger Panther WITH 12.8 CM PAK 8C L/55

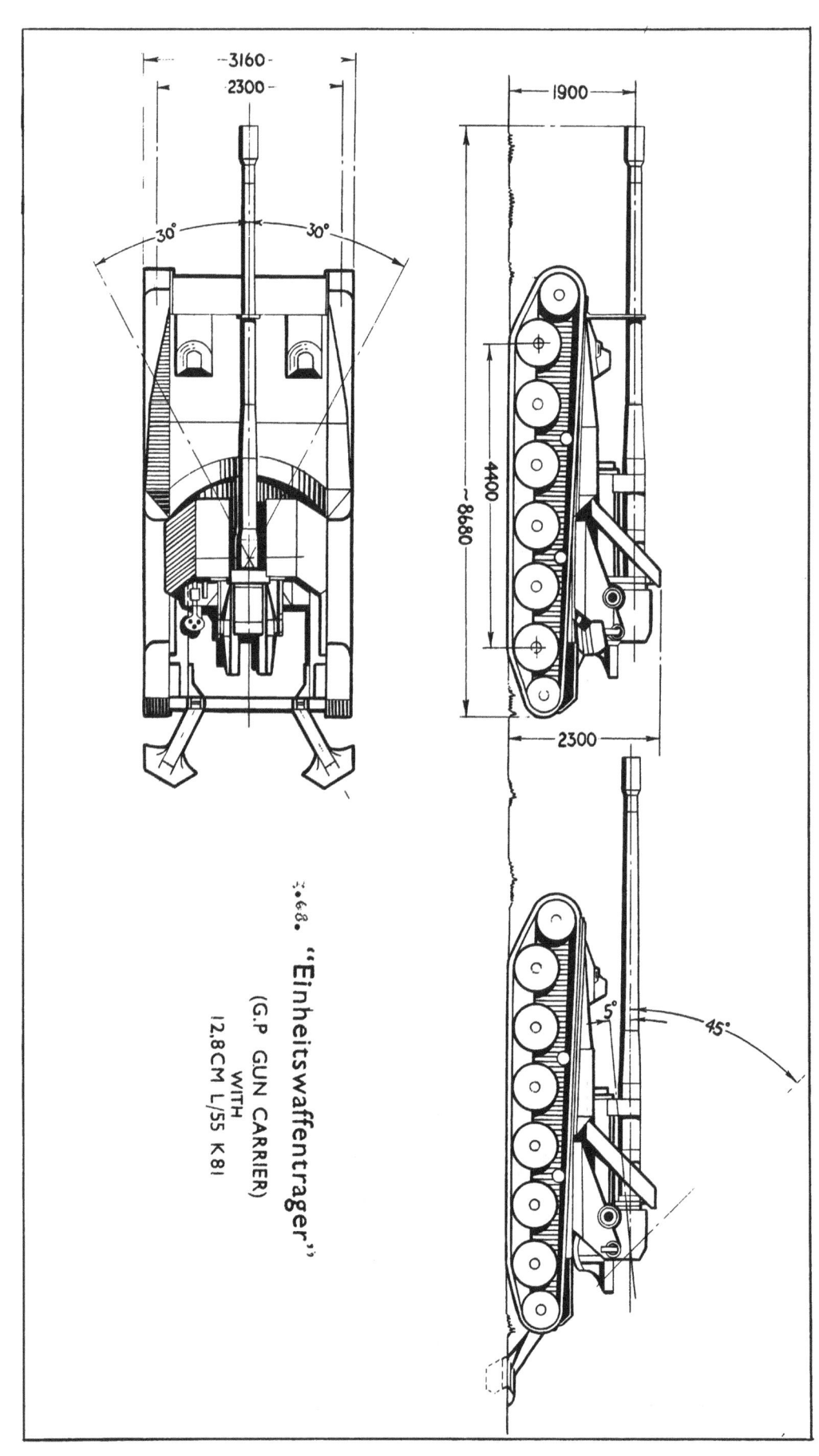

5.68. "Einheitswaffenträger"
(G.P GUN CARRIER)
WITH
12.8 CM L/55 K81

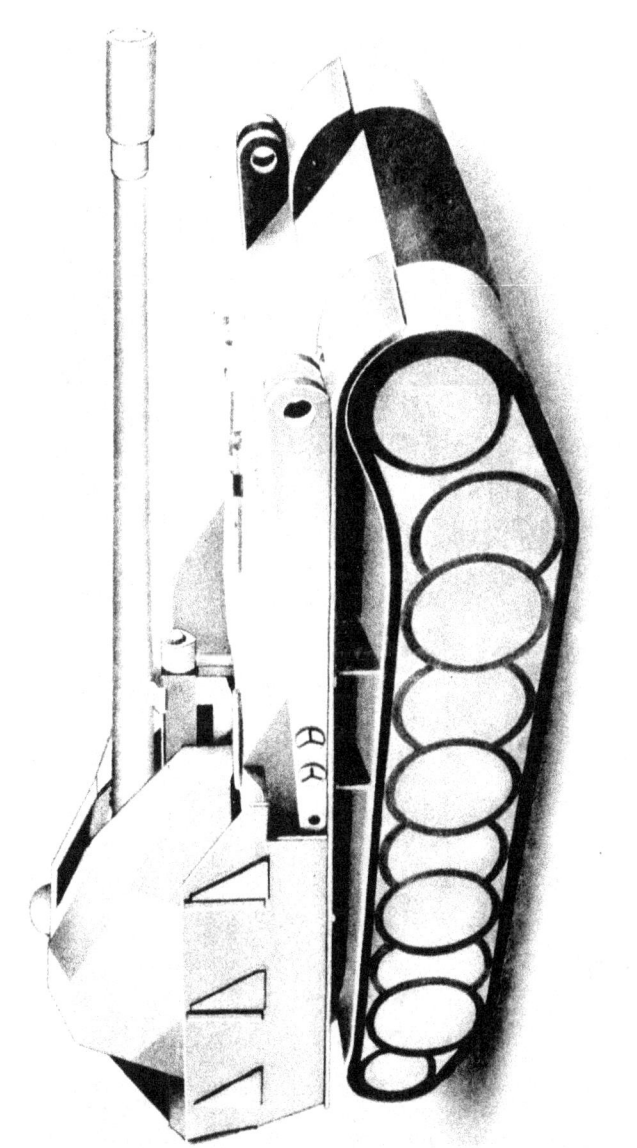

Fig.69. Mock-up of 'Grille' 15 by Krupp, mounting 15 cm. s.F.H.43 or 12.8 cm.K.43.

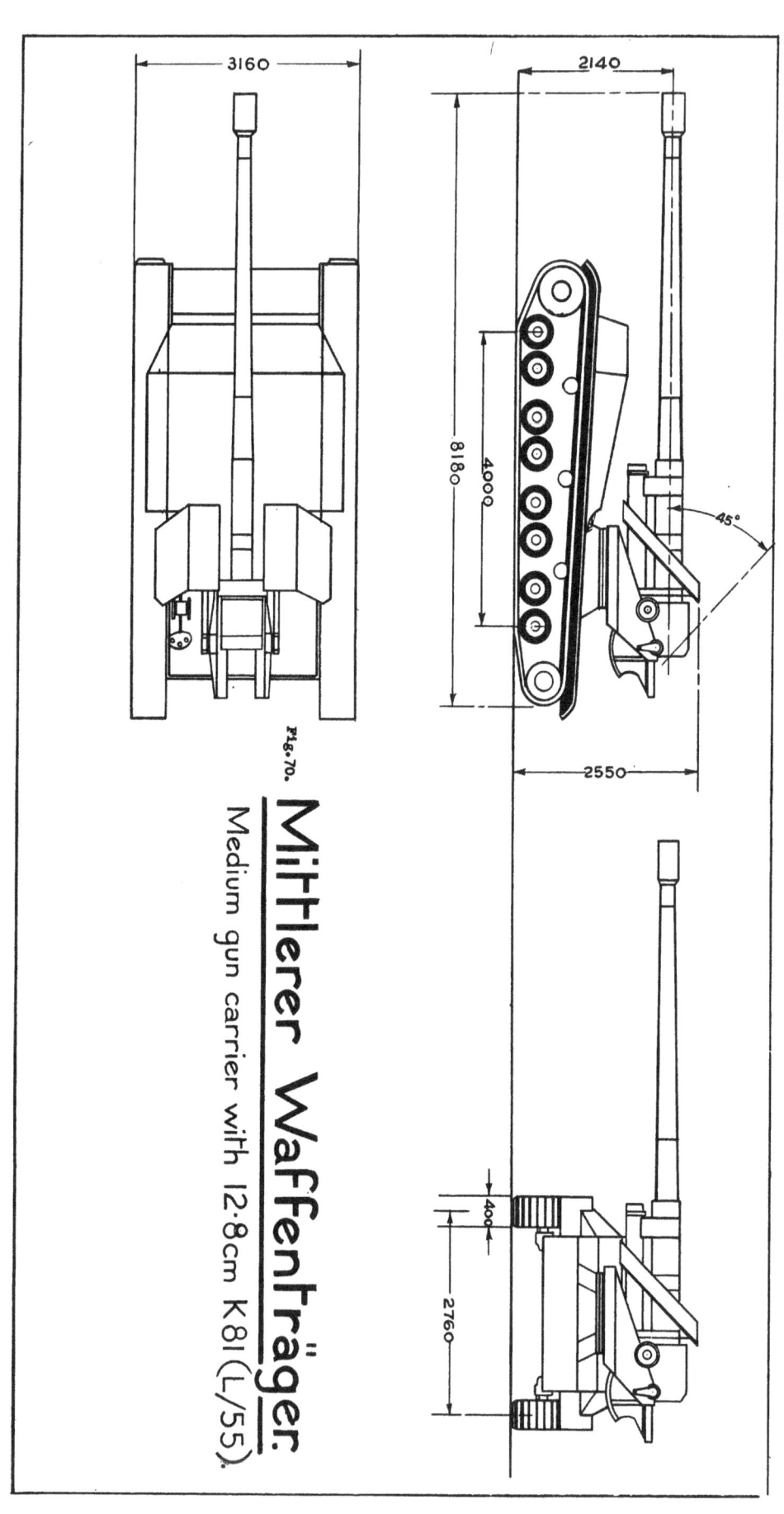

Fig. 70.

Mittlerer Waffenträger.

Medium gun carrier with 12·8cm K81 (L/55).

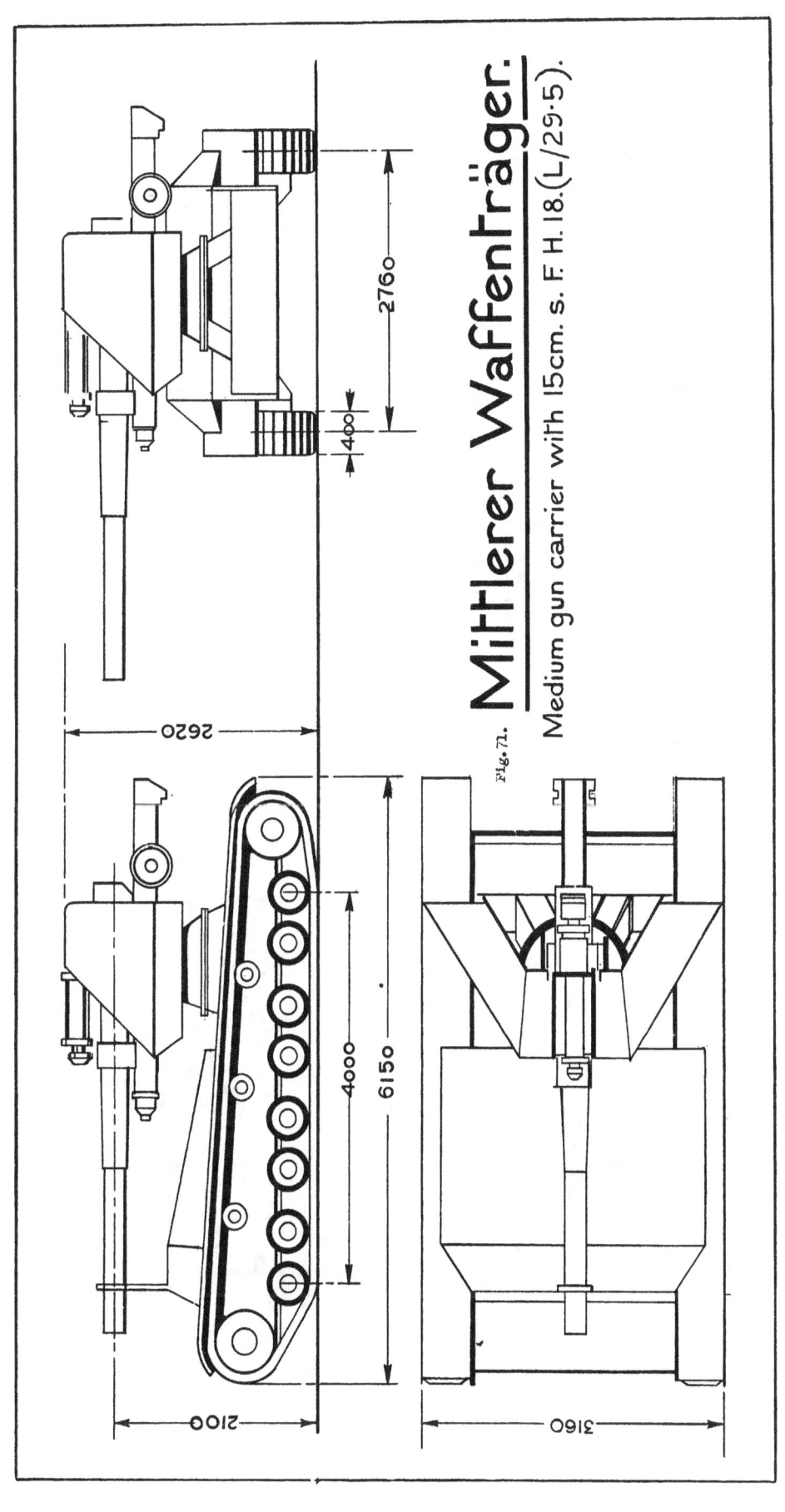

Fig. 71. **Mittlerer Waffenträger.**
Medium gun carrier with 15 cm. s. F.H. 18. (L/29·5).

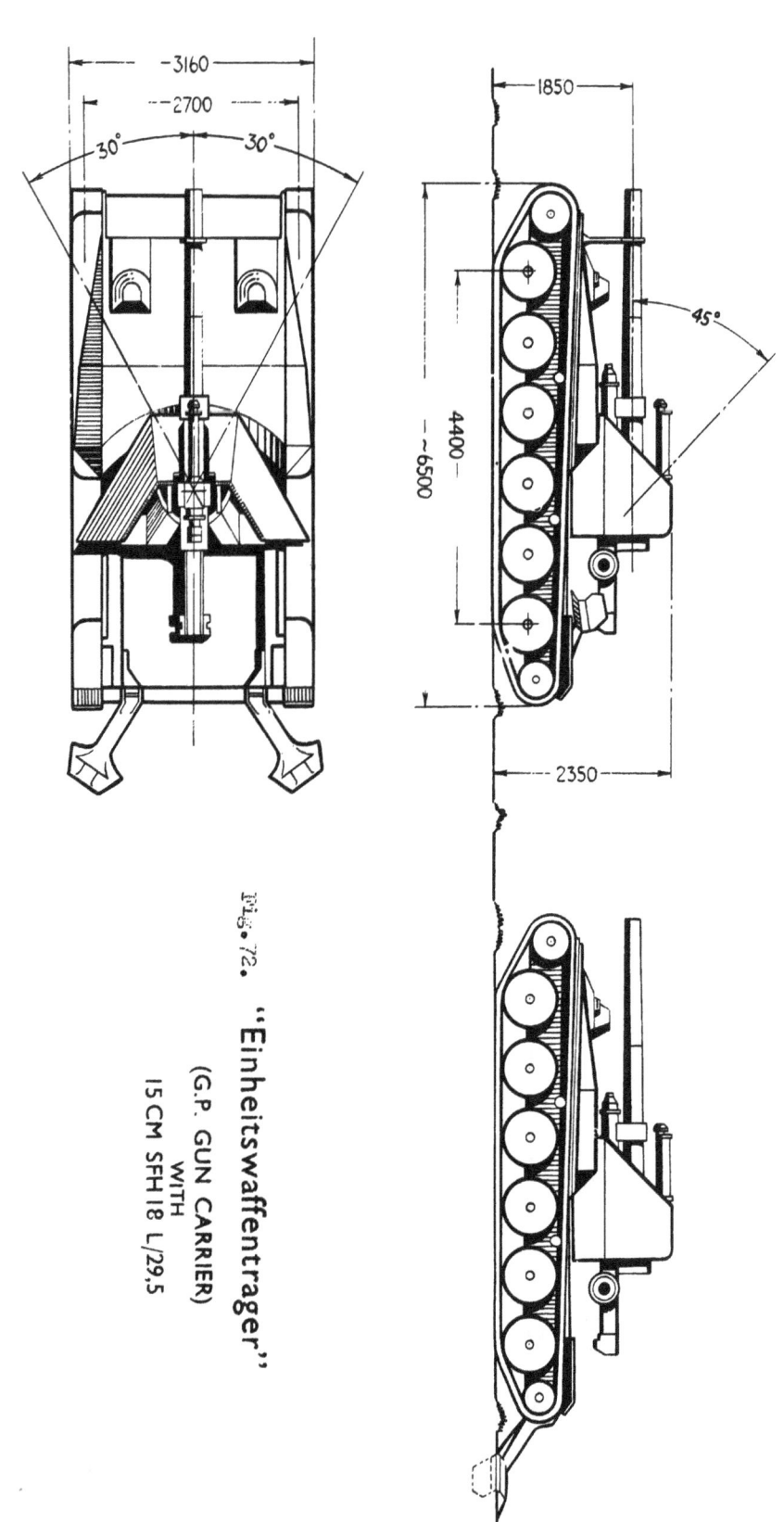

Fig. 72. "Einheitswaffentrager"
(G.P. GUN CARRIER)
WITH
15 CM SFH 18 L/29.5

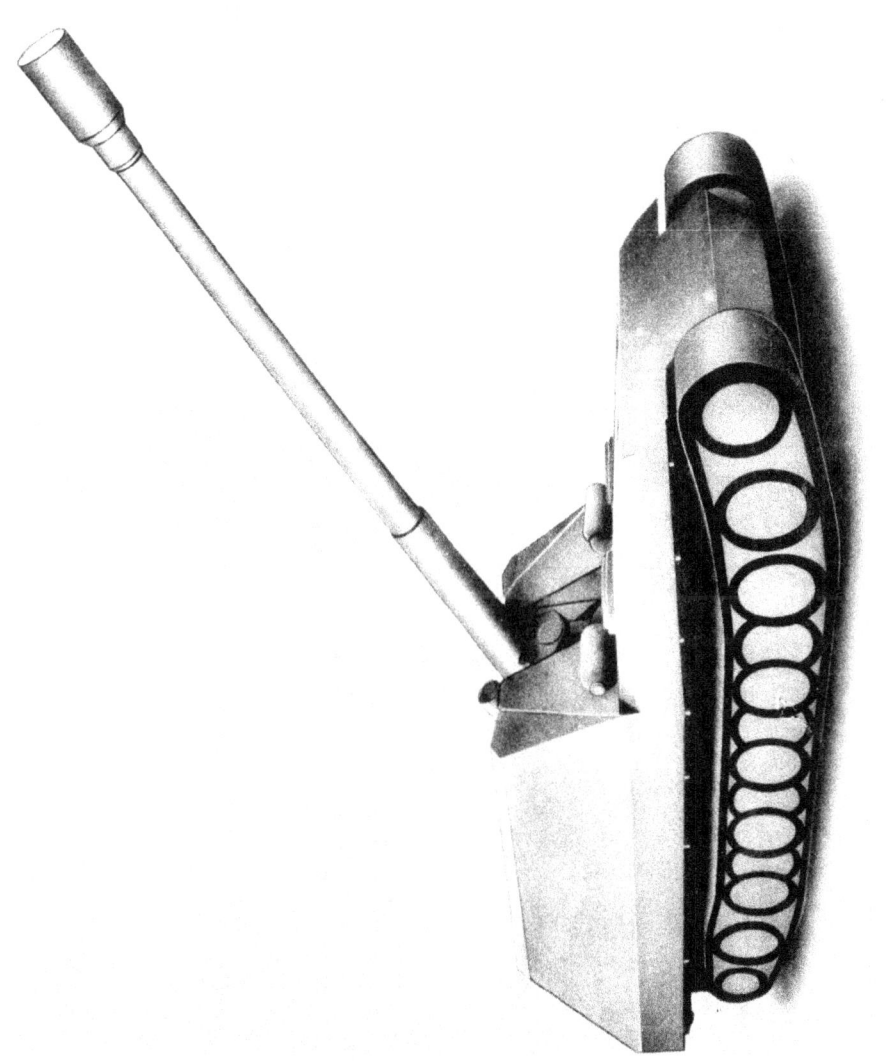

Fig.73 Mock-up of 'Grille' 17/21 - Waffenträger for 17 cm.K or 21 cm. Mrs.

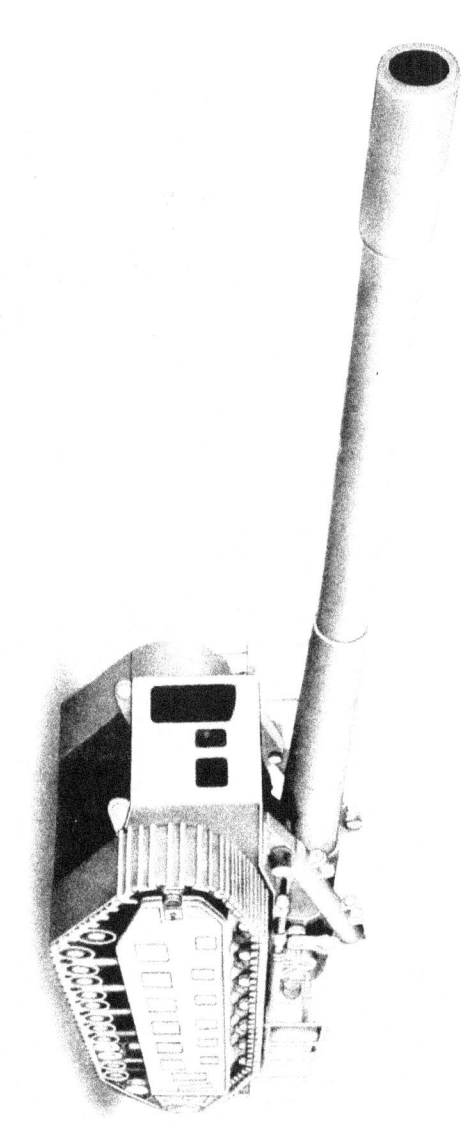

Fig.74. Krupp prototype of Naval mobile 28 cm. Coast Defence Gun – R.2.

SECTION THREE - ARMOURED CARS

INDEX TO SECTION THREE

1. Introduction.
2. Development history of vehicles taken into service.
3. Descriptions and outline specifications of basic chassis.
4. Unsuccessful Projects.
5. Photographs and specifications of vehicles taken into service.
6. Table of leading data.
7. Bibliography.

SECTION THREE - ARMOURED CARS

PART I

1. Introduction

This section will deal solely with the German wheeled armoured cars, the semi-tracked types being covered under a separate section of this publication.

As with tanks and S.P. guns, each type of armoured car was distinguished by a 'Sonderkraftfahrzeug' number (abbreviated to Sd.Kfz.), indicating that it was a special purpose Army vehicle and serving to identify it in the Ordnance Vocabulary. In addition, the fact that it was an armoured car was indicated by the abbreviation Pz.Sp.Wg., standing for Panzerspähwagen (Armoured Car). The German nomenclature also distinguished any vehicle which had more than four wheels by the inclusion of the words '6 rad' or '8 rad' indicating a 6- or 8-wheeled vehicle respectively.

As armoured cars were produced on a relatively small scale as compared to tanks and S.P. guns, correspondingly little development and production data has come to light. The scope of this section will be limited, therefore, to a chronological account of the types introduced into service, together with photos and specifications and approximate dates of introduction. Photos and outline specifications are included in Chapter 5.

2. Development history.

If British tanks and S.P. guns were consistently outgunned by their German equivalents, it is true to say that the reverse was the case with British and German armoured cars. The Germans held the belief that speed, lightness and manoeuvrability were the criterions of good armoured car design, and to this end sacrificed both fire power and armour protection, the latter right through the war and the former until the introduction of the high velocity 5 cm tank gun 39/1 mounted on the new 8-wheeled armoured car chassis in mid-1944. This was both the first and, as it turned out, the last German attempt to mount a gun of calibre larger than 2 cm. in a turret with 360° traverse on a true armoured car. While it is true that the 2.8 cm. heavy A.Tk. rifle 41 (2.8 cm. s.Pz.B.41) had been mounted on the 4-wheeled armoured car Sd.Kfz.221 as far back as 1942, the low velocity 7.5 cm. K.37 (L/24) had been mounted on the old version of the 8-wheeled armoured car (Sd.Kfz.233) in 1943, and the low velocity 7.5 cm K.51 (L/24) and high velocity 7.5 cm. Pak 40 (L/46) had been mounted on the new 8-wheeled car chassis (Sd.Kfz.234) in 1944 and 1945 respectively, these vehicles must be classified as self-propelled guns rather than as armoured cars by virtue of their limited-traverse mountings. As such, they are mentioned in Section II of this publication, 'Self-Propelled Equipments'.

The first armoured car taken into service with the German Army was the Kfz.13, a light, four-wheeled vehicle introduced about 1934 and already obsolete by the outbreak of war. Little is known of this vehicle, as no specimen was ever captured, neither were many documents dealing with it ever found. It was, however, apparently unique among German armoured cars in that it was not mounted on a standard Army car chassis. The superstructure was open-topped, and the armament consisted only of one 7.92 mm. M.G.13 on a pedestal mounting in the fighting compartment, with a light bullet-proof shield. A crew of 2 was carried. A wireless version of this vehicle (known as the Kfz.14) was also produced.

By the outbreak of war, German policy had changed and two complete ranges of armoured cars, one a light and the other a heavy series, had taken the place of the Kfz.13, now relegated to training uses. The new series of light cars (Sd.Kfz. 221 series) were all based on the Auto-Union A.G. Werk Horsch 801 4-wheeled general purpose chassis (Einheitsfahrgestell I für s.Pkw. also Einheitsfahrgestell II für s.Pkw.), also used as a basis for certain light lorries and personnel-carrying vehicles, while the heavy (Sd.Kfz. 231) series had as a basis a six-wheeled Büssing NAG chassis known as the A5P. Corresponding vehicles in the two series mounted similar armament, but differed slightly in armour protection, the light series having an armour basis of 5-8 mm. and the heavy series, one of 5-15 mm. The light series was retained in production right through the war, but the various six-wheeled vehicles were replaced by a new heavy series based on an 8-wheeled Büssing NAG chassis between mid-1940 and mid-1941. The six-wheeled vehicles were then used for training purposes and the 8-wheeled cars assumed the Sd.Kfz. numbers of their six-wheeled counterparts, thus rendering necessary '6 rad'/'8 rad' distinguishing suffixes in the ordnance vocabulary nomenclature, mentioned in '1' above.

The 8-wheeled (Sd.Kfz. 231) series were in turn rendered obsolete at the beginning of 1944 by the introduction of a new 8-wheeled series, incorporating a Tatra diesel engine and several other improvements such as increased armour protection and armament, bearing the Sd.Kfz. series number 234. The final development of this latter chassis came with the mounting on it of the 7.5 cm. Pak. 40, to Hitler's personal order, in November, 1944.

3. Descriptions and Outline Specifications of Basic Chassis.

   (i) Light chassis (S.D.Kfz. 221 series - Horsch 801)

   This chassis, serving, as it did, as a basis for several light lorries and personnel-carrying vehicles, has been fully described in the section of this publication dealing with Wheeled Vehicles. Description in this section will, therefore, be limited to outline specifications of the various armoured car versions (Sd.Kfz. 221, 222, 223, 260 and 261) listed in '5' below.

   Outline Specification of Sd.Kfz. 221 chassis.

   Power Plant
     Maker   Auto-Union
     Type   Horch V-8 petrol, water-cooled.
     Output   75 B.H.P. at 2000 r.p.m.

   Clutch
     Dry, single plate type.

   Gearbox
     Crash type, giving 5 speeds forward and 1 reverse.

   Drive
     From gearbox output shaft to front and rear differentials, for all four wheels. Rear differential integral with gearbox on early models, separate on later models.

   Suspension
     Independent, each assembly consisting of two unequal length radius arms and 2 coil springs side by side.

Wheels and tyres

Detachable pressed steel 3-piece type with 210 x 18 low pressure, cross country bullet-proof tyres.

Dimensions of chassis with armoured body.

Overall length	15 ft. 6 in.
" width	6 ft. 6½ in.
Ground clearance	10 in.
Wheelbase	9 ft. 3 in.
Track	5 ft. 5 in.

Performance

Max. speed (roads)	46 m.p.h.
Average speed (roads)	27 m.p.h.
Radius of action (roads)	175 miles
" " " (cross country)	125 miles
Trench	
Step	
Fording depth	2 ft.
Gradient	19°

(ii) 6-wheeled heavy chassis (Büssing NAG A5P)

The chassis frame is composed of pressed steel 'V'-section side-members, with pressed steel cross-members, while an auxiliary frame is provided to take the engine and gearbox. The individual joints are reinforced by means of butt straps. The engine, mounted at the front of the vehicle, is a water cooled 6 cyl., in-line Büssing petrol engine, with an output of 100 BHP at 3000 r.p.m., driving, through a two plate clutch, a 6-speed gearbox mounted centrally on the chassis. An additional direction-change gearbox is also provided, making available the full range of gears in forward and reverse directions. The drive is taken from the gearbox via universally-jointed shafts to all three axles. The front wheels are single and the rear wheels double, all sprung on semi-elliptic springs and fitted with cross-country bullet-proof tyres. Steering is on the front single axle only, but may be accomplished from either a front or rear steering wheel. The rear steering wheel, normally disengaged, is automatically engaged by the selection of reverse in the direction-change box. A duplicate set of main controls is also provided for the rear driving position. For improved cross-country performance chains may be placed round the rear pairs of wheels and wide rims fitted inside the front wheels. A hand brake with mechanical linkage operating on the 4 back wheels and a foot brake with cable and hydraulic control of all 6 wheels are provided. Armoured cars on this chassis, described in Chapter 5 below, are the Sd.Kfz.231, 232, and 263 (A.C.V.)

Outline Specification of Sd.Kfz.231 (6 rad.) chassis.

Power Plant
Maker	Büssing N.A.G.
Type	6 cyl. water cooled petrol.
Output	100 B.H.P. at 3000 r.p.m.

Clutch
Dry, 2-plate type.

Gearbox
Crash type giving 6 m speeds. Additional direction - change box, making available all six speeds for forward and reverse.

Drive
To all three axles, with inter-wheel and inter-axle differentials.

Steering
Front wheels only, from front or rear driving position.

Suspension
Independent for front axles. Rear wheels on each side coupled in bogie pairs by semi-elliptic springs, centrally-pivoted.

Wheels and tyres.
Detachable, 3-piece pressed-steel disc wheels, with cord-reinforced low-pressure bullet-proof tyres.

Dimensions of chassis with armoured body
Overall length	18 ft. 4 in.
" width	6 ft.
Ground clearance	8 in.
Wheelbase	11 ft. 2 in.
Track	5 ft. 7 in.

Performance
Max. speed (roads)	50 m.p.h.
Radius of action (roads)	156 miles
" " " (cross country)	93 miles
Trench	
Step	
Fording depth	2 ft.
Gradient	12°

(iii) 8-wheeled heavy chassis (Büssing NAG - SD.Kfz. 231 series)

The chassis frame, which is of light construction due to the rigidity of the armoured hull, serves mainly as the assembly foundation for all the components of the vehicle and is composed of two parallel 'Z' - section side-members joined by two main tubular cross-members which also serve as the pivots on which rock the four suspension springs. Auxiliary light cross-members of channel section and the four final drive gearboxes, very rigidly attached to the side members, give additional strength

A Büssing water-cooled V8 petrol engine is mounted at the front of the frame, giving an output of 155 B.H.P. at 300 r.p.m., and the drive is taken via a dry 2-plate clutch and a short jointed coupling shaft to a centrally mounted 3-speed gearbox which incorporates an auxiliary high-low ratio operated by a separate lever. There are, in effect, therefore, 6 speeds available by the use of two levers, and these may be used for forward or reverse travel by the use of a foot-pedal operated direction-change box. From the gearbox, the drive is taken fore and aft to two reduction boxes, one each for the front and rear bogies, each of which is located between, and transmits the drive to, the two axles of a bogie via a Z.F. cam-type differential or compensating gear of the free-wheel type. All four axles are thus driven and are also steered. Due to the differences in the radii of the circles described by the front and rear and the intermediate wheels on full lock, a De Lavaud inter-axle differential is housed in each of the two reduction boxes. Each of the eight road wheels is linked to the frame by two swinging links. One above the other and the upper of these links are connected in 2 bogie pairs per side and sprung on single inverted semi-elliptic springs, pivoted to the frame.

The four-axle steering system has been additionally complicated by the provision of front and rear steering wheels and columns. In addition the other main driving controls are duplicated front and rear. Wheels are of conventional pressed-steel disc three-piece type, carrying tyres of low pressure, cord-reinforced, cross-country type with a self sealing internal coating to the inner tubes, of red plastic rubber. Armoured cars based on this chassis, all of which (with the exception of the 7.5 cm. S.P. gun Sd.Kfz.233) are described in chapter 5 are:- Sd.Kfz.231 (8 rad), 232(8 rad), 233 (8 rad), 7.5 cm. S.P.) and 263 (8 rad) (A.C.V.).

Outline specification of Sd.Kfz.231 (8 rad) chassis.

Power Plant
- Maker: Büssing N.A.G.
- Type: 90° V8 cyl. water-cooled petrol O.H.V.
- Output: 155 B.H.P. at 3000 r.p.m.

Clutch
Dry 2-plate type.

Gearbox
Constant mesh helical gear type giving 3 speeds. An additional range is provided by an auxiliary high-low box and all six speeds are available in forward and reverse directions by means of a direction-change box.

Drive
Via two reduction boxes to all 8 wheels. Inter-wheel and inter-axles differentials are incorporated.

Steering
On all 8 wheels, from front or rear driving positions.

Suspension.
Semi-independent, with semi-elliptic springs coupling front and rear pairs of wheels on each side.

Wheels and tyres
3 piece pressed steel disc wheels, mounting cord-reinforced, low pressure bullet-proof cross-country tyres.

Dimensions of chassis with armoured body
- Overall length: 19 ft. 0½ in.
- Overall width: 7 ft. 3 in.
- Ground clearance: 11 in.
- Wheelbase (overall): 13 ft. 5¼ in.
- Track (axle shafts horizontal): 6 ft. 4½ in.

Performance
- Max. speed (roads): 53 m.p.h.
- Average speed (roads): 33 m.p.h.
- Max. speeds (cross country): 19 m.p.h.
- Radius of action (roads): 187 miles
- "   "   " (cross country): 106 miles
- Trench: 4 ft. 1 in.
- Step: 1 ft. 7 in.
- Fording depth: 2 ft.
- Gradient: 27°

(iv) 8-wheeled heavy chassis (Büssing NAG - Sd.Kfz. 234 series)

The chassis is identical to the earlier version except that it mounts a V-12, four stroke, air cooled Tatra diesel engine, with an output of 217 B.H.P. at 2250 r.p.m. in place of the V-8 Büssing petrol engine. An additional external recognition feature of this chassis is the long single mudguard on each side, compared to the two small mudguards per side (each covering two wheels) of the earlier series. Other differences, described in (5) are limited to armour thicknesses, turret design and armament. Armoured cars based on this chassis are the Sd.Kfz.234/1 (2 cm.), 234/2 (5 cm.Kw.K.39/1), 234/3 (7.5 cm. K.) and an S.P. 7.5 cm. Pak 40 (Sd.Kfz.No. unknown) of which the Sd.Kfz.234/1 and 234/2 are described in (5) below.

4. Unsuccessful Projects

Due to the relatively small allocation of firms to the design and building of armoured cars and the greater interest of the Heereswaffenamt in the design and development of tanks and self-propelled guns, comparatively little information on projected designs and unsuccessful projects has come to light. In fact, it is probable that, apart from one or two 'private ventures' by small firms outside the armoured car production 'ring', no further armoured car projects were officially contemplated before the end of the war.

Of the 'private ventures', the most persistently pushed and therefore the one about which the most is known, was a project by Hans Trippel of Trippelwerke, Molsheim for a light 4-wheeled amphibious armoured car known as "Schildkröte" (Turtle), based on the Trippel amphibious passenger car S.G.6. Three prototypes of this vehicle were produced, their design and production being spread over a long period (1941 - Oct 42) due to delays in the granting of the priorities required to obtain material for their construction. These prototypes differed slightly from each other in armament, engine and armour arrangement, but were all based on the S.G.6 chassis, described in the 'Wheeled Vehicles' section of this publication. Armament varied from one 7.92 mm. M.G. 81 on the Schildkröte I to a 20 mm M.G. 151 or 7.92 mm. M.G. 81 with coaxial 7.92 mm. M.G. 34 on the Schildkrote II and a 20 mm. M.G. 151 only on the Schildkrote III. Armour basis on the Schildkrote I was 7 - 7.5 mm. and was increased to 10 mm. for subsequent prototypes. None of these designs was successful, however, and the idea appears to have been reluctantly dropped after the end of 1942. A photograph of the Schildkröte III is included for information.

The Austro-Daimler 'wheel cum-tracks' vehicle was also used in small numbers, as an armoured and unarmoured vehicle. The armoured version of which a photo is included, was known as the 'le.gep. Beob. Kw. Sd.Kfz.254.'

5. Outline Specifications of Vehicles taken into Service

(i) le.Pz.Sp.Wg.Sd.Kfz.221 (light armoured car)

Wt. in action	3 tons 19 cwt.
Crew	2
Armament	One 7.92 mm. M.G.34 Sight - Open sight on gun
Ammunition	2,000 rds.

/Armour

Armour
   Hull
      Front)
      Sides) 8 mm.
      Rear)
      Glacis) 6 mm.
      Roof   )
   Turret
      Front)
      Sides) 8 mm. at 35°
      Rear)

Dimensions
   Overall height   5 ft. 11 ins.

Communication
   No wireless, by flag only.

Identification
   Turret is roofless and is of 7-sided, truncated pyramid form, with wire mesh anti-grenade screen over the fore part only.

(ii) le.Pz.Sp.Wg.Sd.Kfz.222 (light armoured car)

Wt. in action	4 tons 14 cwt.
Crew	3
Armament	One 2 cm. Kw.K.30 or Kw.K.38 with coaxial 7.92 mm. M.G.34 in 10-sided turret.
	Elevation -4° to + 87° Sights T.Z.F.3a and Fliegervisier 38 for A.A.
Ammunition	2 cm. 220 rds. 7.92 mm. 2,000 rds.
Armour	As for Sd.Kfz.221 above.
Dimensions	Overall height (to top of wire mesh anti-grenade screen) 6 ft. 9 ins.
Communication	W/T receiver and transmitter

Identification
   Roofless turret is ten-sided and of truncated pyramid form. Raised wire mesh anti-grenade screen covers whole of turret. Distinctive main armament.

(iii) le.Pz.Sp.Wg.(Fu)Sd.Kfz.223 (light armoured car (wireless))

Wt. in action	4 tons 6 cwt.
Crew	3
Armament	One 7.92 mm. M.G.34
	Elevation -10° to + 69° Sight - Open sight on gun
Ammunition	1,200 rds.

Armour — As for Sd.Kfz.221 above.

Dimensions — Overall height 5 ft. 11½ ins.

Communication
Long range W/T transmitter and receiver. Horizontal rectangular hinged rail aerial can be raised or folded downwards and backwards to give clear field of view.

Identification
9-sided truncated pyramidal turret, open at the top and covered at the front by hinged wire mesh anti-grenade screen. Rectangular folding horizontal aerial, of rail type.

(iv) kl.Pz.Fu.Wg.Sd.Kfz.260 (Small armoured wireless car)

Wt. in action — 4 tons 4 cwt.

Crew — 4

Armament) — None
Ammunition)

Armour — 8 mm. basis

Dimensions — Overall height 5 ft. 10 ins.

Communication — R/T and W/T transmitter and receiver.

Identification
No turret and no armament. Waterproof covering over turret opening. Rod type aerials.

(v) kl.Pz.Fu.Wg.Sd.Kfz.261 (Small armoured wireless car)

Wt. in action — 4 tons 5 cwt.

Crew — 4

Armament) — None
Ammunition)

Armour — 8 mm. basis

Dimensions — Overall height 5 ft. 10 ins.

Communication — R/T and W/T transmitter and receiver

Identification
As for Sd.Kfz.260 above except rectangular horizontal folding rail aerial (as fitted to Sd.Kfz.223) is provided.

(vi) s.Pz.Sp.Wg.Sd.Kfz.231 (6 rad) (heavy 6-wheeled armoured car)

Wt. in action — 5 tons 18 cwt.

Crew — 4

Armament — One 2 cm. Kw.K.30 and coaxial 7.92 mm. M.G.34 in turret.

Armour — Front 14 mm.
Sides 8 mm.

Dimensions   Overall height   7 ft. 4 ins.

Communication
W/T transmitter and receiver with rod type aerial sometimes fitted.

Identification
Enclosed armoured rotating turret, rod type aerial.

(vii) **s.Pz.Sp.Wg.(Fu)Sd.Kfz.232** (6 rad) (Heavy 6-wheeled armoured car wireless))

Wt. in action	6 tons 3cwt.
Crew	4
Armament	As for Sd.Kfz.231 (6 rad) above
Armour	
Dimensions	Overall height (to top of aerial) 9 ft. 6ins.

Communication
R/T and W/T transmitter and receiver with curved horizontal grid aerial (fixed) above car.

Identification
Rotating enclosed turret, distinctive grid aerial above car.

(viii) **s.Pz.Fu.Wg.Sd.Kfz.263** (6 rad) (heavy 6-wheeled armoured wireless car)

Wt. in action	5 tons 15 cwt.
Crew	5
Armament	One 7.92 mm. M.G. 13 firing forward in fixed turret.
Armour	As for Sd.Kfz.231 (6 rad) above.
Dimensions	Overall height to top of aerial 9 ft. 6 ins.

Communication
R/T and W/T transmitter and receiver, with grid type aerial as on Sd.Kfz.232 (6 rad) above.

Identification
Armament of one M.G. mounted in fixed turret. Aerial as on Sd. Kfz. 232 (6 rad).

(ix) **s.Pz.Sp.Wg.Sd.Kfz.231** (8 rad) (heavy 8-wheeled armoured car)

Wt. in action	8 tons 3 cwt.
Crew	4
Armament	One 2 cm. Kw.K.30 or Kw.K.38 with coaxial 7.92 mm. M.G.34 in turret.
	Elevation -10° to +26°
	Traverse 360°
	Sight T.Z.F.6.

Ammunition   2 cm.   180 rds.
                   7.92 mm. 2,100 rds.

Armour
  Hull
    Front   8 mm at 28°
    Sides   8 mm (10 mm rear) at 40° upper and 37° lower
    Rear   8 mm at 28°
    Roof   5 mm at 71° (front) and 83° (rear)
  Turret
    Front   8 mm at 25°
    Sides   8 mm at 28°
    Rear   8 mm at 30°
    Roof   5 mm at 78° (front) and 88° (rear)

Dimensions Overall height 7 ft. 10 in.

Communication
    R/T transmitter and receiver with rod type aerial.

Identification
    Turret with 360° traverse, conspicuous main armament with coaxial M.G., and vertical rod type aerial.

(x)   s.Pz.Sp.Wg.(Fu)Sd.Kfz.232 (8 rad) (Heavy 8-wheeled armoured car (wireless))

Wt. in action   8 tons 7 cwt.

Crew   4

Armament   ⎫
Ammunition ⎬ As for Sd.Kfz.231 (8 rad) above.
Armour   ⎭

Dimensions Overall height, to top of aerial 9 ft. 6 in.

Communication
    R/T and W/T transmitter and receiver with curved horizontal grid type aerial.

Identification
    As for Sd.Kfz.231 (8 rad) above except for horizontal grid aerial in place of vertical rod.

(xi)   s.Pz.Fu.Wg.Sd.Kfz.263 (8 rad) (heavy 8-wheeled armoured (wireless car)

Wt. in action   7 tons 19 cwt.

Crew   5

Armament One 7.92 mm. M.G. 34 firing forward from fixed cab.

Ammunition 1000 rds. of 7.92 mm.

Armour
    As for Sd.Kfz.231 (8 rad) above, except angles of turret side plates which conform to upper hull sides and are integral with them.

Dimensions   Overall height to top of aerial 9 ft. 6 in.

Communication
R/T and W/T transmitter and receiver with grid aerial as on Sd.Kfz.232 (8 rad) above.

Identification
Long, fixed, turret-like superstructure, integral with upper hull sides. Armament of one M.G. Horizontal curved grid aerial above car.

(xii) s.Pz.Sp.Wg.Sd.Kfz.234/1 (8 rad) (2 cm) (heavy 8-wheeled armoured mounting 2 cm. gun).

Wt. in action   10 tons 8.5 cwt.

Crew   4

Armament
One 2 cm. Kw.K.38 and coaxial 7.92 mm M.G. 42 in 6-sided open topped turret with raised mesh anti-grenade screen.
   Elevation   0° to +75°
   Traverse   360°

Ammunition   2 cm. 280 rds.

Armour
  Hull
    Front   25 mm.
    Sides   8 mm.
    Rear   15 mm.
  Turret
    Front   30 mm.
    Sides)
    Rear)   8 mm.

Dimensions   Overall height 6 ft 10½ in.

Communication
W/T transmitter and receiver with rod type aerial.

Identification
Single mudguard each side. 6 sided open-topped turret with wire mesh anti-grenade screen. Rod type aerial.

(xiii) s.Pz.Sp.Wg. (5 cm) Sd.Kfz.234/2 (8 rad) (heavy 8-wheeled armoured car mounting 5 cm. gun.)

Wt. in action   10 tons 16 cwt.

Crew   4

Armament
One 5 cm. Kw.K.39/1 (L/60) with coaxial 7.92 mm. M.G. 42.
   Elevation   -7° to +25°
   Traverse   360°
   Sight   T.Z.F.46

Ammunition   5 cm. 55 rds.

Armour
  Hull   as for Sd.Kfz.234/1 above.

Turret
- Front   30 mm. at 20°
- Sides   10 mm. at 20°
- Rear   10 mm. at 2°
- Roof   10 mm horizontal
- Mantlet   40-100 mm. rounded.

Dimensions Overall height 7 ft. 6 in.

Communication
R/T and W/T transmitter and receiver with rod type aerial.

Identification
High, rounded roofed-in turret with flat front, mounting long gun with double baffle muzzle brake. Remainder as for Sd.Kfz.234/1 above.

6. TABLE OF LEADING DATA OF OPERATIONAL GERMAN ARMOURED CARS

	VEHICLE	(a) Weight (b) Crew (c) Speed (rds) (d) Radius of action (rds)	ARMAMENT	ROUNDS CARRIED	ARMOUR THICKNESS IN mm. Hull Front	Side	Turret (a) Front	(b) Side	DIMENSIONS (a) Length (b) Width (c) Height (d) Clearance	ENGINE	COMMUNICATION	REMARKS
1.	Lt.-4-wheeled Armoured Car (Sd.Kfz.221) le.Pz.Sp.We.	(a) 4.6 tons (b) 2 (c) 50 m.p.h. (d) 200 miles	One 7.92 mm M.G.34 One 9 mm. M.P.38 or 40 One 27 mm. signal pistol Six stick hand grenades	1200 — 12	(a) 30 (nose plate only) (b) 8		(a) 8 (b) 8		(a) 15 ft 7 in (b) 6 ft 6 in (c) 6 ft (d) 10 in	Auto Union (Horch V-8) 89 B.H.P., petrol	Flag	Turret in the form of a seven-sided truncated pyramid, with a wire mesh grid over fore part only.
2.	Lt.-4-wheeled Armoured Car (Sd.Kfz.222) le.Pz.Sp.We.	(a) 4.8 tons (b) 3 (c) 50 m.p.h. (d) 180 miles	One 2 cm. Kw.K.30 or 38 One 7.92 mm. M.G.34 coaxial in turret One 9 mm. M.P.38 or 40 One 27 mm. signal pistol Six stick hand grenades	90 1300 — 12	As for Serial 1				As for Serial 1	As for Serial 1	W/T R/T Intercom Flag	Standard light armoured car and used in Div. recce units. Turret is in the form of a shallow truncated ten-sided pyramid. A hinged wire-mesh anti-grenade cage is fitted on top. Overall height including wire-mesh cage is 6 ft 9 in. Two mechanically fired smoke projectors are fitted, one each side of turret. Hull and chassis as for Serial 1.
3.	Lt.-4-wheeled Armoured Car (Sd.Kfz.223) le.Pz.Sp.We. (fu)	(a) 4.4 tons (b) 3 (c) 50 m.p.h. (d) 200 miles	As for Serial 1	As for Serial 1	As for Serial 1		As for Serial 1		As for Serial 1	As for Serial 1	W/T R/T (long range) Intercom Flag	A horizontal rectangular aerial is supported above the car on 4 uprights which can be folded downwards and backwards, giving the gunner a clear field of fire. In both positions the grid resembles a railing round the top of the car. Turret is similar to Serial 1 as are hull and chassis.
4.	Lt.-4-wheeled Armoured Wireless Car (Sd.Kfz.260) Kl.Pz.Fu.Wg.	(a) 4.2 tons (b) 4 (c) 50 m.p.h. (d) 200 miles	None	None	(a) As for Serial 1 (b)		No turret		(a) (b) As for Serial 1 (c) 5 ft 10 in (d)	As for Serial 1	W/T R/T Intercom Flag	No turret – opening covered by waterproof covers. Hull and chassis as for Serial 1. Rod aerial.
5.	Lt.-4-wheeled Armoured Wireless Car (Sd.Kfz.261) Kl.Pz.Fu.Wg.	(a) 4.25 tons (b) 4 (c) 50 m.p.h. (d) 200 miles	None	None	(a) As for Serial 1 (b)		No turret		(a) (b) As for Serial 1 (c) As for Serial 4 (d)	As for Serial 1	W/T F/T (long range) Intercom Flag	As Serial 4, except folding rectangular and horizontal rail aerial fitted (as on Serial 3).
6.	6-wheeled Armoured Car (Sd.Kfz.231) s.Pz.Sp.We. (6 rad)	(a) 6 tons (b) 4 (c) 45 m.p.h. (d) 160 miles	One 2 cm. Kw.K.30 or 38 One 7.92 m. M.G.34 coaxial in turret	200 1500	(a) 15 (b) 8		(a) 15 (b) 8		(a) 18 ft 5 in (b) 6 ft 1 in (c) 7 ft 4 in (d) 8 in	Bussing NAG 6 cyl. 100 B.H.P., petrol	W/T Flag Intercom	Vehicle may be driven from either end (max. speed in reverse direction 20 mph). Mounting for A.A. M.G. on turret roof.
7.	6-wheeled Armoured Car (Sd.Kfz.232) s.Pz.Sp.We. (Fu) (6 rad)	(a) 6.2 tons (b) 4 (c) 45 m.p.h. (d) 160 miles	As for Serial 6	As for Serial 6	As for Serial 6		As for Serial 6		(a) 18 ft 5 in (b) 6 ft 1 in (c) 9 ft 6 in (d) 8 in	As for Serial 6	W/T R/T Intercom Flag	Similar to Serial 6, but with long range wireless equipment. No mounting for an A.A. M.G. on turret roof. Overhead frame aerial.
8.	6-wheeled ACV (Sd.Kfz.263) Pz.Fu.Wg. (6 rad)	(a) 5.7 tons (b) 5 (c) 45 m.p.h. (d) 160 miles	One 7.92 mm. M.G.34	—	As for Serial 6		As for Serial 6		(a) 18 ft 4 in (b) 6 ft (c) 9 ft 6 in (d) 8 in	As for Serial 6	R/T W/T Intercom Flag	An A.C.V. similar in construction to Serial 6, but with a fixed turret and no mounting for an A.A. M.G.
9.	Hy 8-wheeled Armoured Car (Sd.Kfz.231) s.Pz.Sp.We. (8 rad)	(a) 8 tons (b) 4 (c) 50 m.p.h. (d) 165 miles	One 2 cm. Kw.K.30 or 38 One 7.92 mm. M.G.34 coaxial in turret One 9 mm. M.P.38 or 40 One 27 mm. signal pistol Six stick hand grenades	180 2100 — 192 12	(a) 30 (b) 8		(a) 30 (b) 8		(a) 19 ft 3 in (b) 7 ft (c) 7 ft 10 in (d) 9 in	Bussing NAG V-8 155 B.H.P. petrol	R/T Intercom	Standard heavy armd. car and used in Div. recce units. Eight titanium tetrachloride smoke generators are carried 4 on each front mudguard. Rod type aerial.

TABLE 6 – (contd.)

VEHICLE	(a) Weight (b) Crew (c) Speed (rds) (d) Radius of action (rds)	ARMAMENT	ROUNDS CARRIED	ARMOUR THICKNESS IN mm.				DIMENSIONS (a) Length (b) Width (c) Height (d) Clearance	ENGINE	COMMUNICATION	REMARKS
				Hull		Turret					
				(a) Front (b) Side		(a) Front (b) Side					
10. Hy 8-wheeled Armoured Car (Sd.Kfz.232) s.Pz.Sp.Wg. (Fu) (8 Rad)	(a) 8.4 tons (b) 4 (c) 50 m.p.h. (d) 165 miles	As for Serial 9	As for Serial 9	As for Serial 9				(a) 19 ft (b) 7 ft 3 in (c) 9 ft 6 in (d) 9 in	As for Serial 9	R/T W/T (Long range) Intercom	Similar to serial 9 except for wireless equipment. Overhead frame aerial.
11. Hy 8-wheeled A.C.V. (Sd.Kfz.263) Pz.Fu.Wg. (8 Rad)	(a) 8 tons (b) 5 (c) 50 m.p.h. (d) 165 miles	One 7.92 mm. M.G.34 One 9 mm. M.P.38 or 40	1000 192	As for Serial 9				As for Serial 8	As for Serial 9	R/T W/T (Long range) Intercom	The M.G.34 may not be carried. Chassis is similar to Serial 9. Turret is fixed and slightly larger than Serial 9 and 10. Overhead frame aerial.
12. Hy 8-wheeled Armoured Car (Sd.Kfz.234/1) s.Pz.Sp.Wg. (2cm)	(a) 10.4 tons (b) 4 (c) 50 m.p.h. (d)	One 2 cm. Kw.K.38 One 7.92 mm. M.G.42 coaxial in turret	480	(a) 30 (b) 8		(a) 30 (b) 8		(a) 19 ft 9 in (b) 7 ft 10½ in (c) (d) 1 ft 2 in	Tatra V-12 diesel engine air-cooled giving 217 BHP at 2250 rpm	R/T W/T Intercom	Long single mudguard each side, as opposed to two mudguards per side of serials 9 – 11 incl. Open topped 6-sided turret of truncated pyramid form, with folding wire mesh anti-grenade screen over turret top.
13. Hy. 8-wheeled Armoured Car mounting 5 cm gun/Sd.Kfz.234/2) s.Pz.Sp.Wg. (5 cm)	(a) 11.5 tons (b) 4 (c) 50 m.p.h. (d) 372 miles	One 5 cm Kw.K.39/1 (L/60) One 7.92 mm M.G.42 coaxial in turret. Two sets of 3 smoke generator dischargers, one each side of turret.	55	(a) 30 (b) 9		(a) 30 (b) 10		(a) 22 ft 4 in (b) 7 ft 10½ in (c) 7 ft 6 in (d) 1 ft 2 in	As for Serial 12	R/T W/T Intercom	Totally enclosed, rotating, tank-type turret of horseshoe plan with flat front. Bell-shaped gun mantlet. 5 cm gun has double baffle muzzle brake. Rod aerial. Otherwise as for Serial 12.

7. Bibliography

German manufacturers' files etc., held on behalf of B.I.O.S., Group V by M.C. of S., School of Tank Technology.

German vehicle handbooks, held by F.V. Wing, M.C. of S.

Examination reports by: U.S. Ord. Tech. Int. Sect., E.T.O.
(Tech. Int. Reports).
M.I.10, G.H.Q., M.E.F. (Int. Summaries).
G.S.I. (Tech.), 21 Army Group. (Tech. Int. Summaries).
Department of Tank Design, Ministry of Supply.
M.C. of S., S.T.T.
Dennis Bros., (8 wheeled Armoured Car Sd.Kfz.231 and 263) on behalf of D.T.D.

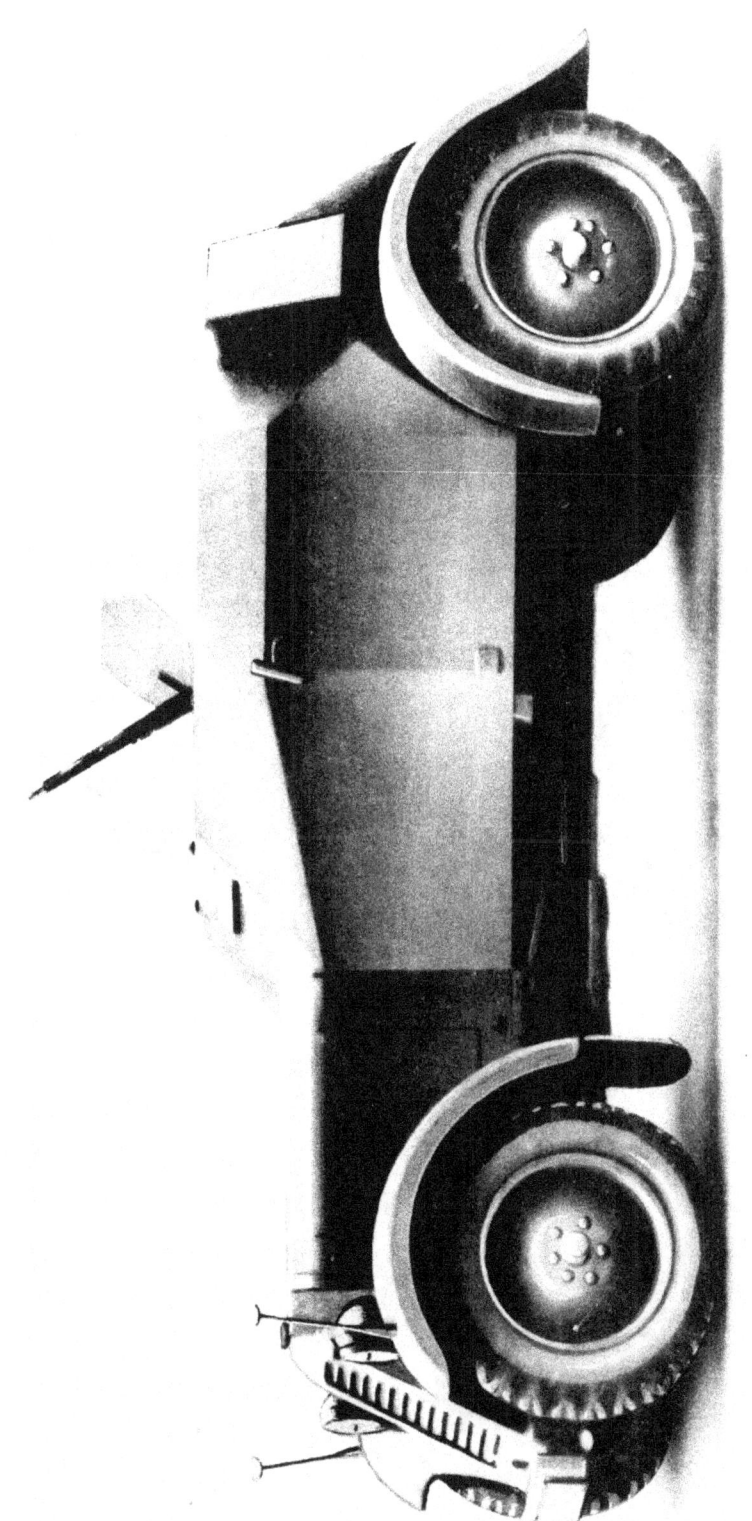

Fig 1. Light Armoured Car Kfz. 13.

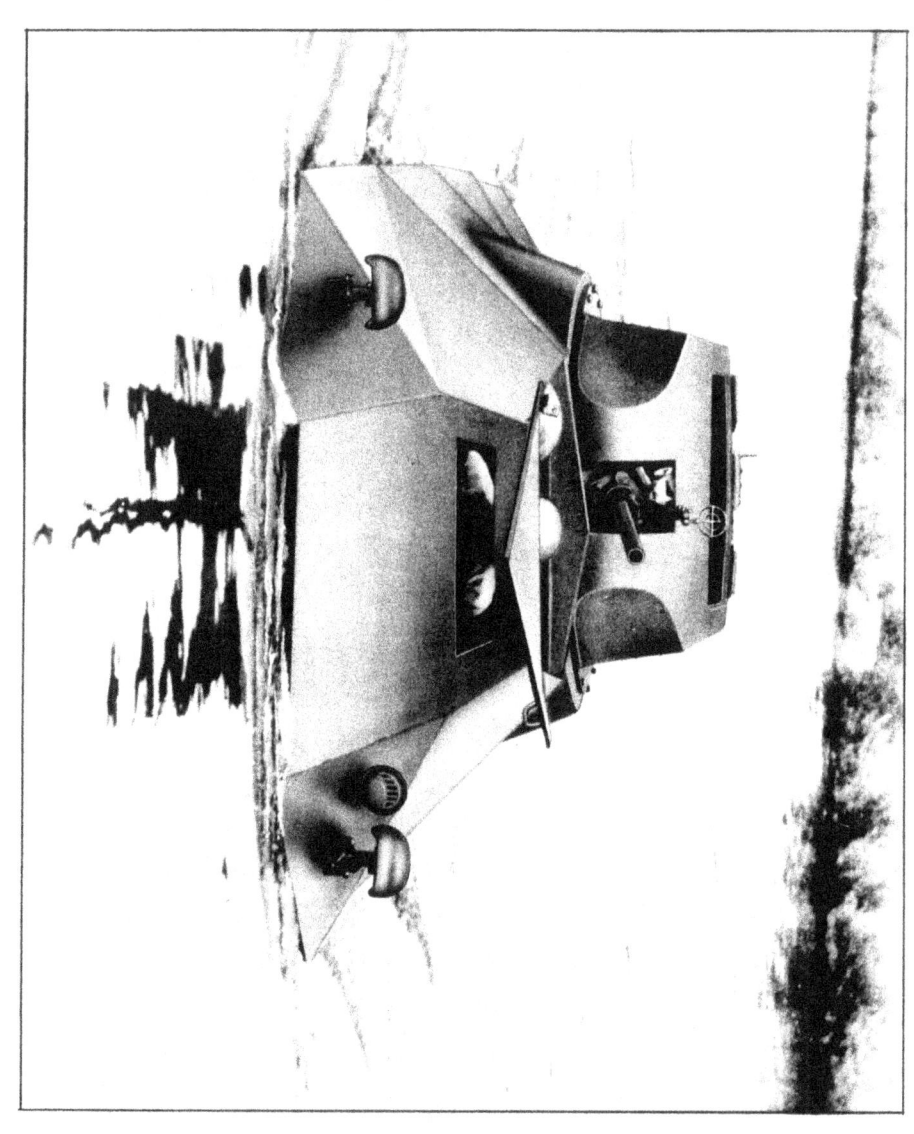

Fig. 2. Trippel Amphibious Armoured Car' Schildkröte III' (Turtle III).

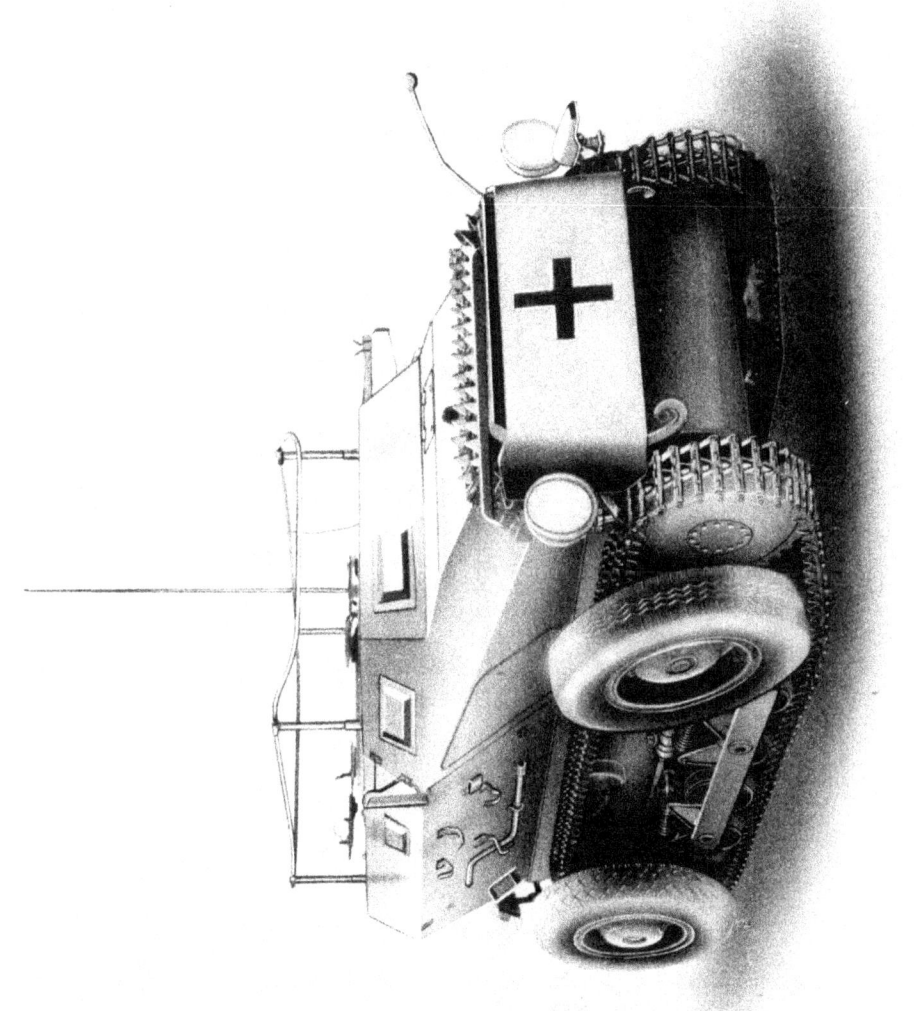

Fig.3. Austro-Daimler Wheel-cum-Track vehicle Sd.Kfz. 254 (armoured version-le.gep.Beob.Kw).

Fig. 4. Light Armoured Car Sd.Kfz. 222. (le.Pz.Sp.Wg.)

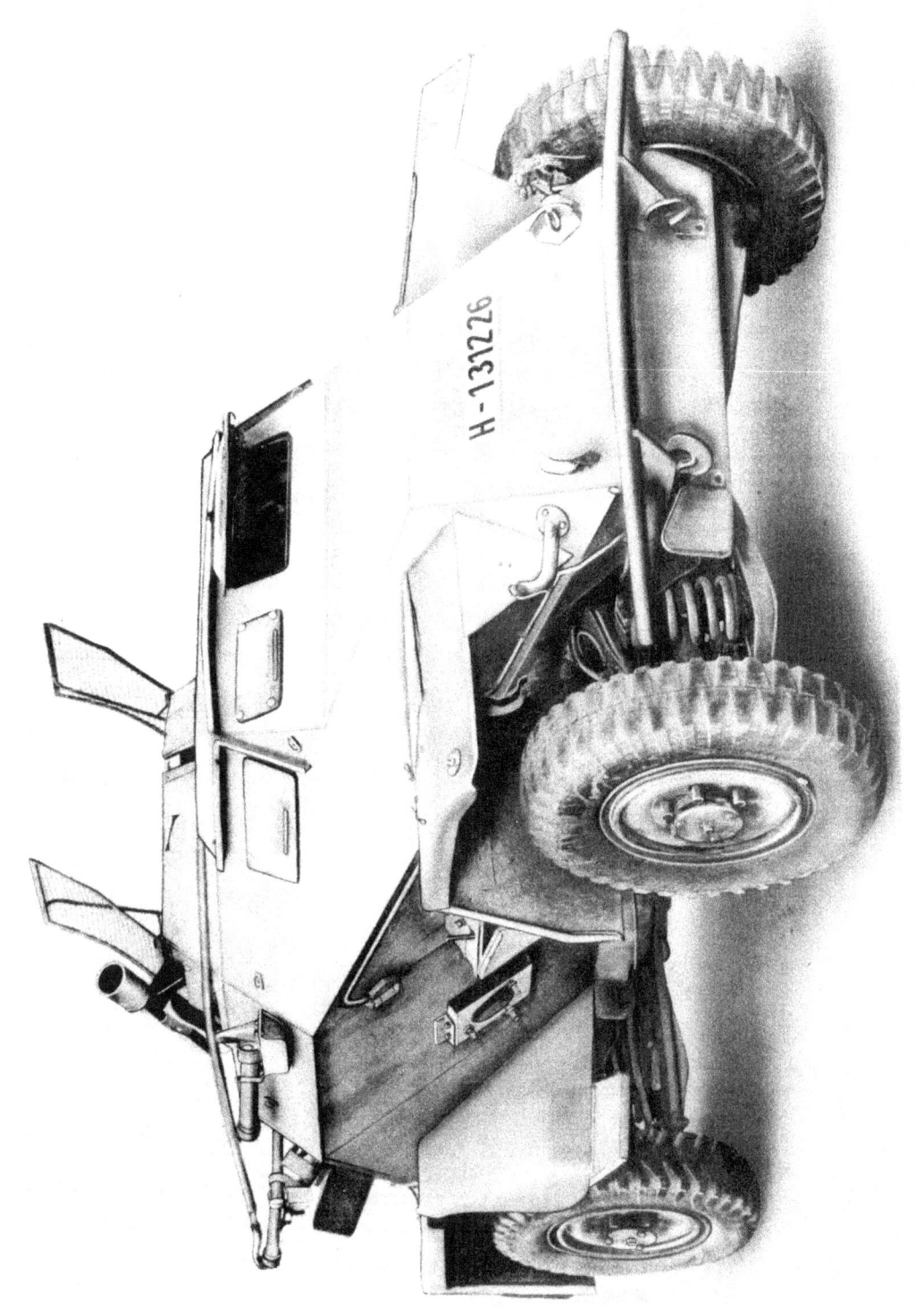

Fig.5.Light Armoured Car (Wireless), Sd.Kfz.223 (le.Pz.Sp.Wg.(Fu.)).

Fig. 6. Light Armoured Wireless Car Sd.Kfz.260. (Kl.Pz.Fu.Wg.)

Fig.7. Light Armoured Wireless Car Sd.Kfz.261 (kl.Pz.Fu.Wg.)

Fig.8. Heavy 6-wheeled Armoured Car Sd.Kfz.231 (6 rad.)

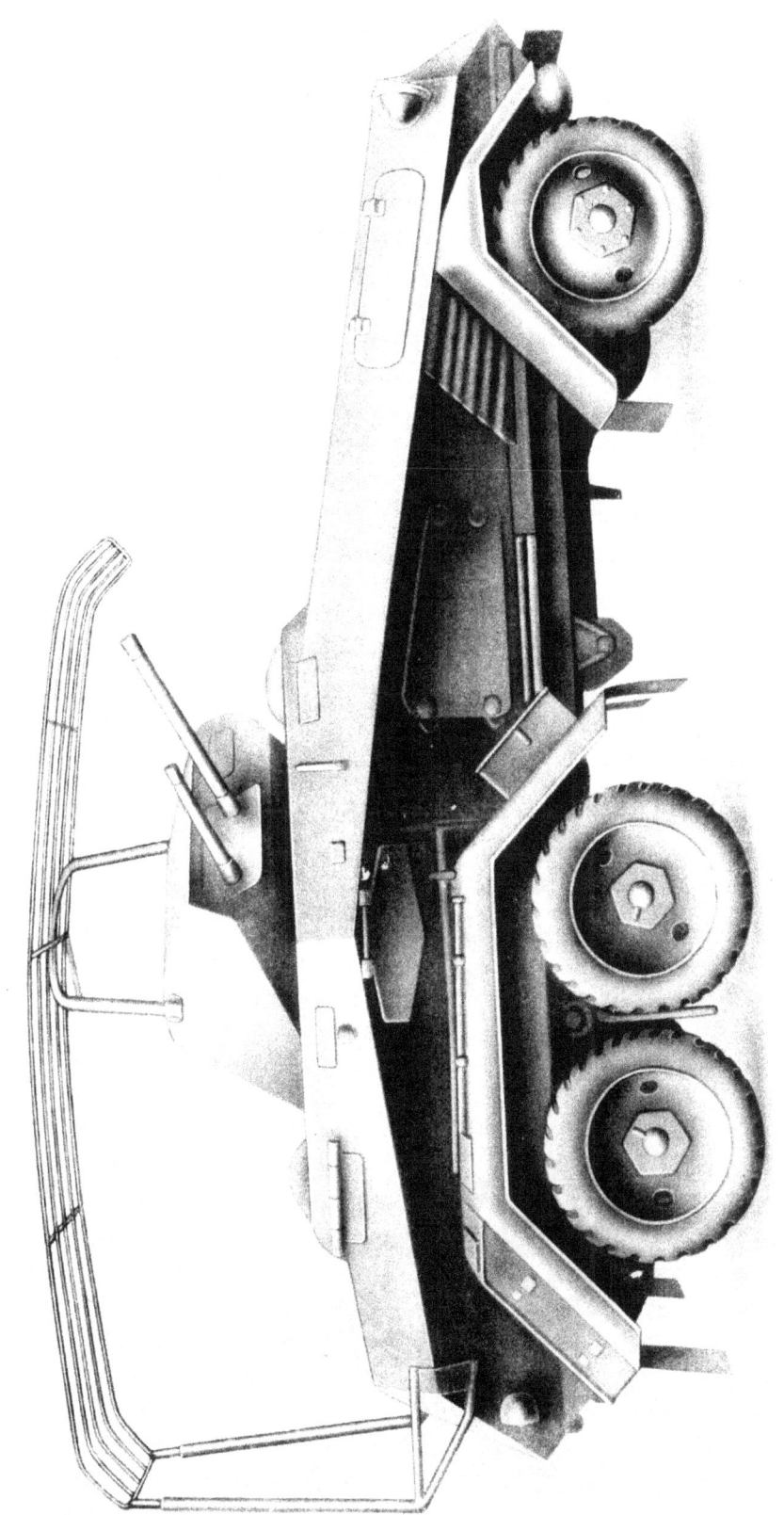

Fig.9. Heavy 6-wheeled Armoured Car Sd.Kfz.232 (6 red.).

Fig. 10. Heavy 6-wheeled Armoured Wireless Car Sd.Kfz.263 (6 rad).

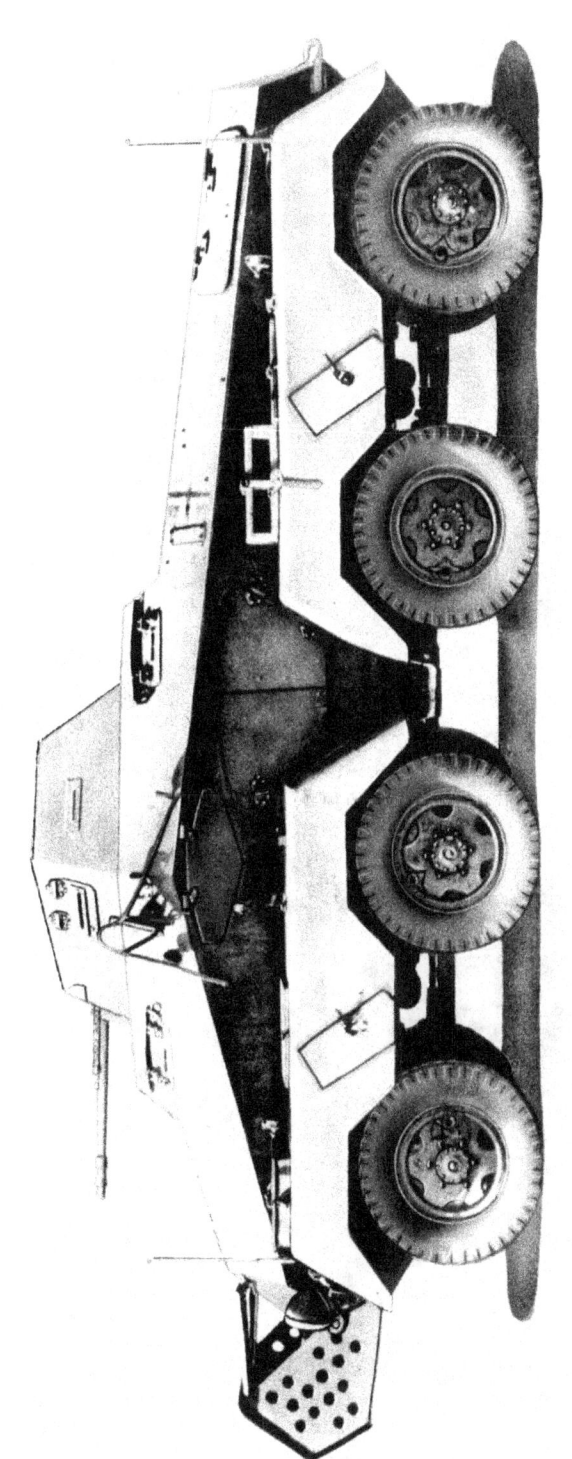

Fig.11. Heavy 8-wheeled Armoured Car Sd.Kfz.231 (8 rad.).

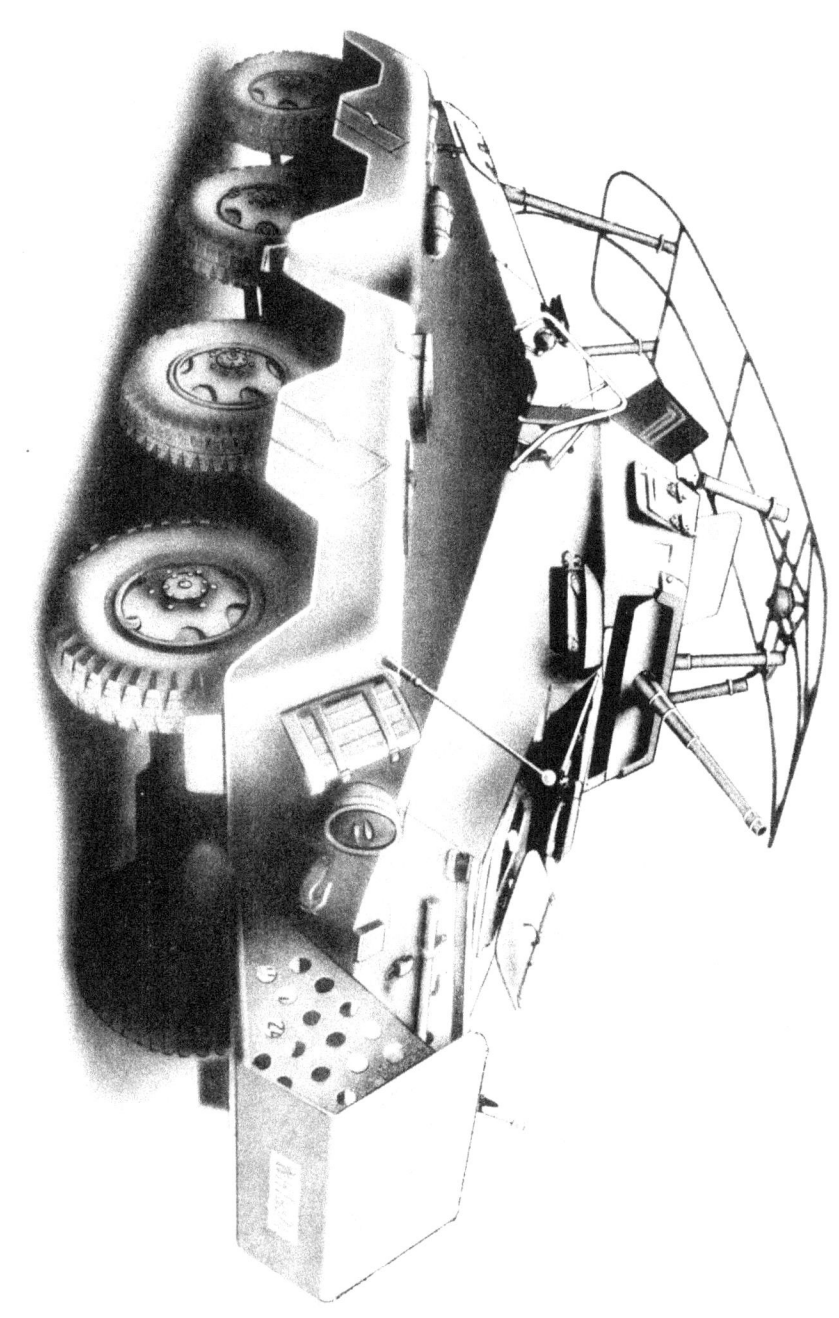

Fig.12. Heavy 8-wheeled Armoured Car (Wireless) Sd.Kfz.232 (8rad.).

Fig. 13. Heavy 8-wheeled Armoured Wireless Car Sd.Kfz.263(8 rad).

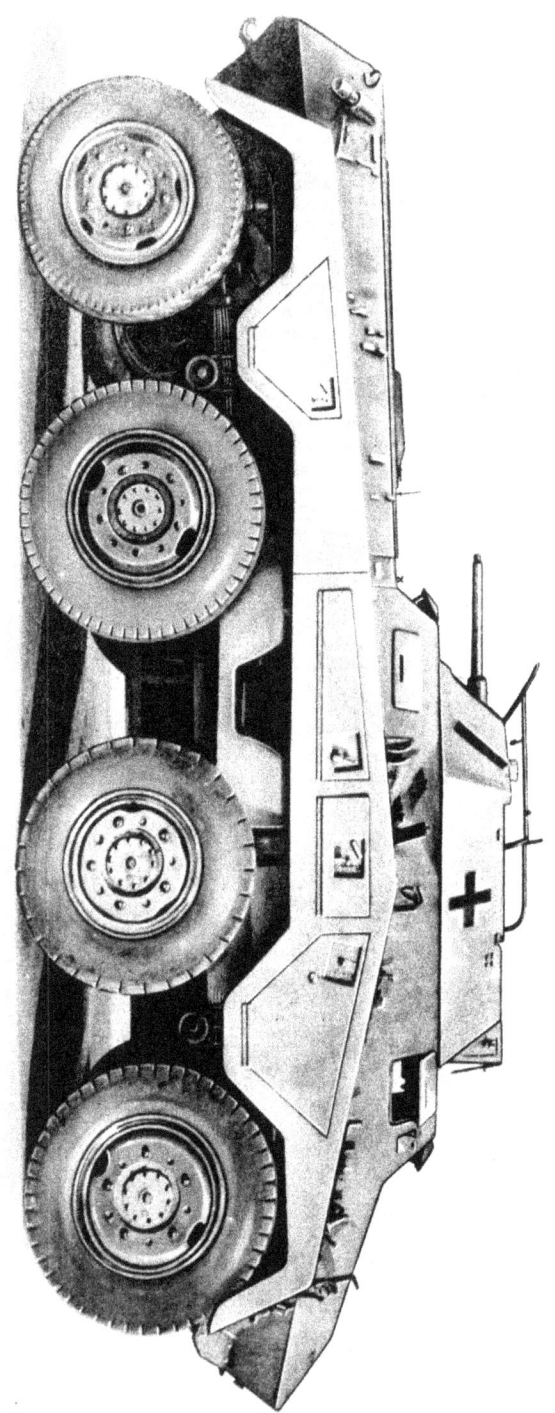

Fig. 14. Heavy 8-wheeled Armoured Car (2 cm.) Sd.Kfz.234/1.

Fig. 15. Heavy-8-wheeled Armoured Car mounting 5cm.Kw.K.39/1(L/60), Sd Kfz.234/2.